Computing Supplementum 3

Parallel Processes and Related Automata

Parallele Prozesse und damit zusammenhängende Automaten

Editors/Herausgeber: W. Knödel, H. J. Schneider

Springer-Verlag
Wien New York

Prof. Dr. Walter Knödel
Institut für Informatik
Universität Stuttgart
Federal Republic of Germany

Prof. Dr. Hans Jürgen Schneider
Institut für Mathematische Maschinen und Datenverarbeitung
Universität Erlangen-Nürnberg
Federal Republic of Germany

With 61 Figures

Library of Congress Cataloging in Publication Data. Main entry under title: Parallel processes and related automata = Parallele Prozesse und damit zusammenhängende Automaten. (Computing: Supplementum; 3.) Essays in honor of W. Händler. English or German. Contents: Beth, T. Geometric parallelism enforces parallel algorithms. – Böhme, J. F. Vektorprozessoren zur Sonar-Feldverarbeitung. – Hellmold, K. U. and Schmidt, B. Parallelstruktur des Simulators GPSS-FORTRAN. – [etc.] 1. Parallel processing (Electronic computers) – Addresses, essays, lectures. 2. Machine theory – Addresses, essays, lectures. 3. Händler, Wolfgang, 1920 – . I. Knödel, Walter, 1926 – . II. Schneider, Hans Jürgen, 1937 – . III. Händler, Wolfgang, 1920 – . IV. Title: Parallele Prozesse und damit zusammenhängende Automaten. V. Series: Computing (Wien): Supplementum; 3. QA76.6.P353.001.64.80 – 26697

ISSN 0344-8029
ISBN-13:978-3-211-81606-6   e-ISBN-13:978-3-7091-8596-4
DOI: 10.1007/978-3-7091-8596-4

Preface

The third supplement volume of "Computing" deals with parallel processes and thus with a highly topical area of informatics. As both the first supplement volumes were concerned with numerical questions, the entire subject, the cultivation of which "Computing" purports, is now broadly outlined in the supplement volumes too.

The reason for the simultaneous production of so many papers on the same subject was the 60th birthday of Prof. Dr. Wolfgang Händler, an eminent specialist in the field of parallel processing. It was the wish of his friends, colleagues and collaborators that Herr Händler be honoured by the gift of a volume which would have as its centre of interest the area of research that he represents. In this volume, parallelism is focused upon from various angles and an attempt has been made, through new results, to bring it a little further. It is obvious from a glance at the bibliographies of the papers contributed, in which many of Herr Händler's publications are referenced, that he was never far from the writer's minds.

After studying naval architecture at the Technical University in Danzig (1941 – 1944), and a period of military service in the navy, Herr Händler then studied mathematics and physics at the University of Kiel (1946 – 1948). His first post was in the research department of the North-West German Radio. From 1957 – 1959 he worked on the TR 4 development project at Telefunken in Backnang and during this time he obtained his doctorate at the Technical University of Darmstadt. In 1959, he became the scientific assistant of Prof. Dr. Johannes Dörr at the University of Saarbrücken, in 1962 he obtained his inauguration (Habilitation), and in 1963 he was called to the Technical University of Hannover as associate professor. Since 1966, he has held the chair at the Friedrich-Alexander University Erlangen-Nürnberg where he built up the Institute of Informatics within the then newly-established technical faculty.

As one of the editors, Herr Händler is closely associated with "Computing". His fellow editors and Springer-Verlag, Vienna, were therefore all too ready to take up the idea of publishing a collection of pertinent papers. Our thanks are due to both and all credit is due to the publishers who, in addition to their patient co-operation, were particularly obliging with regard to the date of publication.

The signatories, together with the authors of this volume, wish Herr Händler a very happy 60th birthday on December 11th, 1980. May the problems dealt with in this volume encourage him to carry on further research.

W. Knödel and **H. J. Schneider**

Vorwort

Der vorliegende dritte Supplementband von „Computing" befaßt sich mit parallelen Prozessen und behandelt damit ein hochaktuelles Gebiet der Informatik. Da die beiden ersten Supplementbände numerische Fragen zum Gegenstand hatten, ist nunmehr das Gesamtgebiet, dessen Pflege sich „Computing" zum Ziel gesetzt hat, auch in den Ergänzungsbänden in großen Zügen angesprochen.

Unmittelbarer Anlaß für das gleichzeitige Entstehen so vieler Arbeiten zu einem geschlossenen Problemkreis war der 60. Geburtstag von Prof. Dr. Wolfgang Händler, einem weithin anerkannten Fachmann auf dem Gebiet der Parallelverarbeitung. Es war der Wunsch seiner Freunde, Kollegen und Mitarbeiter, Herrn Händler ein Geschenk zu verehren, das die von ihm vertretene Forschungsrichtung in den Mittelpunkt stellt, sie von verschiedenen Seiten beleuchtet und versucht, sie durch neue Ergebnisse ein Stück weiterzubringen. Daß dabei das persönliche Gedenken an den Jubilar nicht zu kurz gekommen ist, lehrt ein Blick auf die Literaturverzeichnisse der Beiträge, in denen sich viele Veröffentlichungen von Herrn Händler wiederfinden.

Nach dem Studium des Schiffbaus (1941 – 1944) an der Technischen Hochschule in Danzig, dem Militärdienst bei der Marine und dem Studium der Mathematik und Physik (1946 – 1948) an der Universität Kiel war Herr Händler zunächst in der Forschungsabteilung des Nordwestdeutschen Rundfunks beschäftigt. Von 1957 – 1959 arbeitete er im Rahmen der TR 4-Entwicklung bei Telefunken in Backnang und promovierte während dieser Zeit an der Technischen Hochschule Darmstadt. 1959 wurde er wissenschaftlicher Assistent bei Prof. Dr. Johannes Dörr an der Universität Saarbrücken, habilitierte sich dort 1962 und wurde 1963 als außerordentlicher Professor an die Technische Hochschule Hannover berufen. Seit 1966 lehrt er als Ordinarius an der Friedrich-Alexander-Universität Erlangen-Nürnberg, wo er im Rahmen der damals neugegründeten Technischen Fakultät das Institut für Mathematische Maschinen und Datenverarbeitung (Informatik) aufbaute.

Herr Händler ist durch seine Tätigkeit als Herausgeber besonders mit „Computing" verbunden. Die übrigen Herausgeber und der Springer-Verlag in Wien haben daher den Gedanken an eine Sammelveröffentlichung einschlägiger Arbeiten bereitwillig aufgegriffen. Wir haben beiden dafür zu danken, und wir müssen es dem Verlag hoch anrechnen, daß er zusätzlich zu allen guten Diensten auch in der Frage des Herstellungstermins größtmögliches Entgegenkommen gezeigt hat.

Die Unterzeichneten wünschen gemeinsam mit den Autoren dieses Bandes Herrn Händler alles Gute zu seinem 60. Geburtstag am 11. Dezember 1980. Mögen ihn die behandelten Probleme zu weiteren Untersuchungen anregen.

W. Knödel und **H. J. Schneider**

Contents/Inhalt

Computing, Suppl. 3, 1 — 8 (1981)
© by Springer-Verlag 1981

Geometric Parallelism Enforces Parallel Algorithms

Th. Beth, Erlangen

Abstract — Zusammenfassung

Geometric Parallelism Enforces Parallel Algorithms. The connections between parallelisms in Geometry and Complexity are demonstrated in examples of error-correcting codes: For this purpose linear codes, whose duals — the control spaces — are generated by indicence structures with parallelism, are given by their encoders and decoders. The decoders are parallel processing units according to the parallelism in the incidence structure.

Geometrische Parallelismen führen zu parallelen Algorithmen. Die Beziehungen zwischen Parallelismen in Geometrie und Komplexitätstheorie werden an Beispielen fehler-korrigierender Codes erläutert: Zu diesem Zweck werden lineare Codes, deren Dualräume — die Kontrollräume — von Inzidenzstrukturen mit Parallelismus erzeugt werden, durch Codierer und Decodierer angegeben. Die Decodierer sind parallel arbeitende Einheiten, entsprechend dem Parallelismus der Inzidenz-Struktur.

1. Introduction

Being one of the main concepts of Geometry and Combinatorial Theory parallelisms of Combinatorial and Geometric Structures have been investigated very thoroughly [4], [5]. The concept of parallelisms in the theory of complexity of Algorithms have become of major interest in Computer Science when the availability of fields of processors made the idea of parallel processing realizable. A connection between these two concepts has not been obvious until very recently. An intensive study of Associative Filing Systems [6], [9] shows that the geometric properties of Affine Spaces over $GF(2)$ lead to good Associative Filing Schemes.

In this paper it will be shown that the Geometric Properties of incidence structures with parallelism permit the installation of an associative memory, which is the basis of the construction of an array of processors realizing parallel algorithms.

These ideas which have been sketched by Händler [8] will be developed by considering examples of error-correcting-codes whose implementation by usual hardware "chips" is demonstrated.

2. Basics

2.1 Definition. A *finite incidence structure* $\mathcal{D}$ is a triple $\mathcal{D} = (X, \mathcal{B}, \mathcal{N})$ where X and B are disjoint finite sets and $\mathcal{N}$ is a relation in $X \times \mathcal{B}$. The elements $x \in X$ are called *points* of $\mathcal{D}$ and the elements $B \in \mathcal{B}$ are called *blocks* of $\mathcal{D}$. A point $x \in X$ is said to be incident with a block $B \in \mathcal{B}$ iff $(x, B) \in \mathcal{N}$, denoted by $x \mathcal{N} B$.

Probably the most classical examples of such an incidence structure are given by the affine spaces $AG(n, q)$ of dimension n over $GF(q)$, where the class of blocks is given by the set of k-dimensional affine subspaces for some $k \in [1:n-1]$. These examples give rise to another definition by observing that parallelisms of affine subspaces can be defined in general.

2.2 Definition. Let $\mathcal{D} = (X, \mathcal{B}, \mathcal{N})$ be an incidence structure. An equivalence relation $\|$ on $\mathcal{B}$ is called *parallelism*, iff each equivalence class $\mathcal{B}' \subseteq \mathcal{B}$ forms an incidence structure $\mathcal{D}' = (X, \mathcal{B}', \mathcal{N}|_{X \times \mathcal{B}'})$ whose blocks partition the set X. The equivalence classes of a parallelism are called *parallel classes*.

In the sequel incidence structures of a certain type play an important role so that it is necessary to introduce their common properties.

2.3 Definition. A *Steiner System* $S(t, k, v)$ is an incidence structure $(P, \mathcal{B}, \in)$ with $|P| = v$ points, $\mathcal{B} \subseteq \binom{P}{k}$ i.e. blocks of size k, such that each t-subset $T \in \binom{X}{t}$ is contained in exactly one block of B. An important class of such Steiner Systems we shall be concerned with is the class of affine spaces $AG(n, 2)$ of dimension n over $GF(2)$ where the set of blocks is given by the affine planes in this space:

2.4 Lemma. *Let $Q_n = (GF(2)^n, \mathcal{P}, \in)$ be the incidence structure on the n-dimensional vectorspace $GF(2)^n$ whose class $\mathcal{P}$ of blocks is given by the set of 2-dimensional affine subspaces of $GF(2)^n$. Q_n is an $S(3, 4, 2^n)$.*

Proof. The proof is immediate since any 3 points in $GF(2)^n$ define a plane of 4 points uniquely.

In addition to their canonical parallelism property another concept of these incidence structures is needed.

2.5 Proposition. Let $(P, \mathcal{B}, \in)$ be an $S(t, k, v)$. For $i \in [0:t]$ let $I \subseteq X$ be a set of cardinality $|I| = i$. Then the number of blocks $B \in \mathcal{B}$ with $I \subseteq B$ is given by

$$\lambda_i = \frac{\binom{v-i}{t-i}}{\binom{k-i}{t-i}}.$$

Proof. Cf. [5].

2.6 Example. For an $S(3, 4, 2^n)$

$$\lambda_0 = |B| = \tfrac{1}{3} 2^{n-2} (2^n - 1)(2^{n-1} - 1)$$
$$\lambda_1 = \tfrac{1}{3}(2^n - 1)(2^{n-1} - 1)$$
$$\lambda_2 = 2^{n-1} - 1$$
$$\lambda_3 = 1.$$

2.7 Observation. In $Q_n = (GF(2)^n, \mathcal{P}, \in)$ the following holds: Let $P, P' \in \mathcal{P}$. Then either $P \cap P' = \emptyset$ or $|P \cap P'| = 2$ and $P \triangle P' \in \mathcal{P}$.

Proof. This is clear from the underlying geometry.

This observation can very efficiently be used in coding theory. Therefore we make some definitions.

2.8 Definition. Let $n \in \mathbb{N}$, $k \in [1:n]$. A (binary) *linear (n, k)-code C* is a k-dim. linear subspace $C \leqslant GF(2)^n$.

A $(k \times n)$-matrix G is called *generator matrix of C* if $(GF(2)^n)G = C$, i.e. if its row space is C. Let $C^{\perp}$ be the linear space orthogonal to C. $C^{\perp}$ is called the *dual code* of C.

The transpose H^t of a generator matrix H of $C^{\perp}$ is called a *control matrix* of C.

In the sequel we shall be concerned with the development of decoding procedures which permit an efficient implementation based on their geometric structure.

2.9 Definition. Let $\mathscr{D} = (X, \mathscr{B}, \mathscr{N})$ be an incidence structure. The *incidence matrix N* of D is the matrix

$$N: \quad X \times B \to GF(2)$$

given by

$$N(x, B) = \begin{cases} 1 & \text{iff } x \mathscr{N} B \\ 0 & \text{otherwise.} \end{cases}$$

The row space of N (over $GF(2)$) is called the *code generated by $\mathscr{D}$*.

2.10 Example. The code H_n generated by Q^n is the extended Hamming Code $(2^n, 2^n - n - 1)$. A proof can be found in [4], [12].

The codes are used to transmit $(2^n - n - 1)$-bit words over a binary symmetric channel [1] which generates at most 1 bit-error per transmitted word of length 2^n. A very efficient implementation for the encoding and decoding procedure for these codes is well known [3], [10], if the data are received sequentially. The purpose of this paper is to develop decoding procedures on the basis of finite geometrical structures whose properties allow an acceleration of known decoding procedures. This shall be demonstrated first for the extended Hamming Codes.

2.11 Theorem. $H_n = H_n^{\perp}$.

Proof. $H_n = \text{span}\langle 1_P | P \in \mathscr{P} \rangle$ where

$$Q_n = (GF(2)^n, \mathscr{P}, \in).$$

Since $|P \cap P'| = 0$ or 2 for $P, P' \in \mathscr{P}$ it follows that $\mathbf{c} \cdot \mathbf{c}' = 0$ for any $\mathbf{c}, \mathbf{c}' \in H_n$.

2.12 Corollary. *The blocks of Q_n can be used as control equations for H_n.*

Under the assumption that by transmitting code words of H_n through a binary symmetric channel which "adds" at most 1 bit-error per word of length 2^n this error can be corrected. If a sequential procedure is not possible, e.g. due to different run times, frequency hopping etc., another procedure can be suggested as follows.

Let $\mathbf{u} = \mathbf{c} + \mathbf{e}$ be a received word, $\mathbf{c} \in H_n$ and $\mathbf{e}$ an unknown 1-bit-error-word of length 2^n. How to find $\mathbf{e}$? For each coordinate $i \in [1:2^n]$ take the blocks B_i containing the ith point in Q_n to construct a test $\mathbb{T}_i$:

1*

If this coordinate is not in error, the scalar products $\mathbf{u} \cdot \mathbf{1}_{B_i}$ will result in 1 for all $(2^n - 1)(2^{n-1} - 1)/3 = \lambda_1$ blocks B_i.

If this coordinate is not in error, the scalar products $\mathbf{u} \cdot \mathbf{1}_{B_i}$ will result in 1 for only $2^{n-1} - 1 = \lambda_2$ blocks B_i.

Thus a threshold procedure can be suggested: Whenever for some $i \in [1:2^n]$ a test $\mathbb{T}_i$ gives at least 2^{n-1} "1"'s the ith coordinate is in error and the received word can be corrected.

Observing that the set of control-equations is a Q_n with parallelism the following parallel processor can essentially increase the speed of this algorithm:

Let

$$M = \frac{(2^n - 1)(2^{n-1} - 1)}{3}.$$

Let $\{B^1, \ldots, B^M\}$ be a partition of P into parallel class B^i, $|B^i| = 2^{n-2}$ for each $i \in [1:M]$.

This partition gives rise to construct a processing unit based on associative memories. But since the codes H_n are single-error-correcting the fast decoding procedure described in [3], [10] can be made no faster by tricks coming from their geometric structure.

But for a large class of codes, the Reed-Muller-Codes, this method is applicable as well as for the extended binary Golay-Code. This will be discussed in the following sections.

3. Presentation of the Results

3.1 Definition. Let $n \in \mathbb{N}$. For a vector $\mathbf{x} = (x_1, \ldots, x_n) \in GF(2)^n$ the set supp $\mathbf{x} = \{i \in [1:n] | x_i = 1\}$ is called the *support of* x. The cardinality $wgt(\mathbf{x}) = |\text{supp}(\mathbf{x})|$ is called the weight of $\mathbf{x}$.

Let $k \in [1:n]$. A linear (n, k)-code over $GF(2)$ is said to be *e-error-correcting*, if

$$\min_{\substack{\mathbf{c} \in C \\ c \neq 0}} wgt(\mathbf{c}) \geqslant 2e + 1.$$

3.2 Definition. Let C be a linear f-error-correcting (n, k)-code such that $C^\perp$ is the code generated by an incidence structure, called *control structure*, $\mathcal{D} = (P, \mathcal{B}, \mathcal{N})$. C is said to *threshold decodable by* $\mathcal{D}$ iff there exists an integer $T \in \mathbb{N}$ such that for each $p \in P$ and for any vector $\mathbf{e} \in GF(2)^n$ with $wgt(\mathbf{e}) \leqslant f$ the number of blocks B with $p \mathcal{N} B$ and $\mathbf{e} \cdot \mathbf{1}_B = 1$ exceeds T iff $p \in \text{supp}(\mathbf{e})$.

Therefore codes which are threshold decodable by incidence structures $\mathcal{D}$ can be used in a similar manner as demonstrated in Sect. 2. Under these codes those are of special importance whose control structure $\mathcal{D}$ possesses a parallelism.

3.3 Definition. A threshold decodable linear code is said to be *parallel threshold decodable* if its control structure possesses a parallelism.

3.4 Theorem. *Let C be a parallel threshold decodable linear (n, k)-code over $GF(2)$. Then there exists a natural parallel decoding algorithm for C.*

Proof. Suppose C is f-error-correcting. Let $\mathbf{u} \in GF(2)^n$ be the received word which is the sum of a code word $\mathbf{c}$ and an error-word (unknown) $\mathbf{e}$ with $wgt(\mathbf{e}) \leqslant f$.

Let $\mathscr{D} = (P, \mathscr{B}, \mathscr{N})$ be the control structure of C. Let $\{\mathscr{B}^1, \ldots, \mathscr{B}^M\}$ be the set of parallel classes of $\mathscr{D}$.

Let

$$L = \max_{i \in [1:M]} |\mathscr{B}^i|.$$

Define an $M \times L$-array A of vectors which are the indicator functions of the blocks of D, so that each row i of A consists of a parallel class $\mathscr{B}^i$ of $\mathscr{B}$. This array can be used as $\mathscr{N}$ parallel associative memories, where in each row i at most N scalar products $(\mathbf{u} \cdot \mathbf{1}_{B^i})_{B^i \in \mathscr{B}^i}$ can be computed simultaneously since each $p \in P$ is in exactly one block B^i of $\mathscr{B}^i$.

This procedure will be repeated for each row while a counting register counts the number of 1's obtained in the scalar products after being assigned to corresponding points $p \in P$ by the coordinate allocator of each row.

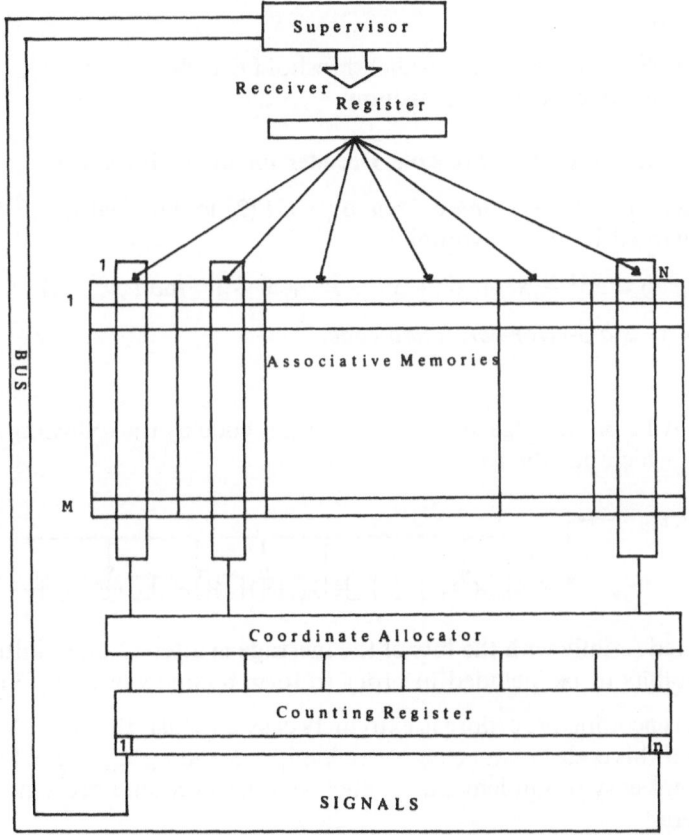

Whenever a counter in the register meets the threshold T it gives a signal to the supervisor which will switch off the processors whenever a sufficient number of signals has arrived.

3.5 Corollary. *The time complexity of the parallel threshold decoding procedure reduces by a factor M^{-1} compared to the time complexity of the threshold decoding procedure presented in Sect. 2, where each coordinate and each block has to be tested.*

3.6 Remark. In general M^{-1} is not necessarily a constant. In affine plane codes for example $M \approx \sqrt[2]{|P|}$ where $|P|$ is the number of coordinates of the codewords.

The condition of being parallel threshold decodable is met by many important classes of codes. Two examples shall be mentioned here:

3.7 Theorem. *Reed-Muller-Codes of length 2^m, $m \in \mathbb{N}$, are parallel threshold decodable.*

Proof. Cf. [11] and observe that the control structure of an $(m - k)$th order *RM*-code is the incidence structure generated by the k-dimensional affine subspaces of $GF(2)^m$.

3.8 Theorem. *The extended binary $(24, 12)$-Golay-Code is parallel threshold decodable.*

Proof. Cf. [12].

The actual implementation of a parallel threshold decoder for the $(24, 12)$-Golay-Code is demonstrated in the next section.

4. A Parallel Threshold Decoder for the Golay Code

4.1 Definition. The *(23, 12)-Golay-Code* over $GF(2)$ is the ideal $G < {}^{GF(2)[x]}\!/_{x^{23}-}$ which is generated by the polynomial

$$g(x) = x^{11} + x^9 + x^7 + x^6 + x^5 + x + 1 \quad \mod x^{23} - 1.$$

4.2 Theorem. *G is a 3-error-correcting code.*

Proof. [3].

4.3 Remark. A 12-bit message **m** is encoded in this code by the following feed-back shift-register which has the form

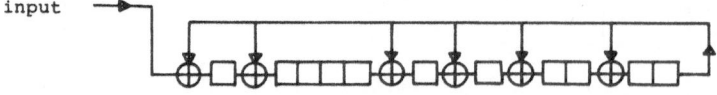

which being fed serially with the bits of the message **m** after 12 time shifts contains the 11 controlbits to be included in order to form a code word, cf. [3].

Although the encoding procedure is extremely easy and fast, the possible decoding procedures for this code are not easy: Berlekamp's decoding algorithm [10] is very refined and not easy to implement. A much simpler decoding procedure shall be presented here.

For this purpose the 12-bit message is to be encoded in a slightly different manner by adding a 24th parity-check coordinate, hence encoding the message $\mathbf{m} \in GF(2)^{12}$ in the extended binary (24, 12)-Golay Code $\bar{G}$.

4.4 Theorem. *For the extended binary (24, 12)-Golay Code $\bar{G}$ the following properties hold*:

(i) $\bar{G} = \bar{G}^{\perp}$.
(ii) *The control structure $\mathscr{D}$ of $\bar{G}$ is an $S(5, 8, 24)$ with parallelism.*

Proof. Cf. [2].

Thus we have to study the properties of the Steiner System $S(5, 8, 24)$.

4.5 Theorem. *Let $\mathscr{D} = (P, \mathscr{B}, \in)$ be an $S(5, 8, 24)$. Then*

(i)
$$\lambda_0 - |\mathscr{B}| = 759$$
$$\lambda_1 = 253$$
$$\lambda_2 = 77$$
$$\lambda_3 = 21$$
$$\lambda_4 = 5$$
$$\lambda_5 = 1.$$

(ii) *B can be partitioned into 253 parallel classes $(\mathscr{B}^i)_{i \in [1:253]}$.*

Proof. Cf. [2], [10].

4.6 Corollary. *Let $\mathbf{e} \in GF(2)^{24}$ with wgt $\mathbf{e} \leqslant 3$. Let $\mathscr{B}_p = \{B \in \mathscr{B} | p \in B\}$.*

The vector $(\mathbf{e} \cdot \mathbf{1}_B)_{B \in \mathscr{B}_p}$ has weight ω according to the following table

$$\omega = \begin{cases} 253 & \text{if } wgt(\mathbf{e}) = 1 \\ 176 & \text{if } wgt(\mathbf{e}) = 2 \\ 141 & \text{if } wgt(\mathbf{e}) = 3 \end{cases} \text{ and if } p \in \text{supp}(\mathbf{e})$$
$$\begin{cases} 125 & \text{if } wgt(\mathbf{e}) = 3 \\ 112 & \text{if } wgt(\mathbf{e}) = 2 \\ 77 & \text{if } wgt(\mathbf{3}) = 1 \end{cases} \text{ and if } p \notin \text{supp}(\mathbf{e}).$$

4.7 Corollary. *$\bar{G}$ is parallel threshold decodable.*

Proof. Take the threshold $T = 133$ and design a parallel algorithm according to Section 3.

4.8 Construction. A parallel threshold decoder for the extended (24, 12)-Golay Code can be designed as follows:

For the 253 × 3-array of 24-bit-words take 9(256 × 8)-bit-PROMs such that the 3 24-bit words of 1 parallel class can be retrieved at a time. The coordinate allocators can be taken as multiplexers and the counting registers as a set of binary counters of standard type. The supervisor can easily be realized in standard LSI-chips or − more comfortably − in a small microprocessing unit.

4.9 Concluding Remark. The concept described here is presently being developed in the laboratory of the author's institution.

References

[1] Augustin, U.: Noisy channels (Lecture Notes in Mathematics). Berlin-Heidelberg-New York: Springer (to appear).
[2] Beth, Th.: A note on the resolvability of the Steiner systems $S(5, 6, 12)$ and $S(5, 8, 24)$. Le Matematiche (to appear).
[3] Beth, Th., Strehl, V.: Materialien zur Codierungstheorie. Berichte des IMMD Erlangen **11** (1978).
[4] Cameron, P.: Parallelisms of complete designs. London Math. Soc. Lecture Notes, Vol. 23. Cambridge University Press 1976.
[5] Dembowski, P.: Finite geometries. Berlin-Heidelberg-New York: Springer 1968.
[6] Grammer, F.: Über assoziative Block-Designs. Diplomarbeit, Erlangen, 1978.
[7] Händler, W.: Aspects of parallelism in computer architecture, in: Mathematics and computers in simulation, Transactions of IMACS **19**. North-Holland 1977.
[8] Händler, W.: Personal communication.
[9] Rivest, R. L.: Partial match retrieval algorithms. SIAM J. Comp. **5**, 19 – 50 (1976).
[10] Sloane, N. J. A.: A short course on error-correcting codes. (C.I.S.M. Lectures, No. 188.) Wien-New York: Springer 1975.
[11] van Lint, J. H.: Coding theory (Lecture Notes in Mathematics). Berlin-Heidelberg-New York: Springer 1971.
[12] von Eichhorn, K.: Steiner-Systeme, Codes and affine Räume. Berichte des IMMD, Erlangen, **10** (1977).

Dr. Th. Beth
Institut für Mathematische Maschinen
und Datenverarbeitung
Universität Erlangen-Nürnberg
Martensstrasse 3
D-8520 Erlangen
Federal Republic of Germany

Computing, Suppl. 3, 9—24 (1981)
© by Springer-Verlag 1981

Vektorprozessoren zur Sonar-Feldverarbeitung

J. F. Böhme, Wachtberg-Werthhoven

Zusammenfassung — Abstract

Vektorprozessoren zur Sonar-Feldverarbeitung. Diese Arbeit soll zunächst einen Einblick in einige Aufgaben und Methoden der passiven digitalen Sonar-Feldverarbeitung, wie Beamforming, Spektralanalyse über Frequenz und Winkel, und gewisse Feinauflösungsmethoden geben. Die entsprechenden Berechnungsprobleme werden zusammengestellt und passende Algorithmen angedeutet, wenn mit Vektorprozessoren gerechnet wird. Wir diskutieren einige Vektorprozessoren, die in rechnerkontrollierten Systemen von Forschungslabors zur Sonar-Feldverarbeitung benutzt werden. Unterschieden wird zwischen aufwendigeren Vektorprozessoren, in denen der größte Teil des Gesamtrechenaufwandes bewältigt wird, und kleineren Prozessoren, bei denen die Aufgaben auf mehrere parallel arbeitende Prozessoren verteilt werden. In kurzer Form wird über Software-Hilfsmittel zum Programmieren von Feldverarbeitungsmethoden und über erste Realisierungen von höheren Signalverarbeitungssprachen berichtet.

Vector Processors for Sonar Array Processing. The paper reviews some problems and methods of digital array processing of passive-sonar signals as beamforming, spectral analysis over frequency and angle and high-resolution estimation. The corresponding computational problems are collected. We indicate suitable algorithms if vector or array processors do the computing. We discuss some vector processors used in computer-controlled systems for passive-sonar array processing by research laboratories. It is discriminated between medium scale processors accomplishing nearly the total computation and small processors for distributed computing in parallel. We briefly report software aids for programming of array processing algorithms and implementations of high-level signal-processing languages.

1. Einleitung

Einer Definition von W. S. Liggert folgend ist passive Feldverarbeitung Interpretation von Geräuschen und geräuschähnlichen Signalen, die mit Hilfe eines Feldes von Sensoren, das heißt von Hydrophonen im Falle von Sonar, empfangen werden. Sonar ist eine Abkürzung für sound navigation and ranging. Typische Aufgaben einer passiven Sonar-Anlage, die solche Feldverarbeitung durchführt, sind die Entdeckung und Vermessung von Geräuschquellen, wie sie fahrende Schiffe darstellen, im Störgeräusch, das aus allen Richtungen empfangen wird. Zum Beispiel ist man interessiert an der Richtung der Geräuschquelle und an ihrer Spektralverteilung, um weitere Schlüsse zur Identifikation ziehen zu können.

Aus statistischer Sicht sind die passiven Feldverarbeitungsprobleme Aufgaben der multivariaten Zeitreihenanalyse. Als Prozeßmodelle für die Sensorausgaben dienen gewöhnlich homogene Wellenfelder, die durch Spektralverteilungen über Frequenzen und Winkel gekennzeichnet sind. Die Abschätzung dieser Spektralverteilungen, in denen die Geräuschquellen diskrete Anteile im Winkelspektrum liefern, ist die zunächst wichtigste Aufgabe der Analyse.

In diesem Aufsatz interessieren Forschungssonarsysteme, mit denen mehrere Feldverarbeitungsaufgaben zum Beispiel zur Verfahrensklärung durchgeführt werden sollen. Flexibilität und unterschiedliche Genauigkeitsanforderungen verlangen digitale Systeme. Die Sensorausgaben werden daher gleichartig bandgefiltert und gegebenenfalls moduliert, parallel abgetastet und digitalisiert. Wenn man als Beispiel von 128 Sensoren ausgeht und Bandbreiten von 1 kHz betrachtet, so erhält man am Eingang des Rechnersystems zur Feldverarbeitung mindestens 256 000 Wörter pro Sekunde, die bis auf eine konstante Verarbeitungszeit in Realzeit abgearbeitet sein wollen.

Die von den meisten Sonar-Forschungslabors verwendeten robusten Rechensysteme, die zeitweise auch an Bord eines Schiffes installiert werden müssen, bestehen aus einem Minirechner zur Ablaufsteuerung, intelligenten Eingabeprozessoren und doppelten Datenpuffern, wobei gleichzeitig der eine geladen und der andere entladen oder bearbeitet wird, einem oder mehreren Vektorprozessoren zur Durchführung der numerischen Aufgaben, einem großen und schnellen Zwischenspeicher und intelligenten Displayvorrichtungen, die die Darstellung der aktuellen Analyseergebnisse und die der Geschichte der beispielsweise letzten zehn Minuten erlaubt. Bedingt durch die großen Datenraten versucht man im System, die Transfers von Daten und die von Instruktionen, Kontrollinformationen etc. über verschiedene Busse durchzuführen.

Wie sich weiter unten ergeben wird, könnte man die anfallenden typischen „number-crunching"-Probleme gut mit Hilfe von großen Skalar- oder Vektorrechnern, wie CDC Star 100, TI-ASC, Cray I, Burroughs SP oder Cyber 203, behandeln. Dies wird auch gelegentlich getan, wenn es möglich ist, den großen Datenstrom bis in den Großrechner zu bewältigen. Diese Möglichkeit soll hier nicht näher behandelt werden.

Aber auch Systeme auf der Basis des Erlanger GPA, vergleiche [11], könnten wohl mit hinreichendem Aufwand an die in Frage stehenden Aufgaben angepaßt werden. Entsprechendes gilt für das Projekt USP, vergleiche [9]. Statt einer Diskussion dieser sicherlich interessanten Fragestellungen wollen wir uns auf Vektorprozessoren konzentrieren, die schon zweckentsprechend eingesetzt werden, und insbesondere auf solche, die auch kommerziell erhältlich sind.

Im nächsten Abschnitt werden dem Leser einige typische passive Sonar-Feldverarbeitungsmethoden vorgestellt und ihre Eigenschaften diskutiert. Es sind dies Spektralanalyse über Frequenz und Winkel, Beamforming, Feinauflösungsmethoden, wie adaptives Beamforming, Maximum-Entropie-Winkelschätzung, Hauptkomponentenzerlegung im Frequenzbereich und Zeitreihenanalyse von Beamsignalen zum Detektieren und Parameter Schätzen. Anschließend werden die resultierenden Berechnungsprobleme und passende Algorithmen beleuchtet. Da sich diese Probleme in der Regel in nebeneinander und nacheinander ausführbare Vektoraufgaben zerlegen lassen, sind Vektorprozessoren zweckmäßige Rechner. Wir wollen einige Vektorprozessoren, die in Sonar-Feldverarbeitungssystemen eingesetzt werden, beschreiben und Systemkonfigurationen einiger Forschungslabors andeuten. Dabei behanden wir einmal aufwendigere Vektorprozessoren, die fast den gesamten numerischen Aufwand allein bewältigen, und zum anderen kleinere Vektorprozessoren, von denen mehrere parallel rechnend eingesetzt werden. Die Arbeit wird abgeschlossen mit einigen Anmerkungen über Software-Hilfsmittel und höhere Signalverarbeitungssprachen.

Studien der vorliegenden Art über zweckmäßige Rechnerstrukturen für digitale Signalverarbeitungsaufgaben sind häufiger durchgeführt worden, erwähnt seien [1], [3] und [4]. Eine vorläufige Version dieser Arbeit erschien als Technischer Bericht des Forschungsinstituts für Hochfrequenzphysik der FGAN in 5307 Wachtberg-Werthhoven.

2. Feldverarbeitungsmethoden

Ähnlich wie in [7] sollen die Wellen, die die Geräusche übertragen, mit Hilfe eines homogenen Wellenfeldes charakterisiert werden. Die Ausgabe eines Sensors, an einer Stelle gekennzeichnet durch den Vektor x_j, werde beschrieben durch einen diskreten stochastischen Prozeß $y_j(m)$ ($|m| = 0, 1, 2 \ldots$), von dem wir den Erwartungswert $Ey_j(m) = 0$ und Stationarität annehmen. Sei $r_{nj}(m - \bar{m}) = Ey_n(m) y_j(\bar{m})$ die Kovarianz zwischen zwei Sensorausgaben. Wir nehmen weiter an, daß die Kreuzspektraldichte

$$f_{nj}(\lambda) = \sum_{m=-\infty}^{+\infty} r_{nj}(m)e^{-i\lambda m} \tag{1}$$

existiert, gegebenenfalls unter Zuhilfenahme von Diracs Deltafunktion, wobei $\lambda = 2\pi f T$ eine normalisierte Frequenz, f die Frequenz einer Welle und T die Abtastperiode im Sensor ist. Falls zusätzlich Raumstationarität gilt, also $f_{nj}(\lambda)$ bei festem λ nur von $x_n - x_j$ abhängt, so stellt $y_j(m)$ in Abhängigkeit von m und x_j ein homogenes Wellenfeld dar. Schreibt man $h(x_n - x_j, \lambda) = f_{nj}(\lambda)$, so wollen wir annehmen, daß $h(x, \lambda)$ die Spektraldarstellung

$$h(x, \lambda) = \int e^{ik'x} F(\lambda, dk) \tag{2}$$

besitzt. Hierbei wird über den Raum integriert und k als Vektorwellenzahl interpretiert, das heißt $2\pi f/|k|$ ist die Ausbreitungsgeschwindigkeit der Welle mit der Frequenz f und $k/|k|$ ist ihre Wellennormale. Zur Vereinfachung der folgenden Darstellung nehmen wir ein Wellenmodell in der Ebene und eine nahezu konstante Ausbreitungsgeschwindigkeit c an. Die Existenz einer Dichte voraussetzend können wir dann mit $k' = \lambda(\cos \alpha, \sin \alpha)/(cT)$ schreiben

$$h(x, \lambda) = \int_{-\pi}^{\pi} e^{i\lambda(x_1 \cos \alpha + x_2 \sin \alpha)/(cT)} f(\lambda, \alpha) \, d\alpha, \tag{3}$$

wobei x_1 und x_2 die kartesischen Koordinaten von x und α der Winkel zwischen der negativen Wellennormalen und der x_1-Achse sind. Da

$$r_{jj}(0) = \frac{1}{2\pi} \iint_{-\pi}^{\pi} f(\lambda, \alpha) \, d\lambda \, d\alpha,$$

beschreibt $f(\lambda, \alpha)$ die Verteilung der Leistung des Wellenfeldes über Frequenz und Winkel und heißt Frequenz-Winkel-Spektraldichte.

Analysen der Dichten f oder f_{nj} liefern die gewünschten Informationen. Zum Beispiel werden Spitzen von $f(\lambda, \alpha)$ bei einem Winkel α, die in einem ganzen Frequenzband auftreten, als Leistungsanteile einer diskreten Geräuschquelle mit der Peilung α und der Rest als diejenigen des Umgebungsrauschens angesehen. Die Schätzung von $f(\lambda, \alpha)$ aus endlich vielen Daten, die mit Hilfe eines endlichen Feldes von Sensoren empfangen werden, z. B. $y_j(m)$ $(j = 0, \ldots, N - 1; \ m = 0, \ldots, M - 1)$, ist damit ein grundlegendes Problem der Feldverarbeitung.

Gewöhnlich geht man folgendermaßen vor, um die Frequenz-Winkel-Spektralverteilung abzuschätzen. Für einen festen Winkel α wird $f(\lambda, \alpha)$ durch Frequenz-Spektralanalyse der Wellen aus der Richtung α abgeschätzt. Dazu formt man zunächst ein sogenanntes Beamsignal, indem die Laufzeitunterschiede, die durch das Wandern einer ebenen Welle aus der Richtung α über das Sensorfeld entstehen, kompensiert und anschließend die Sensorausgaben gewichtet aufsummiert werden. Mit der Abkürzung $l(\alpha)' = (\cos \alpha, \sin \alpha)/(cT)$ berechnet man für einen Sensor an der Stelle x

$$y_\alpha(x, m) = \sum_j a(x - x_j)\, y_j(m - l(\alpha)' x_j), \tag{4}$$

wobei angenommen wird, daß die Sensorausgaben hinreichend hoch abgetastet, die Zahlen $l(\alpha)' x_j$ ganz sind und a ein geeignetes endliches Fenster ist. Kurzzeit-Fourier-Transformation mit Hilfe des endlichen Fensters b

$$V_\alpha(x, m, \lambda) = \sum_{\bar{m}} b(m - \bar{m})\, y_\alpha(x, \bar{m}) e^{-i\lambda\bar{m}} \tag{5}$$

und Glättung von $|V_\alpha(x, m, \lambda)|^2$ über Zeit und Raum liefern den Schätzer für die Frequenz-Spektraldichte aus der Richtung α, also

$$P_\alpha(\lambda) = \sum_m \sum_j w(x_j, m)\, |V_\alpha(x_j, m, \lambda)|^2. \tag{6}$$

Hierbei ist w ein endliches nichtnegatives Glättungsfenster mit $\sum_m \sum_j w(x_j, m) = 1$. Dieser Schätzer besitzt im statistischen Sinne, vergleiche [2], [6] und [7], gute Konsistenzeigenschaften, wenn f hinreichend glatt ist, genügend viele Sensoren und Abtastwerte zur Verfügung stehen und schließlich die Fenster passend gewählt werden.

Interessiert man sich für die Spektralverteilung aus wenigen Richtungen, so ist (6) auch hinsichtlich des erwarteten Rechenaufwandes brauchbar. Im anderen Falle wird die Beamforming-Methode ungünstig, da der Aufwand linear mit der Anzahl der Richtungen wächst. Eine günstigere Methode gewinnt man über eine Abschätzung der Frequenz-Wellenzahl-Spektralverteilung in (2) mit Hilfe von mehrdimensionalen diskreten Fourier-Transformationen. Zunächst wird eine Raum-Zeit-Fourier-Transformation durchgeführt,

$$U(m, x, \lambda, k) = \sum_{\bar{m}} \sum_j g(m - \bar{m}, x - x_j)\, y_j(\bar{m}) e^{-i(\lambda\bar{m} + k'x_j)}, \tag{7}$$

wobei g ein endliches Datenfenster ist, und dann $|U|^2$ über m und x geglättet,

$$P(\lambda, k) = \sum_m \sum_j w(x_j, m)|U(m, x_j, \lambda, k)|^2. \tag{8}$$

Damit ist $P(\lambda, \lambda l(\alpha))$ der Schätzer für die Frequenz-Winkel-Spektralverteilung. Die Konsistenzeigenschaften von $P(\lambda, \lambda l(\alpha))$ ähneln denjenigen von $P_{\alpha}(\lambda)$, vergleiche [2]. Genauer gesagt werden in [2] die Eigenschaften der Schätzer (6) und (8) untersucht, wenn das Wellenfeld nur noch semihomogen ist. Die diskrete Fourier-Transformation (7) kann mit Hilfe von FFT-Algorithmen berechnet werden, wenn die Sensororte ein geeignetes Raster bilden. Man erhält auf diese Weise den Schätzer (8) z. B. an den Stellen (λ, k) mit $\lambda = 2\pi j/M$ $(j = 0, \ldots, M - 1)$ und $k = 2\pi(j_1, j_2)/(Kd)$ $(j_1, j_2 = 0, \ldots, K - 1)$, wobei angenommen wurde, daß sich die Sensoren an den Orten $x_j = (j_1 d, j_2 d)$ $(j_1, j_2 = 0, \ldots, K - 1)$ befinden. Die gewünschten Zahlen $P(\lambda, \lambda l(\alpha))$ gewinnt man durch Interpolation. Eine ausführliche Einführung in die bisher angesprochenen Feldverarbeitungsprobleme findet man in [8] und eine Beschreibung einer Realisierung in [22].

Die Lagen der Spitzen der Dichte $f(\lambda, \alpha)$, an denen man besonders interessiert ist, genauer abzuschätzen, gelingt in der oben angedeuteten Weise häufig nicht. Zwei Gründe sind hierfür ausschlaggebend. Zumeist ist die Zahl der verwendeten Sensoren und die Ausdehnung des Sensorfeldes nicht groß genug, um eine ausreichende Winkelauflösung zu erzielen, und zum anderen verbieten Instationaritäten des Mediums große Integrationszeiten. Sogenannte Feinauflösungsmethoden bieten Abhilfe, wenn zusätzliche Modellannahmen akzeptiert werden. Im folgenden wird auf eine Diskussion der statistischen Eigenschaften dieser Methoden verzichtet und auf die entsprechende Literatur verwiesen. Im Hinblick auf das Thema dieser Arbeit werden die Methoden nur kurz beschrieben.

Als erste sei Capons Maximum-Likelihood-Methode erwähnt, vergleiche [7], die auch adaptives Beamforming genannt wird. Zunächst benutzt man als einen Schätzer für $f_{nj}(\lambda)$ in (1)

$$S_{nj}(\lambda) = \frac{1}{K} \sum_{h=1}^{K} Y_{nh}(\lambda) Y_{jh}(\lambda)^* \qquad (k, j = 0, \ldots, N - 1), \qquad (9)$$

wobei der Stern die konjugiert-komplexe Zahl bezeichnet und

$$Y_{jh}(\lambda) = \sum_{m} b((h - 1)\bar{M} - m) y_j(m) e^{-i\lambda m} \qquad (10)$$

und b eine Weite von höchstens $\bar{M}$ Abtastwerten besitzt. Bezeichnet $(s_{nj}(\lambda))$ die Inverse der Marix $(S_{nj}(\lambda))$, so ist der (8) entsprechende Schätzer

$$P_1(\lambda, k) = 1 \bigg/ \sum_{n} \sum_{j} s_{nj}(\lambda) e^{-ik'(x_n - x_j)}. \qquad (11)$$

Um die notwendige positive Definitheit der Matrizen zu erzwingen, wird gegebenenfalls $S_{nj}(\lambda)$ durch $S_{nj}(\lambda) + \varepsilon \delta_{nj}$ ersetzt.

Die Maximum-Entropie-Methode, vergleiche [14], schätzt aus den Daten im Frequenzbereich für jede interessierende normierte Frequenz λ die Koeffizienten 1, $\gamma_1, \gamma_2, \ldots, \gamma_K$ eines rekursiven Prädiktionsfilters. Wenn man annimmt, daß die Sensoren äquidistant mit dem Abstand d auf der x_2-Achse liegen, so ist der (8) entsprechende Schätzer für $k = \lambda l(\alpha)$

$$P_2(\lambda, k) = \sigma^2 d \bigg/ \bigg| 1 + \sum_{j=1}^{K} \gamma_j e^{-ijd\lambda \sin \alpha/(cT)} \bigg|^2 \tag{12}$$

Die Koeffizienten und die Varianz σ^2 des Prädiktionsfehlers werden z. B. mit Burgs Rekursionsformeln aus den komplexen Zahlen

$$Y_j(\lambda) = \sum_{m=0}^{M-1} y_j(m) e^{-i\lambda m} \qquad (j = 0, \dots, N-1) \tag{13}$$

geschätzt. Hierbei wird die Ordnung $K < N$ im einfachsten Fall als bekannt angenommen. Man rechnet für $n = 0, \dots, K-1$ rekursiv nach den Formeln

$$\sigma_1^2 = \frac{1}{N} \sum_{j=0}^{N-1} |Y_j|^2,$$

$$\gamma_{n+1,n+1} = -2 \sum_{j=1}^{N-n-1} \varepsilon_{j+n+1,n}\, \eta_{j,n}^* \bigg/ \sum_{j=1}^{N-n-1} (|\varepsilon_{j+n+1,n}|^2 + |\eta_{j,n}|^2),$$

$$\varepsilon_{j,n} = Y_j + \sum_{m=1}^{n} \gamma_{m,n}\, Y_{j-m} = \varepsilon_{j,n-1} + \gamma_{n,n}\, \eta_{j-n,n-1},$$

$$\eta_{j,n} = Y_j + \sum_{m=1}^{n} \gamma_{m,n}^*\, Y_{j+m} = \eta_{j,n-1} + \gamma_{n,n}^*\, \varepsilon_{j+n,n-1},$$

$$\gamma_{j,n+1} = \gamma_{j,n} + \gamma_{n+1,n+1}\, \gamma_{n-j+1,n}^*,$$

$$\sigma_{n+2}^2 = \sigma_{n+1}^2 (1 - |\gamma_{n+1,n+1}|^2) \tag{14}$$

und setzt $\gamma_j = \gamma_{j,K}$ und $\sigma^2 = \sigma_{K+1}^2$. Auf andere Ansätze mit Prädiktionsfiltern, z. B. [5], soll hier nicht eingegangen werden.

Eine etwas schwieriger zu handhabende Feinauflösungsmethode ist die Hauptkomponentenanalyse im Frequenzbereich, vergleiche [6] und [24]. Man geht z. B. von den Schätzungen $S_{nj}(\lambda)$ in (9) für die Spektraldichtematrix $(f_{nj}(\lambda))$ aus und berechnet für die interessierenden Frequenzen λ aus der Hermitischen Matrix $(S_{nj}(\lambda))$ die größten Eigenwerte und eine orthonormale Basis für den zugehörigen Eigenraum. Der diesem Raum entsprechende Anteil $(\bar{S}_{nj}(\lambda))$ in der dyadischen Zerlegung von $(S_{nj}(\lambda))$ liefert den Schätzer

$$P_3(\lambda, k) = \sum_{n} \sum_{j} w(N-n)\, w(N-j)^* \bar{S}_{nj}(\lambda) e^{-ik'(x_n - x_j)}. \tag{15}$$

Hat man erst einmal eine Richtung gefunden, in der eine Geräuschquelle vermutet wird, so behandelt man ein entsprechendes Beamsignal, z. B. $y_\alpha(0, m)$ nach (4), mit Hilfe geeignet abgewandelter Techniken der statistischen Zeitreihenanalyse [6] weiter, um spezielle Signale der Geräuschquelle zu detektieren und Parameter zu schätzen. Eine Untersuchung solcher Techniken in dem Sinne, wie es die vorliegende Arbeit beabsichtigt, ist in [3] und [4] beschrieben worden und soll deshalb nicht wiederholt werden.

3. Berechnungsprobleme

Der überwiegende Teil der im letzten Abschnitt behandelten Feldverarbeitungsmethoden kann unmittelbar in Standardaufgaben der digitalen Signalverarbeitung zerlegt werden. Diese Aufgaben sind in Büchern wie [15] und [20] ausführlich behandelt worden. Wir wollen uns daher bei der Darstellung der Berechnungsprobleme und der Algorithmen für deren Lösung kurzfassen. Die beschriebenen Feldverarbeitungsverfahren beginnen in einer Überwachungssituation mit Beamforming oder Spektralzerlegungsoperationen, die möglichst schnell und immer wieder ausgeführt werden müssen.

Zu berechnen sind im ersten Fall Ausdrücke wie (4) für mehrere Winkel und gegebenenfalls mehrere Orte sowie in aufeinanderfolgenden Zeitpunkten mit vergrößerten Abständen. Eine direkte Berechnung dieser Formeln ist aus physikalischen Gründen zweckmäßig, wenn die Sensorausgaben breitbandig sind. Wegen des hohen Rechenaufwandes ist bei einer großen Zahl von Beams die Verwendung eines Spezialrechners allein zum Beamformen unumgänglich. Für schmalbandige Sensorausgaben gibt es effektivere Algorithmen, die eine Dezimierung der notwendig zu hoch abgetasteten Daten vornehmen, die dezimierten Daten beamformen und anschließend die Beamsignale interpolieren, vergleiche [16].

Die Spektralzerlegung beginnt mit für alle Sensorausgaben parallel auszuführenden Fourier-Transformationen wie (10), (13) oder mit (7). Wenn man in (7) $g(m, x) = b(m)a(x)$ setzt, könnte man ebenso zunächst die Fourier-Transformationen im Zeitbereich ausführen. Eine ähnliche Aufgabe ist in (5) zu berechnen. Parallele Prozessoren können gut verwendet werden. Der zweite Berechnungsschritt in (7) wäre, für alle interessierenden Frequenzen eine 2-D Fourier-Transformation im Ortsbereich durchzuführen. Vom Rechenaufwand her gesehen ist es allerdings günstiger, die Zeit- und Ortstransformation mit Hilfe einer 3-D Fourier-Transformation simultan zu berechnen. Diese Transformation führt man günstig in einem größeren Vektorprozessor durch. Schnelle Verfahren zur Berechnung der verschiedenen Fourier-Transformationen sind bekanntlich die FFT- und Winograd's Algorithmen.

Die zur Berechnung der Schätzer (6) und (8) verbleibenden Betragsbildungs- und Mittelungsoperationen fallen gegenüber dem Beamformen oder Fourier-Transformieren kaum noch ins Gewicht. Zu erwähnen ist, daß man die Zahlen $P(\lambda, k)$ zu den geforderten Schätzgrößen $P(\lambda, \lambda l(\alpha))$ schnell mit Hilfe von Tabellenspeichern interpolieren kann.

Die nach der Berechnung von (9) oder (13) durchzuführenden rechenintensiven Aufgaben bei den Feinauflösungsmethoden sind die folgenden. Für (11) müssen für die interessierenden Frequenzen je die Hermitische Matrix $(S_{nj}(\lambda))$ invertiert und anschließend für die Winkel von Interesse die quadratischen Formen in den Vektoren mit den Komponenten $z_j(\lambda, \alpha) = e^{-i\lambda l(\alpha)'x_j}$ berechnet werden. Wenn die Zahl der Winkel klein ist, so ist es günstiger, zunächst das lineare Gleichungssystem $\sum_j S_{nj}(\lambda)t_j = z_n(\lambda, \alpha)$ zu lösen und mit $\sum_n t_n z_n(\lambda, \alpha)^*$ den Wert der quadratischen Form zu erhalten. Für mäßige Anzahlen von Winkeln bleibt nur die direkte Berechnung. Für viele Richtungen wird zunächst invertiert, dann die Fourier-Transformation $\sum_j s_{nj}(\lambda)e^{-ik'x_j} = t_n(\lambda, k)$ berechnet, $t_n(\lambda, \lambda l(\alpha))$ interpoliert und

$\sum_n t_n(\lambda, \lambda l(\alpha)) z_n(\lambda, \alpha)^*$ bestimmt. Die Formeln (14) für den Maximum-Entropie-Schätzer können in einem Vektorprozessor direkt und schnell berechnet werden. Es soll hier erwähnt werden, daß Makhoul [13] eine ähnliche Schätzmethode für die Prädiktorkoeffizienten angegeben hat, die jedoch zwei bis viermal so schnell wie die hier zitierte Methode von Burg berechnet werden kann. Da in (12) die Zahl der Prädiktorkoeffizienten nicht groß ist, fällt die Berechnung von (12) gegenüber derjenigen der Koeffizienten nicht ins Gewicht. Die dritte Feinauflösungsmethode auf der Grundlage der Hauptkomponentenanalysen der Hermitischen positiv-semidefiniten Matrizen $(S_{nj}(\lambda))$ ist besonders rechenintensiv. Für wenige ausgewählte Frequenzen sind die größten Eigenwerte und die zugehörigen orthonormierten Eigenvektoren gesucht und eine entsprechend höhere Anzahl von Eigenwerten in fallender Ordnung zu berechnen. Für größere N ist das Verfahren der simultanen Iteration wohl das schnellste für die Aufgabe. Der Programmaufwand ist jedoch beträchtlich. Da die Berechnung mit Hilfe eines nicht großen Vektorprozessors vorgenommen wird, ist die bezüglich des Rechenaufwandes schlechtere Jacobi-Prozedur vorzuziehen, da sie gutartig bezüglich ihrer Konvergenz und ihrer numerischen Eigenschaften ist und sich relativ gut als kompaktes Vektorprogramm realisieren läßt. Den Schätzer (15) berechnet man über die Fourier-Transformierten der verwendeten Eigenvektoren.

Schließlich bleiben die Berechnungsprobleme bei der Signalverarbeitung eines Beamsignales aufzuzählen, wie sie in [3] und [4] in drei Gruppen zusammengestellt worden sind.

(a) Mengen von inneren Produkten, wie eine Matrix von Referenzdaten multipliziert mit einem Vektor von Meßdaten, Kreuzkorrelation zwischen Referenzvektoren und einem gemessenen Vektor,

(b) quadratische Formen für einen oder mehrere gemessene Vektoren mit unterschiedlichen Annahmen über die Kerne, z. B. Toeplitz-Matrizen, und über die Daten, z. B. Schmalbandigkeit,

(c) Sortierprobleme, wie Bestimmung der Ränge von Meßwerten.

Offensichtlich ähneln die Aufgaben aus (a) und (b) den zuvor besprochenen. Benötigt werden hierzu Standardprozeduren für Vektoroperationen und schnelle Fourier-Transformationsalgorithmen. In Abhängigkeit von der speziellen Signalverarbeitungsaufgabe lassen sich gelegentlich beträchtliche algorithmische Verbesserungen vornehmen, die jedoch hier nicht diskutiert werden sollen. Die Ausführung einer Sortieraufgabe aus (c) verlangt datenabhängige Programmsprünge. Bei der Realisierung in Vektorprozessoren wandelt man Standardprozeduren derart ab, daß eine Pipeline-Struktur entsteht (look-ahead programming).

4. Zweckmäßige Vektorprozessoren

Die Architektur der meisten Vektorprozessoren, wie sie in Sonarforschungsinstituten verwendet werden, kann man folgendermaßen beschreiben: Der Vektorprozessor ist ein peripheres System eine Host-Computers und wird von diesem aus initialisiert, mit Programmen und Referenzdaten geladen und bezüglich des globalen Steuerns von Programmen kontrolliert. Der Vektorprozessor besitzt eine

Kontroll-Einheit zur Ablaufsteuerung, die durch einen sehr schnellen Mini- oder Microrechner realisiert wird. Über Eingabe-/Ausgabeprozessoren, wovon einer nur für den Verkehr mit dem Host zuständig ist, gelangen die Referenzdaten und die Meßdaten, z. B. aus den abgetasteten analog/digital gewandelten Sensorausgaben direkt in den Datenspeicher. Intelligentere Prozessoren dieser Art können Formatwandlungen während der sequentiellen Übertragung und programmierbare Abspeicherpläne realisieren. Die Berechnung erfolgt parallel in mehreren Arithmetikprozessoren, die Gleitkomma- oder Blockgleitkommaberechnungen durchführen bei einer Mantissenlänge von mindestens 24 bit. Prozessoren für Punktoperationen und solche für Strichoperationen werden in der Regel paarweise eingesetzt; zumeist existieren ein oder zwei Paare. Als schnelle Zwischenspeicher dienen Felder von Akkumulatoren oder eine gewisse Zahl von Operandenregistern in jedem Arithmetikprozessor. Komplexere arithmetische Aufgaben werden häufig durch Tabellen-Verarbeitung effektiv durchgeführt. Dazu besitzen einige Systeme einen separaten schnellen Tabellenspeicher, der unter anderem eine Cosinus-Tabelle zur Fourier-Transformation enthält. Mehrere Transfers zwischen Ergebnisregistern oder Speicherregistern und Zwischenspeichern oder Operandenregistern können parallel ablaufen. Die Bereitstellung der Daten aus dem in der Regel sehr schnellen Datenspeicher und der Rücktransport der Ergebnisse wird mit Hilfe eines Adreßprozessors erledigt. Grob gesprochen können folgende Aktivitäten parallel ablaufen: Dateneingabe mit Formatwandlung, Datenausgabe, Adreßrechnung, Punktrechnung, Strichrechnung und gewisse Datentransfers innerhalb des Vektorprozessors. Für die meisten der hier interessierenden Berechnungsprobleme läßt sich mit dieser Struktur eine günstige Pipeline-Verarbeitung realisieren. Die ablaufenden Programme befinden sich in einem oder mehreren separaten Programmspeichern je nachdem, ob die Prozessoren synchron oder asynchron betrieben werden. Die beim Sortieren notwendigen datenabhängigen Programmsprünge werden durch Abfrage des Ergebnisregisters des Strichprozessors und Übermittlung des Resultates zum Adreßprozessor durchgeführt. Die Abarbeitung dieser Befehle und die Programmierung einer betreffenden Pipeline-Verarbeitung ist offensichtlich in einem synchronen System weniger problematisch. Aufgerufen werden die Vektorprozessoren in der Regel durch ein im Host ablaufendes Fortran-Programm. Die Hersteller liefern umfangreiche Bibliotheken von in Fortran aufrufbaren Unterprogrammen, mit denen man die üblichen Vektor-, Matrix- und Signalverarbeitungsaufgaben im Vektorprozessor ausführen kann. Mit den von den Herstellern gelieferten Cross-Assemblern, Linkern etc. gelingt es im Host, neue in Fortran aufrufbare Benutzerprogramme zu schreiben. Für die gängigen amerikanischen Minirechner sind Interfaces und passende Driver zu haben.

Nach dieser allgemeinen Beschreibung werden die Eigenschaften einiger spezieller Vektorprozessoren und einige in Sonarlabors installierte Rechnersysteme zur Feldverarbeitung, die diese Vektorprozessoren enthalten, grob skizziert. Auf die Beschreibung spezieller militärischer Entwicklungen wird verzichtet. Als erstes sollen aufwendigere Systeme beschrieben werden, die mit einem schnellen Datenspeicher von mindestens 32 K Wörtern ausgerüstet ungefähr 200 000 DM oder mehr kosten. Anschließend werden zwei Billigsysteme diskutiert, die man z. B. als 2 oder 4 Karten in ein PDP 11-Board stecken kann und die je nach Datenspeicher-größe nicht mehr als ungefähr 50 000 DM kosten. Um eine Vorstellung von der Rechengeschwindigkeit der Vektorprozessoren zu erhalten, wird die von den Herstellern angegebene Rechenzeit für eine mit FFT vollständig ausgeführte Fourier-Transformation eines Feldes von 1024 komplexwertigen Zahlen, die sich im Datenspeicher befinden, angegeben.

Unter den aufwendigeren Systemen wollen wir zuerst die echten Gleitkomma-Rechner diskutieren, die exakt runden und die man daher auch günstig bei der Behandlung anderer umfangreicher numerischer Probleme, die nichts mit Signal-verarbeitung zu tun haben, einsetzen kann.

Der am meisten verkaufte Vektorprozessor dieser Art ist der AP 120 B von Floating Point Systems. Er arbeitet synchron mit einer Taktzeit von 167 ns. Der Rechenzu-stand pro Takt wird durch ein 64-bit-Wort von Befehlen für die parallel auszuführenden Aktivitäten festgelegt. Die Programme befinden sich in einem separaten Programmspeicher mit bis zu 4 K Plätzen. 16 Indexregister stehen dem Adreßprozessor zur Verfügung. Die Wortlänge für das Gleitkommaformat beträgt 38 bit. Der AP 120 B besitzt als Arithmetik-Einheit einen Punkt- und einen Strichprozessor, die im Strom pro Takt ein Ergebnis liefern. Als Zwischenspeicher dienen 2 mal 32 Akkumulatoren, von denen pro Takt zwei als Ergebnisregister für die beiden Arithmetikprozessoren zur Verfügung stehen und zwei weitere zur Versorgung von je einem der beiden Operandenregister dienen. Ein separater Tabellenspeicher steht zur Verfügung, der bis zu 64 K Wörtern ausgebaut werden kann. Für den Datenspeicher ist die obere Grenze 1 M Wörter. Über vier getrennte Datenkanäle können die Arithmetikprozessoren versorgt werden. Eingabe-/Aus-gabeprozessoren, die Formatwandlungen der Daten vornehmen können, und andere, mit denen ein Hintergrundspeicher angeschlossen werden kann, stehen zur Verfügung. Im direkten Speicherzugriff können bis zu 3 M Wörter pro Sekunde geladen werden. Die Fourier-Transformation wird in 4,8 ms ausgeführt. Die von Floating Point Systems gelieferten Software-Hilfsmittel sind sehr umfangreich, insbesondere trifft dies auf die mathematische Bibliothek zu.

Der AP 120 B wird häufig in Forschungslabors mit mittlerer Sonar-Feldverarbei-tungskapazität verwendet. Typische Beispiele sind die Systeme der Admiralty Underwater Weapons Establishment in Portland, U. K., vergleiche [18], und in Deutschland bei Krupp Atlas-Elektronik in Bremen, vergleiche [22], in der Forschungsanstalt der Bundeswehr für Wasserschall- und Geophysik in Kiel oder im FGAN-Forschungsinstitut für Hochfrequenzphysik in Wachtberg-Werthho-ven. Die vielkanaligen analogen Daten werden umgesetzt, gefiltert, parallel abgetastet, A/D-gewandelt, multiplexed und gelangen über einen Eingabe-/Ausga-beprozessor direkt in den Datenspeicher des AP 120 B. Wenn der Speicher groß genug ist, wird mit 2 Blöcken gearbeitet. Einer wird geladen, und im anderen wird die Spektralschätzung so weit wie möglich durchgeführt. Die Ergebnisse werden in einem üblichen Minirechner (z. B. PDP 11/34 oder HP 21 MX) akkumuliert und die Ergebnisse auf Displayvorrichtungen, wie Grauschreibern, dargestellt und in einem Hintergrundspeicher abgelegt. Wenn nach der Inspektion eines Stückes der Zeitentwicklung Feinauflösungsmethoden angewendet werden sollen, muß die Spektralschätzung in Realzeit abgebrochen werden.

Ein anderer bekannter Vektorprozessor ist der MAP 300 von CSPI. Im Vergleich zum AP 120 B besitzt dieses System eine gegensätzliche Struktur. Der MAP 300 ist ein asynchroner Rechner. Unter der Kontrolle eines sehr schnellen Minirechners arbeiten die Prozessoren mit hoher interner Geschwindigkeit voneinander unabhängig. Die Kommunikation untereinander wird durch Setzen und Abfragen von Flags erzielt. Jeder Prozessor wird für sich in relativ einfacher Weise programmiert, wobei zur Erzielung einer guten Pipeline das Zeitverhalten der Prozessoren sehr zu beachten ist. Die Eingabe-/Ausgabeprozessoren, der Adreßprozessor und die Arithmetik-Einheit besitzen eigene Programmspeicher; der Kontrollrechner benutzt als Programmspeicher einen Teil des Datenspeichers. Nicht aktive Programme der Prozessoren sind im Datenspeicher abgelegt und werden vom Kontrollprozessor, wenn nötig, in die einzelnen Programmspeicher geladen. Die Gleitkommawörter sind 32 bit lang. Die mit einer Zykluszeit von 70 ns arbeitende Arithmetik-Einheit enthält zwei Paare von Punkt- und Strichprozessoren. Eine Multiplikation wird in 420 ns ausgeführt und eine Addition doppelt so schnell. Im Strom sind in dieser Zeit also 2 Multiplikationen un 4 Additionen ausführbar. Die Paare führen stets die gleiche Operation durch. Als Zwischenspeicher dienen die 8 Operandenregister eines jeden Arithmetikprozessors. Der Datenspeicher besteht aus drei Teilen mit je höchstens 64 K Wörtern und je einem eigenen Bus. Der Adreßprozessor erzeugt Adreßschlangen, und entsprechend werden Eingabeschlangen aufgebaut, die aus dem Datenspeicher gefüllt werden, wenn die ersten Daten aus der Eingabeschlange in die Operandenregister gelangt sind. Ergebnisse werden in Operandenregister oder in die Ausgabeschlange transferiert usw. Der Eingabe-/Ausgabeprozessor, der die Verbindung zum Host darstellt, kann Formate wandeln. Die anderen sind gut programmierbar zur Realisierung komplizierter Adreßschemata und zum Anschluß von Hintergrundspeichern, Displays, A/D-Wandlern etc. Durch die Dreiteilung des Speichers können kurzzeitig noch größere Ein-/Ausgaberaten als beim AP 120 B erzielt werden. Die Fourier-Transformation benötigt 4,5 ms Rechenzeit. Die existierenden Software-Hilfsmittel und die Programmbibliotheken sind umfangreich. Eigene Assemblerprogramme zu schreiben, ist nicht schwierig im Gegensatz zum Austesten solcher Programme, da der Zustand eines asynchronen Systems nicht definiert ist.

Der MAP 300 ist in das Feldverarbeitungssystem des SACLANTCEN, La Spezia, Italien, vergleiche [21], eingebaut worden. Unter der Kontrolle eines HP 21 MX werden die digitalisierten Sensorausgaben zunächst in einem programmierbaren sehr schnellen Hardware-Beamformer von Plessey in eine größere Zahl von Beamsignalen gewandelt und in einem Pufferspeicher abgelegt. Von dort erhält der MAP 300 die Beamsignale und berechnet den Rest der Frequenz-Winkel-Spektralanalyse oder Zeitreihenanalysen ausgewählter Beamsignale. Der MAP 300 gibt die Ergebnisse in einen weiteren Pufferspeicher, aus dem sich ein zweiter HP 21 MX die Daten zur Displayausgabe und zum Abspeichern in Hintergrundspeicher holt. Das Gesamtsystem garantiert einen hohen Durchsatz, besitzt jedoch sicherlich nicht die Flexibilität ähnlich aufwendiger Systeme, wie sie weiter unten beschrieben werden.

Ein im Vergleich mit den bisher beschriebenen Vektorprozessoren größerer Rechner ist der REAL TIME III MATP von Datawest. Dieses System wird als peripheres System eines Rechners betrieben, über den der gesamte Datenverkehr

2*

läuft. Der Vektorprozessor enthält bis zu vier separate, einzeln programmierbare Arithmetik-Einheiten mit je einem Punkt- und zwei Strichprozessoren. Das System kann ein Programm mit allen vier Einheiten in einer „master und slave"-Weise ausführen, aber auch mit jeder Einheit ein anderes Programm. Die Gleitkomma-Wortlänge ist entweder 32 oder optional 40 bit. Mit einer Arithmetik-Einheit kann die Fourier-Transformation in 3,1 ms und mit vier Einheiten in ca. 1 ms durchgeführt werden. Eine Installation des REAL TIME III MATP in einem Sonar-Labor ist dem Verfasser unbekannt. Wenn der Host geeignet gewählt wird und einen hinreichend schnellen Transport von Daten in den und aus dem Vektorprozessor ermöglicht, könnte man diesen Vektorrechner in großen Sonar-Feldverarbeitungssystemen verwenden.

Als nächstes werden aufwendigere Vektorprozessoren behandelt, die im Blockgleit-komma-Format rechnen und daher in der Regel schneller als die Gleitkomma-Prozessoren sind. In diesem Format wird ein Vektor von reelen Zahlen durch einen Vektor von unnormalisierten Mantissen und einem Exponenten für alle Zahlen dargestellt. Bekanntlich lassen sich übliche Signalverarbeitungsaufgaben in diesem Format numerisch stabil berechnen, wenn die Mantissenlänge nicht zu klein, z. B. 32 bit, und die erwartete Dynamik der Daten nicht zu groß ist, vergleiche [15].

Die vermutlich neueste Entwicklung dieser Art ist der Advanced Digital Signal Processor (ADSP) von Raytheon, vergleiche [12]. Obwohl dieses System zur Zeit noch nicht kommerziell erhältlich ist, diskutieren wir es wegen seiner interessanten Eigenschaften. Zwei unterschiedliche und parallel arbeitende Busse kennzeichnen die Architektur. Der erste Bus dient zur Übertragung von Einzel- und Doppelwör-tern von Daten und Befehlen. Über ihn gelangen die Daten von den Eingabe-/ Ausgabeprozessoren in den Hauptspeicher, verkehrt der Kontrollprozessor mit den anderen Einheiten, wickelt die sogenannte Signalverarbeitungseinheit Trans-porte von Einzeldaten vom und zum Hauptspeicher ab und erhält die Signalverar-beitungseinheit die Instruktionen ihres Programms, das sich im Hauptspeicher befindet. Der zweite Bus ist für Transporte in Form von Datenströmen zwischen dem Hauptspeicher und der Arithmetikeinheit zuständig. Die Signalverarbeitungs-einheit ist ein Pipeline-Prozessor und vereinigt die Funktionen von Adreßprozessor und Arithmetikprozessoren. Bemerkenswert ist ein Akkumulatorfeld von 4 K Wörtern mit 48 bit Wortlänge (32 bit Mantisse, 16 bit Information über die Daten). In diesem Zusammenhang muß auf die beiden wichtigsten Hardware-unterstützten Neuerungen hingewiesen werden: Im Gegensatz zu anderen Vektorprozessoren werden Daten deklariert in Form (Matrix, Vektor, Skalar), Größe, Bereich (komplex, reell, logisch), Packung im Wort und Blockexponent derart, daß die Signalverarbeitungseinheit direkt in ihrer Arbeit unterstützt wird. Zum anderen enthalten die Akkumulatoren die notwendigen Informationen über die einzelnen Daten. Beispielsweise können damit verschiedenartige Daten miteinander ver-knüpft werden, ohne daß der Programmierer darauf eingehen müßte. Die Programmierung von Signal- und Feldverarbeitungsaufgaben wird durch die Trennung von Programm und Deklaration erheblich erleichtert. Der ADSP ist bis zu zehnmal schneller als der weiter unten erwähnte SPS 81; die Fourier-Transformation wird in 0,8 ms durchgeführt.

Der ADSP wurde kürzlich im Signal Processing Evaluation Laboratory im Naval Ocean System Center, San Diego, California, installiert, vergleiche [17]. Die Aufgabe dieses Labors ist die Bewertung von Sonar-Feldverarbeitungsverfahren und von Hardware-Komponenten wie Vektorprozessoren für solche Verfahren. Mit der großen PDP 11/70 als Host-Computer, die auch von anderen Labors mitbenutzt wird, sind verbunden eine rechnergesteuerte sehr komfortable Sonar-datenaufbereitungsstation, die die Eingabedaten liefert, die auf einer großen Platte zwischengespeichert und über einen virtuellen Unibus in die Vektorprozessoren ADSP mit 256 K 32 bit-Wörtern als Hauptspeicher oder SPS 81 zur Verarbeitung gelangen. Umfangreiche Displayvorrichtungen, Hintergrundspeicher und Verbindungen zu Datennetzen stehen zur Verfügung.

Ein zweiter Vektorprozessor dieser Klasse ist der AR 10 von Stein Associates, der auch für Sonar-Feldverarbeitungsaufgaben eingesetzt werden kann. Die Architektur dieses Prozessors ist gekennzeichnet durch einen neuartigen Bus, über den die Prozessoren kommunizieren und die Daten in und aus dem Hauptspeicher transportiert werden. Der Transfer wird in einem transparenten Background-Mode ohne Programmunterbrechungen und Zeitverlust durchgeführt. Die Verteilung der Aktivitäten auf Prozessoren wird im AR 10 folgendermaßen vorgenommen. Eine sogenannte datenabhängige Sektion übernimmt die Datenein- und -ausgabe, die Kontrollfunktionen und einen Teil der arithmetischen Aufgaben, insbesondere Datenabfragen und Verzweigungen. Zwei dieser Sektionen können parallel arbeitend eingesetzt werden. Die Vektoroperationen werden in einem Pipeline-Prozessor durchgeführt, der ein oder zwei Arithmetikeinheiten besitzen kann. Die Wortlänge beträgt 16 bit oder 32 bit. Der Hauptspeicher ist bis zu 256 K 32 bit-Wörter ausbaubar. Die Fourier-Transformation kann in der schnellsten Version des AR 10 in 1,5 ms berechnet werden.

Der SPS 81 von Signal Processing Systems ist eine ältere Entwicklung und war bis vor einigen Jahren das einzige kommerziell erhältliche System. Er ist ein asynchroner Vektorprozessor, der mit 16 und mit 32 bit Datenwortlänge rechnen kann. Über einen schnellen Bus werden Daten und Programme transportiert. Ein Prozessor mit eigenem Programmspeicher übernimmt die Kontrollfunktion, steuert die Arithmetik-Einheit und versorgt sie mit Daten. In diesem Prozessor können bis zu vier verschiedene Aufgaben unabhängig voneinander bearbeitet werden. Die Arithmetik-Einheit enthält vier Multiplizierer und sechs Addierer. Sie verfügt über ein Akkumulatorfeld von 32 Wörtern und einen schnellen Datenspeicher mit 256 Plätzen sowie einen Tabellenspeicher mit einer Cosinus-Tabelle für die Fourier-Transformation bis zu einer Feldlänge von 64 K. Der Hauptspeicher kann in zwei Blöcken bis zu 256 K 32 bit-Wörtern ausgebaut werden. Die Fourier-Transformation von 16 bit-Wörtern wird in 3 ms ausgeführt. Vom Hersteller werden Software-Hilfsmittel zum Programmieren angeboten, jedoch ist es schwierig, eigene Prozessorprogramme zu schreiben und auszutesten.

Von den kommerziell erhältlichen einfacheren Vektorprozessoren sollen hier nur zwei kurz beschrieben werden. Man kann sie, wie schon gesagt wurde, als Karten für die PDP 11-Serie erhalten. Im Prinzip besitzen diese Systeme einen ähnlichen Aufbau wie die schon besprochenen. In der Regel sind sie weniger flexibel, rechnen in Blockgleitkomma mit 24 bit Mantisse, ist ihr Datenspeicher nicht so weit ausbaubar und werden sie über den Host-Computer mit Daten versorgt.

Der MSP-3A von Computer Design and Application ist als ein Billigsystem konstruiert, das speziell die Schmetterlinge in FFT-Algorithmen schnell berechnen kann, und wird auf zwei Karten untergebracht. Der Datenspeicher hat einen Umfang von nur 4 K. Die Programme und die Tabellen sind in PROMs untergebracht. Die Fourier-Transformation erfordert 12,9 ms. Neue Programme für den Prozessor herzustellen, erfordert neue PROMs.

Das Naval Research Laboratory in Washington, D.C., benutzt in seinem auch auf See einsetzbaren und für unterschiedliche Aufgaben konzipierten Sonarfeldverarbeitungssystem mehrere MSP-3A-Prozessoren, vergleiche [10]. Das System wird von einer PDP 11/34 kontrolliert und besitzt neben dem Hauptbus einen Hilfsbus. Über einen größeren Speicher, der Busfenster heißt, können Daten von einem zum anderen Bus gelangen. Der Vorteil der Doppelbusstruktur liegt darin, daß ungefähr doppelt so viel Speicherplatz als mit einem Bus gehandhabt und durch eine geschickte Verteilung der Transfers auf beide Busse die Bandbreite eines Busses nicht so schnell erreicht werden kann. Die Philosophie war nun, die Eingaben gepuffert über den Hilfsbus in die an den Hilfsbus angeschlossenen kleinen Vektorprozessoren zu bringen, einen ersten Teil der Analyse durchzuführen, in einem Speicher am Hilfsbus zwischenzuspeichern, den zweiten Teil mit an den Hauptbus angeschlossenen Vektorprozessoren zu bewältigen und schließlich die Ergebnisse über Displays und in Hintergrundspeicher auszugeben, die ebenfalls an den Hauptbus gekoppelt sind. In einer speziellen Konfiguration sollte in Realzeit mit vollem Durchsatz eine Frequenz-Winkel-Spektralanalyse durchgeführt werden, wobei es auf eine gute räumliche Auflösung ankam. Die Verarbeitung wurde in Stücken von 1024 Punkten aus jedem Kanal durchgeführt. Zwei programmierbare Eingabeprozessoren mit eigenem Speicher führten die doppelte Pufferung aus und gaben die Blöcke aus jedem Kanal nacheinander über den Hilfsbus in einen MSP, der alle Fourier-Transformationen vom Zeit- in den Frequenzbereich ausführt. Die aufwendigere Orts-Winkeltransformation wurde anschließend mit Hilfe von 2 an den Hauptbus gekoppelten MPS bewältigt.

Einen aufwendigen Vektorprozessor der unteren Preisklasse, der als ein 4-Kartensatz für die PDP 11-Serie oder mit eigenem Gehäuse zu haben ist, stellt der AP-400 von Analogic dar. Er könnte gut für verteiltes Rechnen in einem Feldverarbeitungssystem für verschiedenste Zwecke verwendet werden. Dies ist im Gegensatz zum MSP auch dann richtig, wenn für eine hohe Frequenzauflösung im ersten Schritt einer Frequenz-Winkel-Spektralanalyse große Blöcke, z. B. der Länge 16 K, Fourier-transformiert werden müßten. Der AP-400 ist wie die größeren Vektorprozessoren frei programmierbar und besitzt einen Programmspeicher von 2 K Wörtern der Länge 22 bit. Der Datenspeicher hat eine Kapazität von maximal 64 K Wörtern. Die Daten können auch direkt von außen in den Datenspeicher gebracht werden. Interessant ist, daß mit drei Datenformaten gerechnet werden kann: Blockgleitkomma mit 24 bit oder 48 bit Mantisse und 16 bit Exponent und echtes Gleitkomma mit 24 bit Mantisse. Die Fourier-Transformation wird im Blockgleitkommaformat mit 24 bit Mantisse in 7,4 ms ausgeführt.

Beachtenswert ist der Umfang der bereitgestellten Software in bezug auf die Bibliothek und die Programmierungshilfen.

5. Anmerkungen

Wie es weiter oben schon angeklungen ist, kann man beim Programmieren von Vektorprozessoren mit Ausnahme des ADSP keine Daten deklarieren. Der Programmierer hat die Vektoren absolut zu adressieren und kann dann mit symbolischen Namen der Anfangsadressen in Fortranaufrufen operieren. Sein eigentliches Programm besteht dann aus einer Folge von Calls, die die verschiedenen Aktivitäten des Vektorprozessors, wie z. B. eine Fourier-Transformation, vom Host-Computer aus initialisieren. Einige Hersteller liefern Programme, mit denen man Folgen solcher Aufrufe zu einem Unterprogramm verketten kann, das nur eine Initialisierung durch den Host-Computer verlangt und damit viel schneller im Vektorprozessor abläuft als die nicht verkettete Folge. Mit der Möglichkeit der Datendeklarierung und der entsprechenden Hardwareunterstützung beim ADSP können effektive Realisierungen von höheren Signalverarbeitungssprachen für solche Rechner hergestellt werden.

Seit einiger Zeit gibt es Definitionen höherer Signalverarbeitungssprachen und Ansätze von Realisierungen, z. B. SIPROL, [9]. Am weitesten ist man mit der Sprache SPL/I gekommen, vergleiche [23], [19]. Diese Sprache ist zur Produktion von Signalverarbeitungsprogrammen für das U.S.-Militär entworfen worden. Seit 1976 werden Programme in SPL/I für den ASP Vektorprozessor der Navy (IBM) geschrieben, für den entsprechende Compiler und Betriebssysteme für Realzeitbetrieb, z. B. in einer PDP 11-Umgebung existieren. Realisierungen von SPL/I für andere in dieser Arbeit aufgeführte Vektorprozessoren sind dem Verfasser nicht bekannt.

Literatur

[1] Allen, J.: Computer architecture for signal processing. Proc. IEEE **63**, 624 – 633 (1975).

[2] Böhme, J. F.: Array-processing in semi-homogeneous random fields. Proc. Septième colloque sur le traitement du signal es ses applications, Nice, 1979, no. 104.

[3] Böhme, J. F.: Detektion mit Rechnern. Habilitationsschrift, Universität Bonn, 1977.

[4] Böhme, J. F.: Fast signal detection by process computers. In: Parallel Computers – Parallel Mathematics, (Feilmeier, M., ed.), pp. 179 – 182. Amsterdam: North-Holland 1977.

[5] Brandenburg, W.: Spectral analysis using prediction methods. Proc. IEEE Int. Conf. Acoustics, Speech and Signal Processing, Washington, 1979, pp. 155 – 158.

[6] Brillinger, D. R.: Time Series: Data Analysis and Theory. New York: Holt, Rinehart and Winston 1975.

[7] Capon, J.: High resolution frequency-wavenumber spectrum analysis. Proc. IEEE **57**, 1408 – 1418 (1969).

[8] Dudgeon, D. E.: Fundamentals of digital array-processing. Proc. IEEE **65**, 898 – 904 (1977).

[9] Gethöffer, H.: A concept of hardware for digital signal processing. Wie [4], pp. 275 – 279.

[10] Griffin, J. M.: A versatile signal processing system for producing the angular and frequency distribution of acoustic energy in real time. Proc. Conference on Real-Time, General-Purpose, High-Speed Signal-Processing Systems for Underwater Research, SACLANTCEN, La Spezia, 1979, no. 2.

[11] Händler, W.: Aspects of parallelism in computer architecture. Wie [4], pp. 1 – 8.

[12] Janssen, R. A., et al.: Multi-signal processing software on the Raytheon Advanced Digital Signal Processor. Proc. IEEE/AIAA 3rd Digital Avionics System Conference, Fort Worth, Texas, 1979.

[13] Makhoul, J.: Lattice methods in spectral estimation. Proc. RADC Spectrum Estimation Workshop, 1978, pp. 159 – 173.
[14] McDonough, R. N.: Maximum-entropy spatial processing of array data. Geophysics **39**, 843 – 851 (1974).
[15] Oppenheim, A. V., Schafer, R. W.: Digital Signal Processing. Englewood Cliffs, N. J.: Prentice-Hall 1975.
[16] Pridham, R. G., Mucci, R. A.: Digital interpolation beamforming for low-pass and bandpass signals. Proc. IEEE **67**, 904 – 919 (1979).
[17] Pennoyer, B.: NOSC signal evaluation laboratory. Wie [10], no. 4.
[18] Pyett, J. S.: The application of high-speed processors to propagation experiments. Wie [10], no. 6.
[19] Rigsbee, P. A.: A modular signal processing software development system. Wie [10], no. 24.
[20] Schüßler, H. W.: Digitale Systeme zur Signalverarbeitung. Berlin-Heidelberg-New York: Springer 1973.
[21] Seynaeve, R., et al.: SACLANTCEN real-time signal processing system. Wie [10], no. 3.
[22] Wagner, W.: Sonar beamforming with an array processor. Wie [10], no. 28.
[23] Weinztein, S.: Signal processing language and operating system. Wie [10], no. 23.
[24] Ziegenbein, J.: Spectral analysis using the Karhunen-Loeve transform. Wie [5], pp. 182 – 185.

Prof. Dr. J. F. Böhme
FGAN-Forschungsinstitut für
Hochfrequenzphysik
D-5307 Wachtberg-Werthhoven
Bundesrepublik Deutschland

Neue Adresse:
Lehrstuhl für Signaltheorie
Ruhr-Universität
D-4630 Bochum 1
Bundesrepublik Deutschland

Computing, Suppl. 3, 25–39 (1981)

Parallelstruktur des Simulators GPSS-FORTRAN — Entwurf für ein angepaßtes Multiprozessorsystem

K. U. Hellmold und **B. Schmidt**, Erlangen

Zusammenfassung — Abstract

Parallelstruktur des Simulators GPSS-FORTRAN — Entwurf für ein angepaßtes Multiprozessorsystem. Zeitdiskrete Systeme zeichnen sich durch einen hohen Grad an Parallelität aus. Simulationsprogramme, die bei der Modellbildung für zeitdiskrete Systeme eingesetzt werden, erhalten die Parallelität, da bei der Simulation die einzelnen Abläufe des Systems direkt nachgespielt werden.

Um die in Simulationsprogrammen für zeitdiskrete Systeme enthaltene Parallelität auszunutzen, wird eine Rechnerstruktur mit Mikroprozessoren eingesetzt, die sich dem Aufgabenbereich anpaßt.

Zunächst wird die Parallelstruktur beschrieben, die Simulationsprogrammen zugrunde liegt. Hieraus werden Forderungen abgeleitet, die sich auf die Rechnerarchitektur und das Softwaresystem des Simulators beziehen. Es folgt eine ausführliche Beschreibung des Konstitutionskonzepts für das Rechensystem, das diese Forderungen zu erfüllen vermag.

The Parallel Structure of the Simulator GPSS-FORTRAN: A Design for a Matching Microprocessor System. Discrete-time systems are characterized by a high degree of parallelism. Simulation programs that are used to model such systems preserve the parallelism, since they mimic the system's behaviour directly.

In this paper we propose a computer architecture using micro-processors that takes advantage of the parallelism in simulation programs.

First, we describe the parallel structure basic to simulation programs, from which we derive the requirements of a simulator's machine architecture and software system. There we describe in detail the design of a computer capable of meeting those requirements.

1. Die Parallelstruktur eines Rechensystems zur Simulation zeitdiskreter Systeme mit GPSS-FORTRAN

Es soll ein Rechensystem mit Hilfe von Mikroprozessoren entwickelt werden, das sich in bezug auf die parallele Bearbeitung dem Softwaresystem anpaßt. Das bedeutet, daß die Parallelstruktur, die dem Softwaresystem zugrunde liegt, die Architektur des Rechensystems bestimmt.

Das Softwaresystem, das auf der Rechenanlage ablaufen soll, ist das Simulations-paket GPSS-FORTRAN, das sich zur Simulation zeitdiskreter Systeme eignet [1], [2]. Es soll zunächst die dem Simulationspaket GPSS-FORTRAN zugrunde liegende Parallelstruktur aufgedeckt werden. Anschließend wird gezeigt, wie diese Parallelstruktur auf das Rechensystem übertragen werden kann.

1.1. Parallele Aktivitäten in zeitdiskreten Systemen

Um die Parallelstruktur des Softwarepaketes GPSS-FORTRAN beschreiben zu können, ist es zunächst ratsam, die parallelen Aktivitäten zu beschreiben, die in zeitdiskreten Systemen auftreten und die im Simulationsmodell dargestellt werden sollen.

Ein zeitdiskretes System besteht in der Regel aus stationären Systemkomponenten, den Stationen und mobilen Systemkomponenten, den Aufträgen. Die Aufträge wandern zwischen den Stationen hin und her, bauen vor den Stationen Warteschlangen auf, belegen oder verlassen die Stationen.

Beispiel:

* Ein Einkaufszentrum kann als zeitdiskretes System aufgefaßt werden. Die Stationen sind hierbei die Verkaufsstände und Kassen, während die Kunden mit ihren Bedienwünschen als Aufträge gelten.

Abb. 1 zeigt ein Einkaufszentrum mit verschiedenen Verkaufsständen für Obst, Gemüse, Milchprodukte usw. Jeder Kunde verfügt weiterhin über eine Laufliste, die seine Bedienwünsche enthält. Diese Laufliste legt die Reihenfolge fest, in der der Kunde die Verkaufsstände aufsuchen muß und bestimmt, was er dort zu tun hat.

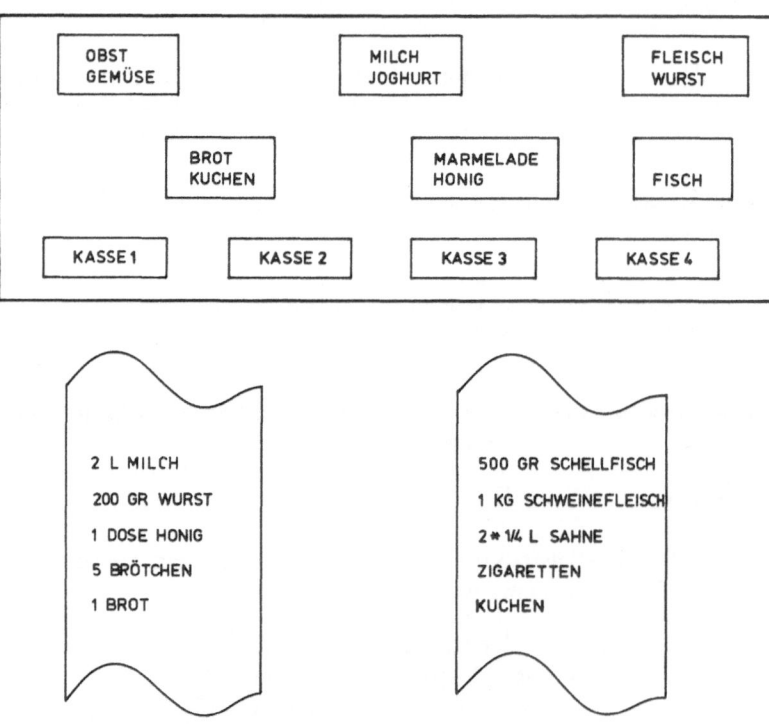

Abb. 1. Das Einkaufszentrum als zeitdiskretes System

Da sich in der Regel in einem Einkaufszentrum zur gleichen Zeit mehrere Kunden zugleich aufhalten, wird ein derartiges System einen hohen Grad paralleler Aktivitäten aufweisen. An jeder Station kann zugleich bedient werden.

Das Strukturschema, das allen Vertretern zeitdiskreter Systeme zugrunde liegt und das durch Abb. 1 veranschaulicht werden sollte, läßt sich in einer Form darstellen, die Abb. 2 beschreibt. Die Stationen hängen hierbei zwischen zwei Schienen. Am Ende der Schienen liegt der Verteiler.

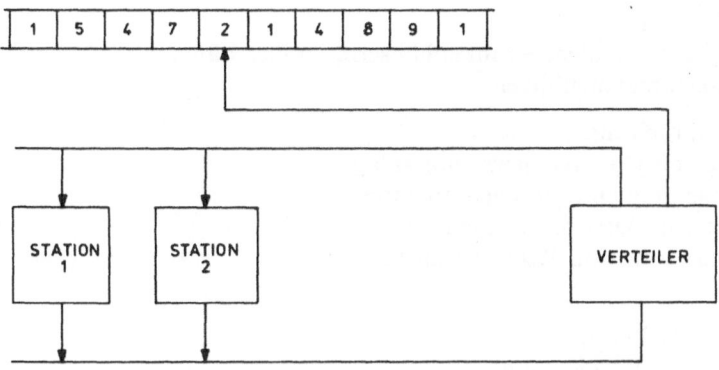

Abb. 2. Das Strukturschema für zeitdiskrete Systeme

Ein Auftrag beginnt seine Lebensgeschichte im System, indem er sich zum Verteiler begibt, der aus der zum Auftrag gehörigen Laufliste die Stationsnummer heraussieht und den Auftrag über die obere Schiene zu der entsprechenden Station schickt.

Alle Aktivitäten, die der Auftrag zu erledigen hat, werden in der Station vorgenommen. Ist der Auftrag fertig bearbeitet, wird er die Station verlassen und sich über die untere Schiene zurück zum Verteiler begeben, der aus der Laufliste wieder eine Stationsnummer bestimmt und den Auftrag erneut auf die Rundreise schickt.

1.2. Die Simulation zeitdiskreter Systeme

Bei der Planung, Organisation und Verwaltung komplexer Systeme ist es erforderlich, das Systemverhalten zu kennen und vorherzusagen. Hierbei hat sich die Modellbildung mit Hilfe der Simulation seit langem bewährt.

Eine Übersicht soll den breiten Einsatzbereich deutlich machen, der die Simulation zeitdiskreter Systeme auszeichnet.

* Verkehrsplanung
  Planung von Bahnhöfen, Hafenanlagen, Flugplätzen, Parkplätzen
  Entwurf von Stadtverkehrssystemen
  Erstellung von Fahrplänen
  Verkehrsampelregelung

* Unternehmensplanung
  Produktionsplanung, Investitionsplanung
  Zeit- und Kostenplanung von Projekten
  Rentabilitätsprüfungen
  Fertigungsablauf, Lagerhaltung
  Dimensionierung einer Werkstatt für die Realisierung bestimmter Auftragsprofile

* Verwaltung
  Wirtschaftsplanung
  Planung von Schulen, Krankenhäusern, Universitäten
  Kapazitätsuntersuchungen

* Datenverarbeitung
  Planung von Datenverarbeitungsanlagen
  Ablaufplanung eines Rechenzentrums
  Entwurf von Betriebssystemen
  Konfigurierung von Rechenanlagen

* Technik
  Geräteentwicklung
  Entwurf von Regelsystemen
  Nachrichtenübertragung

Der breite Einsatzbereich und die zunehmende Bedeutung der Simulation rechtfertigen es, für dieses Aufgabengebiet ein eigenes Rechensystem zu entwerfen. Das gilt umso mehr, als hierbei Entwurfsverfahren zum Einsatz kommen, die allgemein einsetzbar sind.

1.3. Das Konstruktionskonzept des Simulators

Die Simulationstechnik sah bisher ihre Hauptaufgabe in dem Ziel, die in einem zeitdiskreten System parallel ablaufenden Aktivitäten zu sequentialisieren, um sie auf einer Rechenanlage bearbeiten zu können. Alle Softwaresysteme, die zur Simulation zeitdiskreter Systeme angeboten werden, enthalten daher Mechanismen, die es ermöglichen, eigentlich parallele Aktivitäten hintereinander auszuführen.

Die moderne Rechnertechnologie ermöglicht es, den Schritt zur Sequentialisierung wieder rückgängig zu machen und die ursprünglich parallelen Aktivitäten auch parallel auf einem Rechensystem ablaufen zu lassen.

Das Konstruktionsprinzip für ein derartiges Rechensystem entnimmt man Abb. 2. Es bietet sich an, jede Station durch einen eigenen Prozessor zu repräsentieren, der die Bearbeitung des Auftrags übernimmt. Ein Auftrag wird hierbei durch einen Datensatz repräsentiert, der sich entsprechend seiner Laufliste über die Schienen durch das Rechensystem bewegt.

Damit wird in der Simulationstechnik ein völlig neuer Weg beschritten. Da die einzelnen Komponenten, die in zeitdiskreten Systemen vorkommen, in dem hier beschriebenen Rechensystem eine unmittelbare und direkte Entsprechung haben, bewegt sich die Simulation zeitdiskreter Systeme einen deutlichen Schritt in Richtung Analogrechenanlagen.

Vorteile des Konstruktionsprinzips:

* Modularität
  Alle Aktivitäten, die eine Station betreffen, sind zu einer Einheit zusammengefaßt.

* Rekonfigurierbarkeit
  Soll die Anzahl der Stationen erhöht werden, wird eine neue Station zwischen die Schienen gesteckt. Lediglich der Verteiler muß von der Existenz einer neuen Nummer in der Laufliste und von der Anwesenheit einer neuen Station in Kenntnis gesetzt werden. Alle übrigen Stationen bleiben von diesem Vorgang unberührt.

* Strukturierbarkeit
  Gelegentlich erweist es sich als erforderlich, eine Station weiter zu untergliedern und in Teilstationen aufzulösen. Das Konstruktionsprinzip nach Abb. 2 bietet sich für eine derartige Modifikation an, indem man die Schienen, die die Teilstationen verbinden, an den Ein- bzw. Ausgang der ursprünglichen Station ankoppelt (siehe Abb. 3).

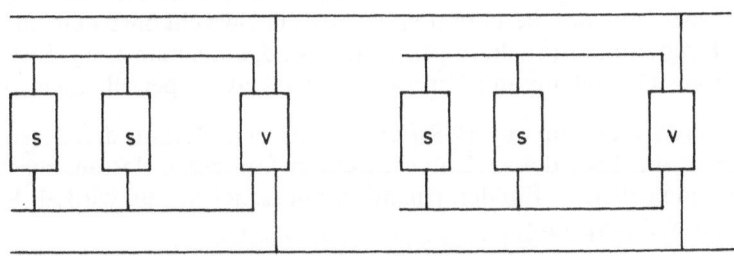

Abb. 3. Erweiterung des Strukturschemas

Die Einfachheit und die Übersichtlichkeit des Konstruktionsprinzips sind die Gewähr für eine wirkungsvolle Realisierung.

1.4. Das Softwarepaket GPSS-FORTRAN

GPSS-FORTRAN ist ein Softwarepaket, das zu den höheren Simulationssprachen [3] zählt. GPSS-FORTRAN eignet sich besonders für ein Rechensystem, das nach Abb. 2 aufgebaut ist, da es Sprachkonstrukte besitzt, die sich unmittelbar auf eine Struktur nach Abb. 2 übertragen lassen.

GPSS-FORTRAN kennt im wesentlichen vier Stationstypen, die sich über die zulässigen Operationen definieren lassen.

a) Bedienstationen (Facilities).
Bedienstationen können von einem Auftrag für einen bestimmten Zeitabschnitt belegt und anschließend wieder freigegeben werden. Ist die Bedienstation belegt,

so bauen neu ankommende Aufträge vor der Bedienstation eine Warteschlange auf. Zulässige Operationen sind Belegen, Bearbeiten und Freigeben.

b) Speicher (Storages).
Speicher sind durch ihre Kapazität und den aktuellen Bestand charakterisiert. Ein Auftrag, der auf einen Speicher läuft, kann nach einer vorgebbaren Strategie eine bestimmte Anzahl von Speicherplätzen belegen. In ähnlicher Weise können durch einen Auftrag Speicherplätze freigegeben werden. Alle Aufträge, deren Speicheranforderungen zum aktuellen Zeitpunkt nicht erfüllt werden können, bauen vor dem Speicher eine Warteschlange auf. Zulässige Operationen sind Belegen und Freigeben von Speicherplätzen.

c) Schranken (Gates).
Schranken dienen der Koordination von Aufträgen. Vor einer Schranke werden alle Aufträge so lange aufgehalten, bis sich der Systemzustand in einer bestimmten, vorgebbaren Weise geändert hat. Zulässige Operationen sind: Prüfen des Systemzustandes, Schließen der Schranke und Öffnen der Schranke.

d) Quellen (Sources) und Senken (Sinks).
Die Quellen und Senken übernehmen das Erzeugen bzw. das Vernichten der Aufträge.

Die Sprachkonstrukte von GPSS-FORTRAN liegen derzeit als FORTRAN-Routinen vor. Von der Beschränkung, daß die Sprachkonstrukte in einer bestimmten Programmiersprache implementiert sind, kann man sich jedoch befreien, wenn man zur Darstellung mit Hilfe abstrakter Datentypen übergeht [4].

Die Datenstrukturen, die in GPSS-FORTRAN eine Station definieren, und die Algorithmen, die über diesen Datenstrukturen operieren, lassen sich zu einem Modul zusammenfassen. Ein derartig abgeschlossener Modul wird als Station im Sinn von Abb. 2 aufgefaßt.

2. Das Multiprozessorsystem

2.1. Die Rechnerkonfiguration

Im folgenden wird ein Rechnerkonzept vorgestellt, das sich durch seine Modularität und Einfachheit auszeichnet und insbesondere zur Lösung der eingangs erwähnten Problemkreise eingesetzt werden kann. Abb. 4 zeigt die wesentlichen Systemkomponenten und deutet an, wie sie zusammengeschaltet sind.

Die zentralen Blöcke STATion, SCHEDuler und SOURce repräsentieren die einzelnen Mikroprozessormodule. Sie kommunizieren miteinander über ihre Ein/Ausgabepuffer IN und OUT, die jeweils durch einen gemeinsamen Datenbus verbunden sind. Man erkennt, daß eine beliebige Anzahl innerer Module der Art STAT von zwei äußeren mit exponierter Funktion eingerahmt werden.

Dieses Konzept basiert auf dem zentralen Gedanken einer losen Koppelung von Modulen, die ihre Aktivitäten durch gezielte Bearbeitung und Weiterleitung von Aufträgen koordinieren.

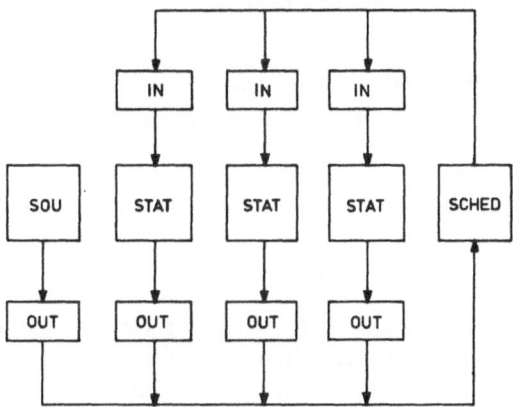

Abb. 4. Rechnerkonfiguration

Die Module gliedern sich in:

a) Stationen: Alle Stationen arbeiten an der dem System übertragenen Aufgabe gleichzeitig. Jede einzelne Station nimmt die ihr zugestellten Aufträge aus dem Eingangspuffer IN entgegen. Sie bearbeitet diese Aufträge entsprechend der ihr zugewiesenen Spezialaufgabe und legt sie abschließend zur Abholung in dem Ausgangspuffer OUT ab.

b) Source: Die Erzeugung der Aufträge übernimmt der Modul Source. Er benötigt zur Erfüllung seiner Aufgabe den Ausgangspuffer OUT, aus dem der Scheduler die neuen Aufträge abholt.

c) Scheduler: Der Scheduler greift die in den Ausgangspuffern lagernden Aufträge in einer vorgeschriebenen Reihenfolge auf und legt sie in den Eingabepuffern derjenigen Stationen ab, die sie weiterbearbeiten sollen.

Der Ausdruck lose Koppelung verdeutlicht die Tatsache, daß die Stationen selbständig und weitestgehend unabhängig voneinander ihre Aufgaben erfüllen. Der Verzicht auf einen allen Stationen gemeinsamen Speicher ermöglicht die unkomplizierte Rechnerstruktur. Die dezentral gehaltenen Daten können dennoch unter den Stationen durch ein Botschaftsystem zugespielt werden. Als Konsequenz muß eine zusätzliche Belastung insbesondere des Schedulers in Kauf genommen werden.

Der Begriff Auftrag steht hier stellvertretend für einen Datensatz, der genau die Informationen enthält, die den Auftrag eindeutig kennzeichnen und seine typischen Eigenschaften beschreiben. Dieser Datensatz wird in der Source generiert und als Auftrag zunächst im zugehörigen Ausgabepuffer abgelegt. Mit der Abholung durch den Scheduler beginnt seine Teilnahme am Ablaufgeschehen. Der erste Transfer endet, wenn seine Daten im Eingangspuffer der Zielstation eingeschrieben sind. Die Station übernimmt die Auftragsdaten, verarbeitet sie und legt sie in ihrem Ausgangspuffer ab, sobald der Auftrag die Station verlassen kann. Wieder greift ihn der Scheduler auf und schickt ihn auf diese Art und Weise so lange von Station zu Station, bis der Auftrag vollständig bearbeitet wurde. Dann wird der zugehörige Datensatz gelöscht.

Dieser Zyklus Station-Scheduler wird von allen existierenden Aufträgen wiederholt durchlaufen, so daß sich in hohem Maße parallele Aktivitäten in den Stationen entfalten können. Wichtig ist, daß sich mehrere Aufträge gleichzeitig in einer Station aufhalten können. Sie müssen sich allerdings in Warteschlangen einreihen und sich gedulden, bis die vor ihnen liegenden Aufträge abgefertigt sind.

2.2. Die Station

Der Prozessor ist das zentrale aktive Element einer Station. Wie in Abb. 5 angedeutet, hat er über den Bus direkten Zugriff zu seinen Speicherblöcken. Ihre Funktion erklärt sich, wenn man den Weg eines Auftrages in der Station verfolgt.

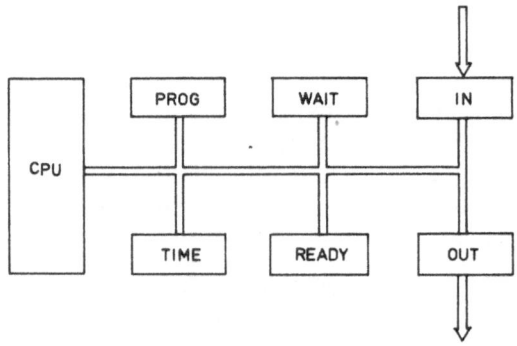

Abb. 5. Aufbau der Station

Als Ausgangssituation wählen wir den Moment, an dem der Scheduler den Auftrag in dem Eingangspuffer IN abgelegt hat. Gleichzeitig wird der Station signalisiert, daß der Auftrag bearbeitet werden möchte. Die Station übernimmt daraufhin die Auftragsdaten in den Speicherbereich WAIT, der alle Aufträge aufnimmt, die noch nicht bearbeitet werden konnten. Sie bilden eine Warteschlange, in die auch der neue eingereiht wird. Ein Auswahlverfahren – die Policy – ermittelt unter ihnen den jeweils dringlichsten Auftrag, der als nächstes bearbeitet wird.

Ist der beobachtete Auftrag an der Reihe, wertet die CPU seine Daten programmgemäß aus und ermittelt die neuen Werte, die den Zustand nach der Bearbeitung kennzeichnen. Im allgemeinen Fall wird dadurch auch die Station selbst Zustandsänderungen registrieren müssen.

Nach welchen Kriterien die Bearbeitung erfolgt, hängt ausschließlich von der Aufgabe ab, die der Station übertragen wurde. Die Tätigkeiten sind im zugehörigen Programm formuliert und schließen die Speicher und Warteschlangenverwaltung mit ein. Der Code des Programms ist im Hauptspeicher PROG abgelegt.

Zum Abschluß der Bearbeitung legt das Programm fest, mit welcher Verzögerung der Auftrag diese Station verlassen soll. Häufig wird die Reihenfolge durch eine

Zeitskala definiert, so daß sich der gesuchte Zeitpunkt aus den Angaben Ankunftszeit + Wartezeit + Verzögerungszeit ermitteln läßt. Schließlich wird der Auftrag dem Speicherbereich READY zugeordnet, denn er wartet jetzt nur noch darauf, die Station verlassen zu können. Befinden sich dort bereits mehrere Aufträge, bilden sie wiederum eine Warteschlange. In dem Ausgangspuffer OUT müssen jeweils die Daten desjenigen Auftrages eingetragen sein, der als nächstes vom Scheduler abgeholt werden muß. Der Zeitpunkt, zu dem dieser Transfer erfolgen soll, wird in das Register TIME geladen, das organisatorisch zum Ausgangspuffer gehört.

Die Bereitstellung des Wartebereiches READY verschafft der Station die wesentliche Freiheit, Aufträge im voraus zu bearbeiten, selbst wenn die anderen Stationen noch nicht in der Lage sind, ihre Auftragsflut zu bewältigen. Dadurch gewinnen die Stationen das nötige Maß an Unabhängigkeit.

Für die Erstellung eines Simulationsmodells lassen sich die Aufgaben einer Station aus den bewährten Sprachelementen, die GPSS-FORTRAN bietet, kombinieren. Eine Facility (Bedienstation) in GPSS-FORTRAN läßt sich beispielsweise durch eine Station nachbilden, wenn eine Warteschlangenverwaltung existiert und die Operationen Belegen der Facility – Bedienen des Auftrages – Freigeben der Facility ausgeführt werden können. Dies entspricht der Unterprogrammfolge POLICY – SEIZE – WORK – CLEAR in GPSS-FORTRAN, die in angepaßter Form auch der Programmspeicher der Station enthält. Die Bedienzeiten müssen gegebenenfalls – wie in GPSS-FORTRAN – durch einen Zufallsgenerator ermittelt werden.

2.3. Die Source

Als Schnittstelle zur Außenwelt des Systems sorgt der Modul Source (Abb. 6) dafür, daß laufend neue Aufträge zur Auslastung der Stationen in das Ablaufgeschehen eingebracht werden. Das Auftragsprofil und die Auftragsfolge sind vom Benutzer in beliebiger Form vorzugeben, um das System den unterschiedlichsten Belastungen aussetzen zu können.

Sämtliche Parameter, die einen Auftrag auszeichnen, z. B. die Kennzahl, die Dringlichkeit, die Größe, Vorschriften hinsichtlich seiner Bearbeitung oder andere Einflußgrößen ermittelt das Programm, dessen Code im Speichersegment PROG

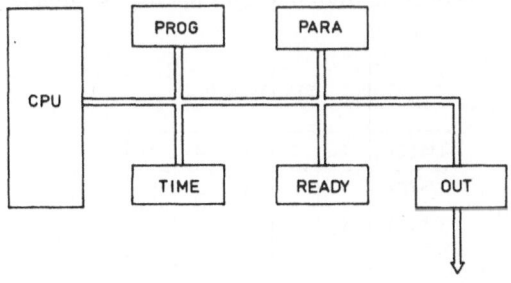

Abb. 6. Aufbau der Source

steht. Dieses Programm wertet dafür die relevanten Benutzerangaben aus, die beim Starten des Systemlaufes in den Speicherbereich PARA eingeschrieben wurden.

Die Parameterwerte werden zu einem einheitlichen Datensatz — dem Auftrag — zusammengestellt und im Speicherbereich READY zur Verfügung gehalten. Die Auftragsfolge definiert, in welchem zeitlichen Abstand die vorbereiteten Aufträge die Source verlassen sollen. Sobald der Ausgabepuffer OUT frei geworden ist, lädt das Programm den nächsten Datensatz aus dem READY-Bereich nach und schreibt die zugehörige Abholzeit ins Register TIME.

2.4. Der Scheduler

In den Ausgangspuffern aller Module warten die abgefertigten Aufträge auf den Transfer zur nächsten Station durch den Scheduler (Abb. 7).

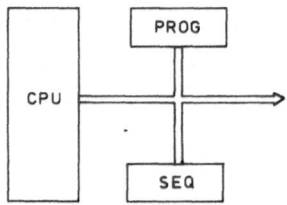

Abb. 7. Der Scheduler

Damit die zeitlich korrekte Verteilung gewährleistet ist, überprüft der Scheduler zunächst sämtliche TIME-Registerinhalte und merkt sich das Register mit dem niedrigsten Zeitwert. Im zugehörigen Ausgabepuffer steht folglich derjenige Auftrag, der weitergeleitet werden muß.

Zur Bestimmung der Zielstation bietet es sich an, dem Scheduler zu Beginn des Systemlaufes eine vom Benutzer erstellte Liste in den Speicher SEQ zu übergeben, die die Stationsfolge (Sequenz) für eine zweckmäßige Bearbeitung der Aufträge enthält.

Für einfachste Fälle, in denen die Stationenfolge starr und eindeutig vorgegeben ist, mögen diese Angaben genügen. Weitaus flexibler läßt sich der Ablauf hingegen gestalten, wenn der Scheduler aus den Auftragsdaten entnehmen kann, wie weit der Auftrag die Liste bereits durchlaufen hat. Das nächste Listenelement verweist dann

	STATIONENFOLGE					
LISTE1	2	3	1	2	1	L
LISTE2	1	3	2	3	L	
LISTE3	1	2	3	L		

Abb. 8. Die Sequenzen

auf die Station, bei der die Bearbeitung fortgeführt werden soll. Am Ende der Liste befindet sich ein Hinweis zum Löschen der Auftragsdaten.

Der Benutzer hat die Freiheit, gleichzeitig mehrere dieser Lauflisten als Alternative anzubieten (Abb. 8). Aus den Auftragsdaten muß dann eindeutig die Entscheidung zugunsten einer der Stationsfolgen möglich sein. Für komplexere Fälle sind bedingte Wiederholungen und Sprünge im Ablauf zugelassen.

Sind die Quell- und Zielstationen des Transfers nach dem geschilderten Verfahren bestimmt, kann der Scheduler die weiteren Auftragsdaten direkt zwischen dem betroffenen Aus- und Eingangspuffer überspielen. Wichtig ist, daß alle Stationen inzwischen ungehindert weiterarbeiten können. Lediglich die Quellstation muß ihren Ausgangspuffer mit dem nächsten Auftrag auffüllen und die Zielstation den Eingangspuffer leeren. Ist dies geschehen, kann der nächste Transfer mit den Suchvorgängen eingeleitet werden.

Die Puffer IN und OUT (inklusive Register TIME) sind die einzigen Speicher, die von zwei Prozessoren in Anspruch genommen werden. Der Scheduler und die jeweilige Station oder die Source greifen abwechselnd auf diese Speicher nur lesend oder nur schreibend zu. Dies kommt einer unkomplizierten Ein-/Ausgabekopplung zugute. Die Puffergröße ist dem Umfang der Auftragsdaten anzupassen.

Die Datenmenge darf ihrerseits ein vernünftiges Maß nicht überschreiten, weil sonst der gemeinsame Datenbus bereits bei mittleren Transferaufkommen zum Engpaß werden kann.

In GPSS-FORTRAN werden die Funktionen des Schedulers entsprechend vom Verteiler und der Ablaufkontrolle (ACTIVI, ACTIVII) übernommen.

2.5. Botschaften

Reale Systeme lassen sich, wie die eingangs erwähnten Beispiele zeigen, in vielen Fällen direkt auf die erläuterte Rechnerstruktur abbilden. Voraussetzung ist, daß ihre Elemente unabhängig voneinander parallele Arbeit leisten.

Andererseits sind aber auch genügend Fälle denkbar, in denen ein Element A seine Arbeitsweise ändert, wenn bei Element B ein spezielles Ereignis, z. B. Überlastung oder Leerlauf, eingetreten ist.

Derartige Abhängigkeiten verlangen den Austausch von Informationen, die als Botschaften — ähnlich wie die Aufträge — durch den Scheduler von Station A zu Station B transferiert werden. Botschaften müssen mit Vorrang behandelt werden und zeitlos ablaufen, denn sie dürfen den Systemzustand nicht verändern. Zur Vereinfachung seien nur gezielte Botschaften, A fragt B und B antwortet A, erlaubt, so daß der Scheduler lediglich den Transfer durchführen muß. Die Programme der Stationen A und B müssen natürlich für das Senden und Empfangen von Botschaften eingerichtet sein.

Man könnte sich auch vorstellen, daß eine Botschaft an mehrere Stationen gleichzeitig gesendet werden soll. Der Scheduler hätte in diesem Falle lediglich dafür zu sorgen, daß alle Eingangspuffer der Empfangsstationen die Daten parallel einlesen.

3*

Grundsätzlich lassen sich mit dieser Methode alle möglichen Abhängigkeiten berücksichtigen, allerdings für den Preis eines spürbaren Aufwandes, so daß mit Bedacht davon Gebrauch gemacht werden sollte. Der Vorteil, den der Verzicht auf den gemeinsamen Speicher einbrachte, wird mit zunehmendem Botschaftenverkehr aufgezehrt. Es wäre schließlich zu prüfen, ob dann andere Rechnerkonzepte geeigneter erscheinen.

2.6. Verwaltungsaufgaben

Das Ablaufgeschehen in den Stationen ist durch stete Zustandsänderungen an den Stationen und den Aufträgen gekennzeichnet. Einerseits interessieren natürlich die Ergebnisse, die die Aufträge durch ihre oftmalige Bearbeitung vor ihrer Vernichtung erbringen. Andererseits ist es besonders aufschlußreich, die Entwicklung an den Stationen oder die Veränderungen an den Aufträgen zu beobachten.

In der Praxis bedeutet dies, die Daten zu sammeln und die Mittelwerte zu berechnen. Dazu sind aber weitere Speicherplätze zur Verfügung zu stellen, die in Tabellenform momentane Zustände oder davon abhängige Größen notieren. Diese Listen werden schließlich regelmäßig oder zu vorgegebenen Zeitpunkten ausgewertet.

Insbesondere interessieren die diversen Wartezeiten vom Eintreffen der Aufträge bis zu ihrer Bearbeitung sowie die Auslastung der Station oder der Verwaltungsaufwand bei Verdrängungsvorgängen, sofern dies vorgesehen ist.

Häufig bilden die statistischen Werte das Kriterium zum Abbruch eines Systemlaufes. Dies ist z. B. der Fall, wenn die mittlere Wartezeit aller Aufträge in einer bestimmten Station im vorgegebenen Konfidenzintervall liegt.

Wesentlich ist, daß die Stationen ihre Verwaltungsaufgaben selbst übernehmen und der Benutzer vorgeben kann, welche Zusammenhänge er ausgewertet haben möchte.

2.7. Bedienung

Damit das System vom Benutzer in seiner ganzen Flexibilität genutzt werden kann, wird es von einem HOST-Computer — der Schnittstelle zwischen System und Benutzer — unterstützt. Er holt sich die Eingabedaten für die Initialisierung der Module von einem geeigneten Datenträger (z. B. Floppy Disk) oder codiert die manuelle Eingabe entsprechend um. Während des Systemlaufes protokolliert der HOST-Rechner die Ablaufdaten und bereitet die Endergebnisse für die Ausgabe auf einem Bildschirm oder Drucker auf.

Das angestrebte Ziel ist die völlige Entlastung des Benutzers von Hard- und Softwareaufgaben, da das Gerät Anwender aus verschiedensten Tätigkeitsbereichen unterstützen soll. Es werden lediglich Kenntnisse hinsichtlich der Systemstruktur verlangt, um die Modulfunktionen und den zeitlichen Ablauf auf das Multiprozessorkonzept übertragen zu können.

Die Module sind für den jeweiligen Anwendungsbereich so vorprogrammiert, daß der Benutzer durch extreme Wahlschalter ihre spezifische Funktion einstellen kann. Übertragbare problemorientierte Programmpakete existieren bereits für herkömmliche Anlagen. Als Beispiel sei von den Simulationssprachen wieder GPSS-FORTRAN zitiert, das die Funktionen der Stationstypen in den Unterprogrammen detailliert beschreibt.

Die eigentliche Arbeit verlangt vom Benutzer die Auflistung der Auftragslast, der Bearbeitungsreihenfolge,. der Verteilungsangaben von Zufallsgrößen und der Ausgabewünsche. Diese Angaben werden auf einem Magnetträger festgehalten und bei der Initialisierung in die dafür vorbereiteten Speicherbereiche der Module (PARA, SEQ) übertragen. Vor jedem Systemlauf kann der Benutzer gezielt einige Angaben variieren, um das Systemverhalten unter verschiedenen Aspekten auszuwerten.

2.8. Erweiterte Systeme

Wenn neue Überlegungen den Ausbau des Systems um eine oder mehrere Stationen erfordern, müssen lediglich die Aus- und Eingabepuffer der neuen Module an die gemeinsamen Datenbusse angekoppelt werden. Natürlich sollen der Station dann auch Aufträge zugestellt werden, so daß seine Existenz in der Laufliste des Schedulers berücksichtigt werden muß.

Die Modularität der Gesamtkonzeption wird besonders deutlich, wenn man dem Scheduler, wie Abb. 9 zeigt, die Speicherblöcke WAIT, READY, IN, OUT und das Register TIME hinzufügt. Nach außen verhält sich der Scheduler mit allen ihm zugeordneten Modulen − ohne die Source − wie eine einzige Station.

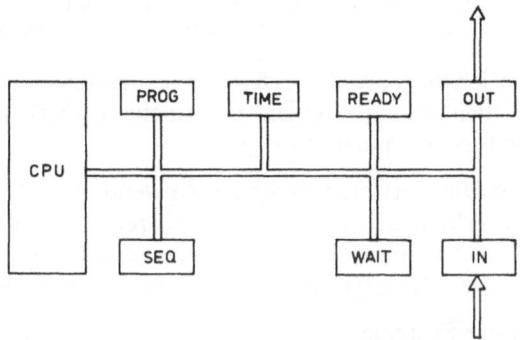

Abb. 9. Der erweiterte Scheduler

Die Aufträge werden nicht mehr vom Modul Source generiert, denn der Scheduler empfängt sie jetzt vom übergeordneten System über seinen Eingangspuffer. Ebenso werden die fertigen Aufträge nach der Bearbeitung nicht gelöscht, sondern in dem READY-Bereich und schließlich im Ausgangspuffer abgelegt. Im Register TIME steht wieder der Transferzeitpunkt.

3. Anwendungsbreite des Systems

Vereinzelt wurde schon betont, daß das vorgestellte Multiprozessorsystem durch

* Einfachheit
* Modularität

* lose Kopplung
* Auftragssteuerung
* Benutzerfreundlichkeit

ausgezeichnet ist. Es leuchtet ein, daß die Summe dieser Eigenschaften mit einem General-Purpose-Konzept unvereinbar ist, sich aber sehr wohl in den Fällen eignet, bei denen die Prozessoranordnung an die natürliche Struktur der Problemstellung angepaßt werden kann. Zusammenfassend sei allgemeiner formuliert, daß sich das Multiprozessorsystem aus einer variablen Menge von aktiven Stationen zusammensetzt, die durch ein vollvermaschtes Wegenetz miteinander verknüpft sind. Es gilt allerdings die Einschränkung, daß der Scheduler quasi im Multiplex-verfahren die Verbindungen nacheinander zwischen einer Sende- und beliebig vielen Empfangsstationen aufbaut. Die von der Source erzeugten mobilen ein-heitlichen Datenblöcke werden in vorgegebener Weise über diese Verbindungen transferiert und steuern die Aktivitäten der Stationen.

Das entscheidende Kriterium für die Anwendung des Systems verbirgt sich hinter der Frage, ob ein ausgewogenes Transferaufkommen zu erwarten ist. Es wird ungünstig beeinflußt durch:

* den Austausch von zu vielen Botschaften
* zu umfangreichen Auftragsdaten
* zu kurzen Bearbeitungszeiten in den Stationen.

Alle drei Situationen führen zu einem Engpaß auf dem gemeinsamen Datenbus und nutzen das System nicht optimal aus. Ist dieser Zustand nicht zu erwarten, läßt sich das beschriebene Konzept vorteilhaft bei parallelisierbaren Problemen anwenden.

Am sinnvollsten werden die Vorteile des Systems genutzt, wenn die Anforderungen in der Mitte zwischen den Extremen mehrfache isolierte Module und eng gekoppelte Module (general purpose) liegen.

Die folgenden Beispiele vertreten typische Anwendungsfälle lose gekoppelter Systeme und lassen erkennen, welcher Einsatzbereich damit umspannt werden kann. Für jeweils einen spezifischen Fall veranschaulichen die aufgeführten Entsprechungen die Begriffe: System − Stationen − Aufträge.

* Simulation diskreter Systeme
  Einkaufsmarkt − Verkaufsstand − Kunde

* Lösen von Differentialgleichungssystemen
  Regelsystem − Regler − Regelgröße

* Steuerung von Stückgutprozessen
  Bahnhof − Gleise − Züge

* Analyse von Netzwerken
  elektrische Schaltung − Bauelemente − Ladungen.

Literatur

[1] Schmidt, B.: GPSS-FORTRAN, Version 2 (Informatik Fachberichte, Band 6). Berlin-Heidelberg-New York: Springer 1978.

[2] Gernoth, B.: Die Simulation zeitdiskreter Systeme mit GPSS-FORTRAN. OR-Spektrum 1 (1979).
[3] Schmidt, B.: Die Simulation zeitdiskreter Systeme — Ein Blick über die Schulter. Informatik-Spektrum 2 (1979).
[4] Guttag, J. V.: Abstract data types and the development of data structures. Comm. ACM 20 (1977).

K. U. Hellmold
B. Schmidt
Institut für Mathematische Maschinen
und Datenverarbeitung IV
Universität Erlangen-Nürnberg
Martensstraße 3
D-8520 Erlangen
Bundesrepublik Deutschland

Computing, Suppl. 3, 41 – 64 (1981)

Einführung in die Methodik der Verkehrstheorie und ihre Anwendung bei Multiprozessor-Rechenanlagen

U. **Herzog** und W. **Kleinöder**, Erlangen

Zusammenfassung – Abstract

Einführung in die Methodik der Verkehrstheorie und ihre Anwendung bei Multiprozessor-Rechenanlagen. Untersuchung, Bewertung und Optimierung des dynamischen Ablaufgeschehens ist die Aufgabe der Verkehrstheorie. Die vorliegende Arbeit gibt eine Übersicht über verkehrstheoretische Problemstellungen bei Rechenanlagen und eine Einführung in die Methodik zur Lösung dieser Aufgaben: Systemstudien, Modellierung, Analyse und Synthese.

Neuartige Probleme bei Multiprozessor-Systemen (Synchronisation von Teilabläufen, Übergabezeiten, optimale Aufgabenverteilung, etc.) werden diskutiert und exemplarisch behandelt.

Traffic Theory and Its Use for Multiprocessor Systems. The field of traffic theory is to investigate, to evaluate and to optimize the dynamic flow of control information and data in computer systems. We first overview traffic problems and demonstrate the methodology for solving this task: Investigation of real systems, modelling, analysis and synthesis.

Modelling multiprocessor systems we have to take into consideration the particulars of these computers (e.g. synchronization of subtasks, overlap and transfer times, optimal partitioning of tasks). We discuss these problems and demonstrate their solution by examples.

1. Einführung

Aufgabe der Rechner-Verkehrstheorie ist die Untersuchung, die Bewertung und die Optimierung des dynamischen Ablaufgeschehens in Rechnersystemen. Ihr Ziel ist eine formale Beschreibung realer Abläufe, die Definition und Bestimmung charakteristischer Leistungsmaße sowie das Bereitstellen von Entscheidungshilfen für den Entwurf optimaler Hardwarestrukturen und Betriebsprogramme.

Verkehrstheoretische Untersuchungen sind notwendig und hilfreich in allen Bereichen der Entwicklung und Anwendung von Datenverarbeitungsanlagen:

bei der Konzeption neuartiger Hardware- und Softwarestrukturen,
bei der Realisierung von Rechnerkomponenten und -familien,
bei der Auswahl einer Konfiguration durch den Planungsingenieur oder
bei der Feinabstimmung eines Rechnersystems durch den Systemanalytiker.

Die klassische Rechner-Verkehrstheorie kann davon ausgehen, daß Vorgänge, die gleichzeitig ablaufen, weitgehend voneinander unabhängig sind. Sie ist anwendbar bei Monoprozessor- und klassischen Multiprozessorsystemen. Ganz anders jedoch bei neuartigen Multiprozessor-Systemen: Hier versucht man einzelne Gesamtaufträge in möglichst viele parallel ablauffähige Teilaufgaben zu zerlegen, die

gleichzeitig auf mehreren Prozessoren bearbeitet werden. Schwierige Koordinie-
rungsprobleme sind die Folge: Teilabläufe müssen synchronisiert werden, Daten
zwischen den einzelnen Prozessoren ausgetauscht werden, etc. etc.

Die vorliegende Arbeit gibt eine Übersicht über verkehrstheoretische Problemstellungen und die Methodik zur Lösung dieser Aufgaben: Systemstudium,
Modellierung, Analyse, Synthese. Neuartige Probleme bei Multiprozessor-Systemen werden diskutiert und exemplarisch behandelt. Erstmals werden Ergebnisse
für die Synthese optimaler Betriebsabläufe vorgestellt.

2. Verkehrstheoretische Problemstellungen

Bei der Leistungsbewertung kann man verschiedene Ebenen verkehrstheoretischer
Problemstellungen unterscheiden: Einerseits kann man das Gesamtverhalten des
Systems untersuchen (globale Verkehrsprobleme); diese globalen Untersuchungen
sind insbesondere für den Operateur und Anwender wichtig. Andererseits benötigt
der Konstrukteur von Hard- und Software zusätzlich eine detaillierte Beschreibung
der internen Abläufe (lokale Verkehrsprobleme).

2.1. Globale Verkehrsprobleme und Leistungsmaße

Gesamtziel verkehrstheoretischer Überlegungen ist es, zu einer vorgegebenen Last
des Rechnersystems eine wirtschaftlich optimale Struktur und Betriebsart zu
finden. Wir untersuchen deshalb die Leistungsfähigkeit jeder einzelnen Kom-
ponente (Prozessor, Speicher, ...), des Verbindungsnetzes (Kommunikation
zwischen den Komponenten) und ebenso die Leistungsfähigkeit des Betriebs-
systems (Verteilung der Benutzeraufgaben, Zuteilung von Resourcen, ...).

Hieraus lassen sich typische charakteristische Größen ableiten, die das Gesamtverhalten beschreiben, z. B.:

Durchsatz des Gesamtsystems, das heißt Anzahl der Benutzeraufgaben, die
pro Zeiteinheit (Minute, Stunde) abgewickelt werden

Antwortzeiten (Mittelwerte und Verteilungsfunktion), das heißt Zeitintervall
zwischen dem Eintreffen einer Anforderung und der Reaktion (Antwort) des
Rechnersystems

Auslastung der Prozessoren, das heißt mittlere Verweilzeit eines Prozessors im
Benutzermodus, Systemmodus bzw. idle-Zustand, bezogen auf die gesamte
Beobachtungsdauer

Auslastung der Speicher und E/A-Einheiten

Anzahl der Seitenzugriffe pro Zeiteinheit

Multiprogramminggrad, etc.

2.2. Lokale Verkehrsprobleme und Leistungsmaße

Hier untersuchen wir das zeitliche Ablaufgeschehen, das Warten, Bearbeiten und
Transportieren von Befehlen und Daten wesentlich detaillierter. Diese Untersuchungen sind notwendig, um eine Feinabstimmung der einzelnen Komponenten

zu erhalten, insbesondere aber auch, damit eine realistische Modellierung des Gesamtablaufgeschehens möglich wird.

Zuerst ist eine genaue Analyse auf Programmebene notwendig:

Antwortzeit für individuelle Benutzerprogramme

Prozentualer Anteil der Rechenzeit für Verwaltung (Overhead), Datentransfer, Benutzerprogramm

Grad der Parallelität einzelner Benutzerprogramme, insbesondere mittlere und maximale Anzahl gleichzeitig bearbeiteter Teilaufgaben, Korrelation zwischen Teilaufgaben etc.

Zweitens ist eine genaue Analyse auf der Ebene von Teilaufgaben erforderlich:

Anzahl von Teilaufgaben, Verteilungsfunktion für Ankunftsabstände und Ausführungszeiten

Anzahl und Ursache der Unterbrechungen sowie Länge der damit verbundenen Verwaltungszeiten

Grad der Parallelität

Einfluß des globalen und der lokalen Betriebssysteme (Koordination, Synchronisation, etc.).

Drittens ist der Datentransfer zwischen den einzelnen Komponenten des Gesamtsystems (Prozessoren, Hauptspeicher, Hintergrundspeicher, etc.) von großer Wichtigkeit:

Anzahl von Blöcken, Ankunftsabstände und Blocklängen
Warteschlangenlängen und Verkehrsengpässe
Ausgewogene Dimensionierung der Pufferspeicher, usw.

Ein sehr wichtiges Gebiet bei Multiprozessor-Systemen ist die Untersuchung der Speicherzugriffskonflikte und deren Einfluß auf einen reibungslosen Betriebsablauf:

Anzahl und Abstandsverteilung der Zugriffe

Anzahl der Konflikte „Prozessor → lokaler Speicher“, „Prozessor → benachbarter Speicher“

Interferenz, das heißt Leistungsminderung der einzelnen Prozessoren durch Zugriffskonflikte bei Daten- und/oder Codesharing.

Auch bei Multiprozessoren sind, wie bei Einzelprozessor-Systemen, zahlreiche Detail-Untersuchungen auf Befehlsebene notwendig:

Relative Häufigkeit von Befehlstypen
Ausführungsdauer – Verteilung
Reihenfolgemessungen
Lebensdauer von Operanden.

2.3. Methodik der Verkehrstheorie

In den vorhergehenden Abschnitten haben wir die Aufgabe der Verkehrstheorie sowie die Vielfalt verkehrstheoretischer Fragestellungen und Untersuchungen diskutiert. Die Vorgehensweise bei der Lösung dieser Aufgaben kann in der folgenden Methodik zusammengefaßt werden (vergleiche Abb. 1):

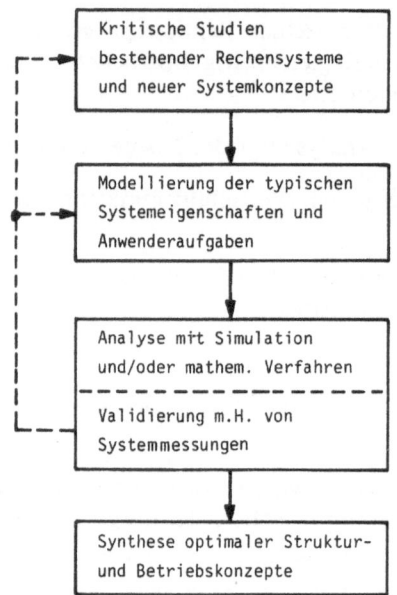

Abb. 1. Methodik der Rechner-Verkehrstheorie

1. Kritisches Studium bestehender Rechnersysteme und neuartiger Struktur- und Betriebskonzepte

2. Modellierung, das heißt formale Beschreibung der wesentlichen Systemeigenschaften und typischer Merkmale der Anwenderprogramme

3. Analyse des Ablaufgeschehens, das heißt Bestimmung charakteristischer Leistungsmaße mit Hilfe der Simulation und exakter oder approximativer mathematischer Verfahren

4. Validierung der Modellierungs- und Analyseergebnisse mit Hilfe von Plausibilitätsbetrachtungen und Systemmessungen

5. Synthese, das heißt Entwurf optimaler Komponenten, Gesamtorganisationen und Betriebsabläufe.

Diese Methodik soll in den folgenden Kapiteln zusammengefaßt und anhand von Beispielen illustriert werden.

3. Multiprozessor-Rechnersysteme

3.1. Allgemeines

Multiprozessorsysteme werden schon seit vielen Jahren geplant und aufgebaut. Zuerst entwickelte man Systeme mit zwei oder drei Prozessoren, wie z. B. die IBM 360/67 oder 370/168, die TR 440 der AEG-Telefunken, die Siemens 7762. Dann baute man Anlagen mit zehn oder mehr handelsüblichen Minicomputern – das C.mmp-Projekt der Carnegie Mellon University ist sicher das bekannteste Beispiel. Heute denkt man daran, hunderte oder tausende von Mikroprozessoren zu einem Rechnersystem zusammenzuschalten.

Parallel zu dieser Entwicklung auf der Hardware-Seite erkennt man auf der Software-Seite die Tendenz, auf den verschiedenen Prozessoren nicht nur unabhängige Programme parallel ablaufen zu lassen; man versucht vielmehr, den in vielen Anwenderprogrammen inhärenten Parallelismus auszunutzen. Mit anderen Worten, jedes Anwenderprogramm wird in Teilaufgaben zerlegt, die zum Teil abhängig, zum Teil voneinander unabhängig sind. Teilaufgaben sind deshalb seriell, zum Teil aber auch parallel ablauffähig. Man ist also in der Lage, nicht nur den Gesamtdurchsatz eines Rechnersystems zu optimieren, sondern auch die Antwortzeit für individuelle Anwenderprogramme zu verkürzen.

Da unsere Untersuchungen durch das Erlanger Mehrprozessor-Projekt EGPA – Erlangen General Purpose Array – angeregt und beeinflußt wurden, beschreiben wir im folgenden kurz die EGPA-Architektur.

3.2. Das EGPA-Projekt, ein hierarchisch organisiertes Mehrprozessor-Feldrechner-System

Hierarchische Strukturen sind häufig in der Natur zu finden, in vielen Bereichen der Zivilisation haben sie sich durchgesetzt. Sie ermöglichen einen klar strukturierten Aufbau komplexer Systeme, begrenzen den Kommunikations- und Koordinierungsaufwand sinnvoll, sind modular erweiterbar und ausfallsicher durch gegenseitige Aushilfe.

Typische Beispiele aus dem Bereich der Rechnerarchitektur sind das Multiprozessor-System an der SUNY [5], die Siemens-Systeme SMS [16], MOPPS [19], X-TREE [2] and EGPA.

Die EGPA-Architektur (Erlangen General Purpose Array [4]) besteht erstens aus einem Feld von Prozessoren (A-Prozessoren), die durch gemeinsame Speicherblöcke (Multiport-Speicher) verbunden sind. Jeder Prozessor kann auf seinen eigenen Speicherblock und auf die seiner Nachbarn zugreifen (vergleiche Abb. 2). Die Ränder des Prozessorfeldes sind zu einem Toroid geschlossen. Aufgabe der A-Prozessoren ist die Bearbeitung von Anwenderprogrammen; üblicherweise arbeiten mehrere A-Prozessoren gemeinsam an einem Problem. Die zweite Ebene von Prozessoren (B-Prozessoren) überwacht je vier A-Prozessoren und führt den Datentransport zwischen den A-Prozessoren und der Peripherie durch. Die dritte Ebene (und eventuell höhere Ebenen) haben globale Verwaltungsaufgaben, wie z. B. die Verteilung von Aufgaben bzw. Teilaufgaben auf das Feld (vergleiche Abb. 3).

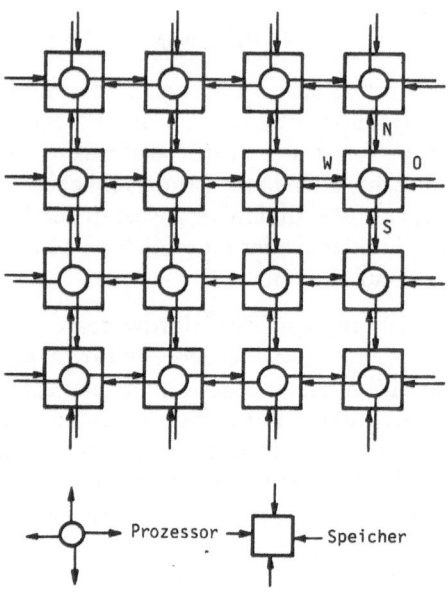

Abb. 2. Zellulare Struktur von EGPA

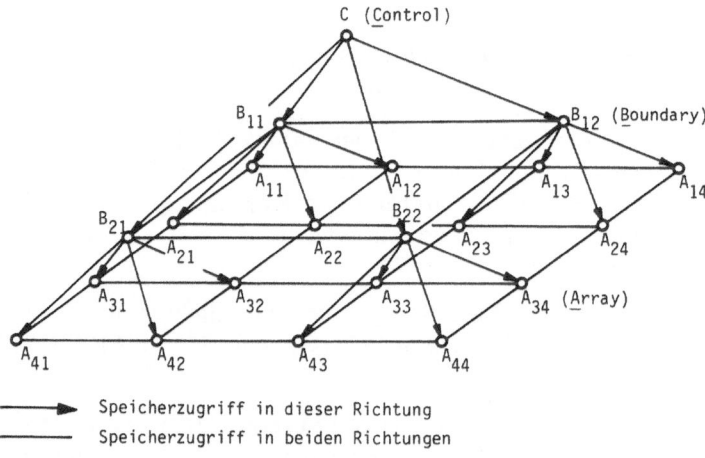

Abb. 3. Erlangen General Purpose Array (EGPA)

Das EGPA-Projekt wird seit dem 1. Januar 1978 durch das Bundesministerium für Forschung und Technologie gefördert; eine Pilotpyramide aus 5 AEG 80 – 60 Rechnern wurde installiert. Für verschiedene Aufgaben aus dem Bereich der Natur- und Ingenieurwissenschaften werden zur Zeit Algorithmen entwickelt und implementiert. Ein leistungsfähiger Meßmonitor steht für Systemmessungen zur Verfügung.

4. Modellierung

4.1. Übersicht

Es gibt verschiedene Möglichkeiten, das Ablaufgeschehen innerhalb eines Rechnersystems zu beschreiben. Die bekanntesten und erfolgreichsten Methoden sind:

1. Die *graphentheoretische Beschreibung* mit Hilfe von Knoten, Kanten und Flüssen. Effektive Algorithmen sind vorhanden, um Verkehrsengpässe und den maximalen Durchsatz zu ermitteln. Die Ergebnisse sind erste Abschätzungen, da das zeitlich schwankende Ablaufgeschehen durch einen konstanten Netzwerkfluß beschrieben wird [3].

2. Die *wahrscheinlichkeitstheoretische Beschreibung* mit Hilfe von Bedienungsmodellen und stochastischen Prozessen. Im Vergleich zur ersten Methode ist eine wirklichkeitstreuere Beschreibung möglich, da zeitlich variierende Belegungen von Übertragungswegen, Pufferspeichern und Bearbeitungseinheiten erfaßt werden. Komplizierte Abhängigkeiten zwischen einzelnen Vorgängen sind nicht oder oft nur mit großem Aufwand erfaßbar.

Die Auswertung derartiger Bedienungsmodelle ist möglich mit Hilfe mathematischer Methoden oder − bei komplizierten Abhängigkeiten − mit Hilfe der Simulation.

Eine Vielzahl von Aussagen über die Leistungsfähigkeit eines Rechnersystems ist möglich: Durchsatz, Auslastung einzelner Komponenten, Antwortzeiten, usw.; Aussagen über Mittelwerte, höhere Momente und Verteilungsfunktionen.

3. Die *Beschreibung mit Hilfe von Auswertenetzen*, detaillierten Flußdiagrammen etc. Hier ist eine sehr genaue Beschreibung des Ablaufgeschehens, auch bei komplizierten Abhängigkeiten möglich. Der Aufwand kann jedoch, insbesondere wenn es sich um größere Teilsysteme handelt, beträchtlich sein. Die Bestimmung charakteristischer Leistungsmaße ist bis heute nur mit Hilfe der Simulation möglich [18].

Bereits aus dieser kurzen Zusammenfassung erkennt man deutlich, wie mit zunehmender Genauigkeit der Beschreibungsmethoden der Aufwand für die Modellauswertung zunimmt. Alle drei Methoden haben ihre Bedeutung in unterschiedlichen Phasen der Systementwicklung. Wir werden uns jedoch im folgenden auf eine ausführlichere Behandlung der wahrscheinlichkeitstheoretischen Modelle beschränken.

4.2. Beschreibung des Ablaufgeschehens mit Bedienungsmodellen und stochastischen Prozessen

4.2.1. Allgemeines

Das dynamische Ablaufgeschehen in Rechnersystemen wird bestimmt

durch den Transport von Daten und Steuerbefehlen zwischen den einzelnen Komponenten

durch die Bearbeitung dieser Daten und Steuerbefehle in den einzelnen Komponenten und durch das Blockieren und Warten von Prozessen an verschiedenen Stellen des Rechners.

Die zeitliche Folge derartiger Transport-, Warte- und Bearbeitungsphasen ist mindestens teilweise deterministisch, auch dann, wenn die Zusammenhänge sehr komplex sind. Aus der Sicht eines Teilsystems scheint die zeitliche Folge der Daten und Befehle jedoch häufig zufällig zu sein, das heißt: dieser zeitliche Ablauf ist beschreibbar als Zufallsprozeß. Die Behandlung derartiger Prozesse ist mit der sehr ausgereiften Theorie der stochastischen Prozesse möglich.

Vollständig erfaßt wird dieses zufällige, stochastische Verhalten durch folgende drei Kriterien:

1. *Ankunftsprozeß*: Der Ankunftsprozeß beschreibt, in welchem zeitlichen Abstand (Ankunftsabstand) die einzelnen Anforderungen eintreffen.

2. *Bedienungsprozeß*: Der Bedienungsprozeß beschreibt die Länge von Bearbeitungs- oder Transportzeiten für die einzelnen Anforderungen.

3. *Systemeinfluß*: Der Einfluß des Systems ist durch die Systemstruktur und die Art der Abfertigung ankommender und wartender Daten oder Befehle festgelegt (Anmerkung: Die Beeinflussung des Ablaufgeschehens durch die Geschwindigkeit von Prozessoren, Speichern, etc. wird fast immer unter Punkt 2 beschrieben).

Mit Hilfe dieser drei Kriterien können qualitative und quantitative Aussagen über die Leistungsfähigkeit eines Rechnersystems und seiner Komponenten gemacht werden.

Abb. 4 zeigt — symbolisch dargestellt — ein einfaches, aber typisches Grundmodell:

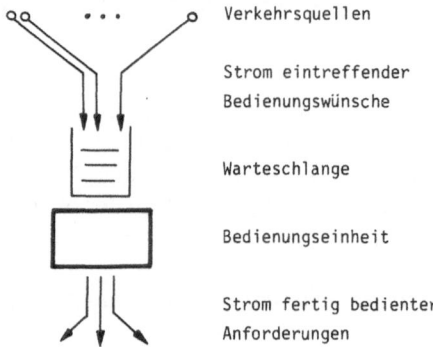

Abb. 4. Grundmodell eines Bedienungssystems mit Warteschlange

Von den Verkehrsquellen (z. B. Terminals, interne Übertragungswege, etc.) wird ein „Strom" von Anforderungen erzeugt. Ist die Bedienungseinheit (z. B. Zentralprozessor, Speicher, etc.) momentan belegt, so wird in einer Warteschlange ein Zeiger gesetzt, der die Ankunft des neuen Bedienungswunsches anzeigt. Die Warteschlange wird in einer bestimmten Reihenfolge (siehe 4.2.3) von der

Bedienungseinheit abgearbeitet. Komplexere Modelle werden in Abschnitt 4.3.2 vorgestellt.

4.2.2. Ankunfts- und Bedienungsprozesse

Die Wahl eines geeigneten Verkehrsmodells ist von weittragender Bedeutung: je realistischer die gewählten Ankunfts- und Bedienungsprozesse sind, desto besser werden die durch Analyse bzw. Synthese erzielten Ergebnisse der Wirklichkeit entsprechen.

Exponential-Verteilung: Die bekannteste Verteilung für Ankunfts- und Bedienungsprozesse ist die negativ exponentielle Verteilung, kurz Exponential-Verteilung genannt. Sie erlaubt nicht nur die Beschreibung vieler Naturereignisse (Zerfall von radioaktiven Präparaten, Brownsche Bewegung von Atomen, etc.), sondern wird auch häufig verwendet, um Zeitabläufe in Transport- und Bearbeitungssystemen (Straßenverkehr, Fernsprech- und Datennetze, Rechnersysteme) zu beschreiben.

Die Verteilungsfunktion $F(t)$ (Wahrscheinlichkeit, daß ein Ankunftsabstand oder eine Bedienungszeit T höchstens die Länge t hat) ist gegeben durch die Beziehung

$$F(t) = P(T \leqslant t) = 1 - e^{-t/t_m} \qquad t \geqslant 0 \tag{1}$$

mit dem Mittelwert

$$E[T] = t_m. \tag{2}$$

Die Exponentialverteilung wird nicht nur verwendet, weil sie häufig das tatsächliche Ablaufgeschehen genau beschreibt; sehr oft wird sie auch deshalb benutzt, da die Behandlung dieser Prozesse noch relativ einfach ist (Markoff-Prozesse, vergleiche [15]).

Konstante Verteilung: Bedienungsprozesse werden häufig besser durch die konstante Verteilung erfaßt (typische Beispiele sind Belegungszeiten von Speichern, Transportzeiten für Befehle oder Daten, etc.). Für die Verteilungsfunktion gilt:

$$F(t) = P(T \leqslant t) = \begin{cases} 1 & t \geqslant t_m \\ 0 & 0 \leqslant t < t_m. \end{cases} \tag{3}$$

Phasen-Verteilungen: Die allgemeine Erlang-Verteilung entsteht durch die Überlagerung von Exponential-Verteilungen und erlaubt es, jede reale Verteilungsfunktion beliebig genau zu approximieren. Für die Verteilungsfunktion gilt:

$$F(t) = \sum_{i=1}^{r} q_i \left(1 - \exp\left(\frac{-t}{t_{m_i}/k_i} \right) \sum_{j=0}^{i-1} \left(\frac{t}{t_{m_i}/k_i} \right)^j (j!)^{-1} \right); \quad t \geqslant 0. \tag{4}$$

Bekannte Sonderfälle der allgemeinen Erlang-Verteilung sind die *Erlang-k-Verteilung* (geeignet zum Modellieren von Zugriffszeiten für Platten-, Trommelspeicher, etc.) und die *Hyperexponential-Verteilung* (häufig benutzt zur Modellierung von Programmablaufzeiten in Teilnehmer-Rechnersystemen). Weitere, nahe verwandte Typen sind die *Cox-Verteilung* und die *stückweise Exponential-Verteilung*. Letztere bildet bereits einen Übergang zu den diskreten Verteilungen, die zum Teil ebenfalls sehr wirklichkeitstreu, analytisch aber meist schwierig zu behandeln sind.

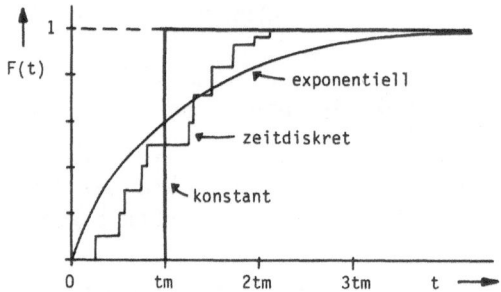

Abb. 5. Drei Beispiele für die Verteilungsfunktion von Ankunfts- und Bedienungsprozessen

4.2.3. Systemeinfluß

Das dynamische Ablaufgeschehen in Rechnersystemen wird sowohl durch die Systemstruktur (Art und Anzahl der Hardware-Komponenten und Verbindungsnetze) als auch durch die Betriebsstrategie (Festlegen der Reihenfolge von Bearbeitungsphasen, Prioritäten, etc.) beeinflußt. Bereits in 4.2.1 wurde ein einfaches Strukturmodell vorgestellt (Abb. 4). Komplexere Modelle werden in 4.3.2, insbesondere aber auch in [6], [8] behandelt.

Von der Vielzahl in der Praxis angewandter Abfertigungsstrategien seien nur die wichtigsten erwähnt. Ausführliche Zusammenstellungen findet man z. B. in [20].

Abfertigung ohne Prioritäten. Eintreffende Anforderungen, die nicht sofort bedient werden können, werden in eine Warteschlange eingereiht. Die bekanntesten Abfertigungsstrategien für gleichberechtigte Anforderungen sind

FIFO: first-in-first-out, das heißt die zuerst eingetroffene Anforderung wird zuerst bedient (bei vielen Echtzeit-Datenverarbeitungsanlagen)

LIFO: last-in-first-out, das heißt die zuletzt eingetroffene Anforderung wird zuerst bedient (z. B. bei Speicherplatzverwaltung)

RANDOM: die wartenden Anforderungen werden in zufälliger Reihenfolge bedient (teilweise in Vermittlungssystemen).

Sind mehrere Warteschlangen mit gleichberechtigten Anforderungen vorhanden, so kommen zu diesen Abfertigungsstrategien noch verschiedene Möglichkeiten zur Auswahl einer bestimmten Warteschlange hinzu.

Abfertigung mit Prioritäten. Bei Prioritäten unterscheidet man interne und externe Prioritäten. *Interne* Prioritäten werden bei an sich gleichrangigen Anforderungen gesetzt, um maximalen Durchsatz oder „gerechte" Wartezeiten zu erzielen. Ein erstes Beispiel ist die SJF-Strategie (shortest-job-first), das heißt die Anforderung mit der kürzesten Bedienungszeit wird zuerst behandelt. Ein zweites Beispiel sind die Zeitscheibenverfahren (round-robin, feedback); sie ermöglichen eine quasi gleichzeitige Bedienung mehrerer Anforderungen und auch bei zunächst unbekannter Gesamtverweilzeit Wartezeiten, die proportional zur Gesamtbedienungszeit sind. *Externe* Prioritäten geben Auskunft über die Wichtigkeit einer Anforderung im Vergleich mit anderen konkurrierenden Anforderungen. Sie sind oft fest vorgegeben (z. B. für Prozesse zur Verwaltung verschiedener Peripheriegeräte), können aber auch wartezeitabhängig sein.

Sowohl Abfertigungsstrategien für interne als auch externe Prioritäten können rein *unterbrechend*, rein *nicht-unterbrechend* oder eine Mischform zwischen beiden Extremen sein.

4.3. Modellierung eines Multiprozessor-Systems

4.3.1. Übersicht

Wie bei klassischen Rechenanlagen wird das Ablaufgeschehen — und deshalb auch die Modellierung — bestimmt durch die Hardwarekomponenten, die Verbindungsstruktur und das Betriebssystem. Zusätzlich spielt jetzt jedoch die Struktur der Anwenderprogramme eine entscheidende Rolle:

Wie ist das Programm in abhängige und unabhängige Teilaufgaben zerlegbar?

Wie werden diese Teilaufgaben auf die einzelnen Prozessoren verteilt?

Wo erfolgt die Koordinierung, welche Datentransfers sind notwendig, wo treten Verwaltungszeiten auf?

Die Klassifizierung der Vielfalt unterschiedlicher Anwenderprogramme, Möglichkeiten für deren Implementierung und die Beschreibung mit Hilfe einer neuen Klasse von Warteschlangennetzen wurde in [6], [8] behandelt. Hier konzentrieren wir uns auf den einfachsten, aber für die Anwendung auch wichtigsten Grundtyp.

4.3.2. Typ-1-Anwenderprogramme, Implementierung und Modellierung

Die Typ-1-Programmstruktur besteht aus eine Schleife, die mehrere Male durchlaufen wird (vergleiche Abb. 6). Nach einer Vorbereitungsphase kann man n unabhängige Teilaufgaben unterscheiden. Der Abschluß eines Schleifendurchlaufs ist möglich, sobald alle n unabhängigen Teilaufgaben fertig bearbeitet sind. Anwenderprogramme entsprechen häufig dieser Grundstruktur:

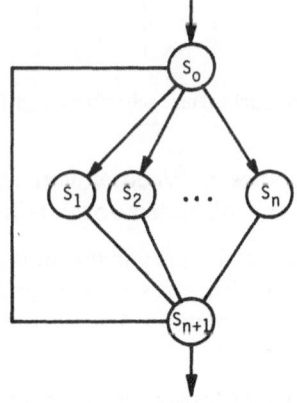

Abb. 6. Typ-1-Grundstruktur eines Anwenderprogramms

Algorithmen für die Lösung linearer algebraischer oder partieller Differential-
gleichungssysteme

Optimierungsalgorithmen

Simulationsprogramme mit Teiltests zur Abschätzung von Konfidenzinter-
vallen

Bildverarbeitungsalgorithmen, etc. etc.

Typ-1-Programme können sehr effektiv auf hierarchisch organisierten Multiprozessor-Systemen mit 2 Ebenen, z. B. auf der EGPA-Pilotpyramide implementiert
werden (vergleiche Abb. 3):

Der B-Prozessor (Kopf der Pyramide) übernimmt den Bearbeitungsschritt S_0.

Nach dieser Vorbereitungsphase übergibt er Steuerinformation und Daten an
die A-Prozessoren (Übergabephase/Startperiode).

Die Teilprogramme S_1 bis S_n laufen unabhängig und parallel auf den
Prozessoren A_1 bis A_n ab.

Das Zusammenfassen und Weiterverarbeiten der Teilergebnisse ist möglich,
sobald alle Teilprozesse abgeschlossen sind. Diese Aufgabe wird wieder vom
B-Prozessor übernommen.

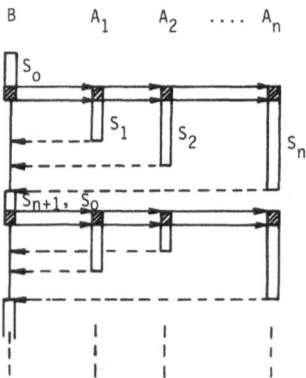

Abb. 7. Ablaufdiagramm (vergleiche Text, schraffiert sind Übergabephasen angedeutet)

Warteschlangenmodelle, die diesen Wechsel von seriellen und parallelen Ab-
laufphasen erfassen, werden im folgenden vorgestellt.

Einprogrammbetrieb. Zunächst nehmen wir an, daß zu einem Zeitpunkt nur ein
Anwenderprogramm von der Multiprozessor-Anlage bearbeitet wird; der zeitliche
Ablauf entspricht deshalb exakt jenem in Abb. 7. Abb. 8 zeigt das entsprechende
Warteschlangenmodell.

Neu eintreffende Anforderungen (Anwenderprogramme) werden in der Eingangs-
Warteschlange zwischengespeichert.

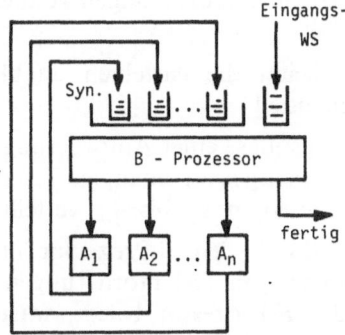

Abb. 8. Warteschlangenmodell für Einprogrammbetrieb

Die erste Anforderung wird, sobald das „innere" System frei ist (Einprogrammbetrieb), vom B-Prozessor übernommen und bearbeitet (FIFO).

Der B-Prozessor erzeugt n unabhängige Teilanforderungen und übergibt diese gleichzeitig an alle A-Prozessoren (zeitlich versetzte Übergabephasen werden in [13] behandelt).

Nach Beendigung jedes unabhängigen Teilablaufs wird in der zugehörigen Synchronisations-Warteschlange eine Marke gesetzt. Sobald alle Teilabläufe beendet sind, werden alle Marken gleichzeitig (symbolisch dargestellt durch eine Synchronisationsklammer) aus den Synchronisations-Warteschlangen herausgenommen und gemeinsam bearbeitet.

Nach dieser Bearbeitungsphase gibt es zwei Möglichkeiten: die Anforderung ist vollständig bedient und verläßt das System oder ein neuer Bearbeitungszyklus (siehe oben) beginnt.

Mehrprogrammbetrieb. Erlaubt man sowohl für den B-Prozessor als auch für die A-Prozessoren Mehrprogrammbetrieb, so werden einzelne Anwenderaufgaben ineinander verzahnt ablaufen. Das entsprechende Warteschlangenmodell sieht nahezu gleich aus wie das in Abb. 8. Zusätzlich gibt es jetzt aber auch vor jedem A-Prozessor eine Warteschlange, in welcher Teilaufgaben unterschiedlicher Programme warten können.

Gemischter Ein- und Mehrprogrammbetrieb. Mehrprogrammbetrieb erlaubt eine effektive Auslastung der wichtigen und teuren Systemkomponenten. Aus Gründen der Einfachheit und Transparenz ist jedoch bei Multiprozessor-Konzepten ein klarer Trend vorhanden, wieder Einprogrammbetrieb einzuführen. Gemischter Betrieb scheint in vielen Fällen ein sinnvoller Kompromiß zu sein: der B-Prozessor arbeitet im Mehrprogrammbetrieb, alle A-Prozessoren im Einprogrammbetrieb. Abb. 9 zeigt das entsprechende Warteschlangenmodell und ist analog zu unserem ersten Modell zu interpretieren:

Gleichzeitig können m unabhängige Anwenderprogramme mit Typ-1-Grundstruktur (kurz Anforderungen genannt) vom „inneren" System bearbeitet werden. Zusätzliche Anforderungen können in der Eingangs-Warteschlange warten.

Der B-Prozessor bearbeitet die einzelnen unabhängigen Anforderungen $(t_1, \ldots, t_i, \ldots, t_m)$ sequentiell.

Ist die serielle Bedienungsphase einer Anforderung t_i durch den B-Prozessor bearbeitet, werden gleichzeitig n_i unabhängige Teilanforderungen erzeugt und an die reservierten Prozessoren A_{i1} bis A_{in_i} verteilt.

Anforderung t_i kann durch den B-Prozessor nur dann weiterbearbeitet werden, wenn alle zugehörigen Teilanforderungen durch die A-Prozessoren bearbeitet sind. Ist der B-Prozessor belegt, warten diese „bereiten" Anforderungen in den Synchronisations-Warteschlangen. Warten mehrere „bereite" Anforderungen, so werden sie nach der FIFO-Strategie bedient.

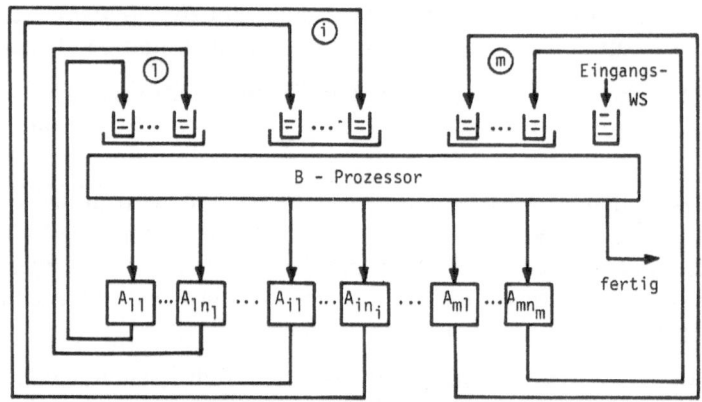

Abb. 9. Warteschlangenmodell für den gemischten Ein- und Mehrprogrammbetrieb

5. Analyse

5.1. Allgemeines

Für die Analyse des Ablaufgeschehens in Rechnersystemen gibt es drei Möglichkeiten: die Verkehrsmessung, die Simulation und die rein rechnerischen Verfahren. Um die Nachteile der einzelnen Methoden nach Möglichkeit zu vermeiden und deren Vorteile zu verbinden, gibt es heute mehrere Ansätze, die Methoden in Programmpaketen zu kombinieren.

Verkehrsmessung. Das Ablaufgeschehen in bestehenden Rechnersystemen kann mit Hilfe systematischer Verkehrsmessungen untersucht und bewertet werden. Gemessen wird mit Hilfe von Software- und Hardwaremonitoren [12] sowohl das globale als auch das lokale Verhalten eines Systems. Um eine hinreichende statistische Aussagesicherheit zu erreichen, sind zeitaufwendige Meßreihen notwendig.

Eine Vielzahl von Aussagen ist möglich, beispielsweise

die Bewertung der Gesamtleistungsfähigkeit einer Rechenanlage, das Aufdecken von Engpässen in Hard- und Software,

die Bestimmung von typischen Verkehrsparametern für die Modellierung,

die Validierung von Simulationsergebnissen und analytischen Berechnungs-
methoden.

Simulation. Bei der Simulation bildet man das zu untersuchende Rechnersystem
sowie das dynamische Ablaufgeschehen mit Hilfe eines Programms nach. Mit
anderen Worten, man entwirft ein Modell des realen Systems und der tatsächlichen
Transport-, Warte- und Bearbeitungsphasen und kann damit — häufig zeitlich
gerafft gegenüber der Wirklichkeit — die Leistungsfähigkeit des Systems untersuchen.

Spezielle Programmiersprachen erlauben eine relativ einfache und schnelle Beschreibung und Bewertung eines Systems. Ein in einer Simulationssprache
programmiertes Grundmodell kann flexibel erweitert und verfeinert werden, bis es
sehr genau dem Verkehrsverhalten des realen Systems entspricht. Typische
Beispiele häufig angewendeter Simulationssprachen sind GPSS, GPSS-Fortran,
SIMULA und SIMSCRIPT, Beispiele für erfolgreiche Programm-Pakete zur
Simulation von Rechnersystemen sind QNET IV, SAMEN und MEM-SIM.

Der Hauptvorteil der Simulation gegenüber den analytischen Verfahren liegt darin,
daß man komplexe Problemstellungen, deren prinzipielle Lösung noch nicht
bekannt ist, in relativ kurzen und gut abschätzbaren Zeiträumen untersuchen kann,
während bei den (genauen) rechnerischen Verfahren eine Lösung nicht immer
gewährleistet ist. Simulation wird häufig auch zur Nachprüfung approximativer
Rechenverfahren eingesetzt. Nachteilig sind die hohen Rechenzeiten bei der
Synthese (siehe unten).

Berechnungsverfahren. Aufgabe eines Systemplaners ist nicht nur die Analyse,
sondern vor allem die Synthese, das heißt der Entwurf wirtschaftlich optimaler
Rechnerstrukturen und Betriebsabläufe. Optimierung ist aber mit Hilfe der
Simulation schlecht möglich; durch systematisches Variieren der Struktur- und
Verkehrsparameter kann man zwar wirtschaftliche Lösungen finden, aber hier
stößt man wegen der enormen Rechenzeiten selbst auf den größten Rechnern bald
auf eine Grenze. Echte Optimierung ist mit sinnvollem Aufwand nur bei den
mathematischen Verfahren möglich.

Die Grundlagen graphentheoretischer und wahrscheinlichkeitstheoretischer Methoden werden in verschiedenen Büchern ausführlich behandelt, siehe z. B. [3],
[15]. Im nächsten Abschnitt wird das Modell eines Multiprozessorsystems mit
Hilfe mathematischer Methoden untersucht.

5.2. Analyse eines Multiprozessor-Systems

Aus didaktischen Gründen konzentrieren wir uns auf den einfachsten Fall, ein
Modell mit Einprogrammbetrieb mit Typ-1-Anwenderprogrammen. Eine Vielzahl
weiterer Ergebnisse für Multiprozessor-Systeme mit zwei oder mehr Ebenen von
Prozessoren findet man in [6, 7, 8, 9, 10, 11, 13].

Gegeben sei ein Bedienungsmodell entsprechend Abb. 8. Neu eintreffende Anforderungen haben exponentiell verteilte Ankunftsabstände. Jede Anforderung bestehe — wieder nur aus Gründen der Übersichtlichkeit — aus einer konstanten Anzahl von c Bedienungszyklen (vergleiche Abb. 10). Die Bedienungszeit der seriellen B-Phase sei beliebig verteilt mit der Verteilungsfunktion $F_B(t)$. Daran anschließend sind während der Übergabephase sowohl der B- als auch alle A-Prozessoren belegt (beliebige Verteilungsfunktion $F_{\ddot{U}}(t)$). Alle n parallelen Teilabläufe sind unabhängig voneinander und gehorchen individuell einer beliebigen Verteilungsfunktion $F_{A_i}(t)$, $1 \leq i \leq n$. (Sind die Verteilungen der Bearbeitungszeiten von Teilabläufen nicht vollständig voneinander unabhängig, so stellt diese Annahme eine Abschätzung nach der sicheren Seite dar).

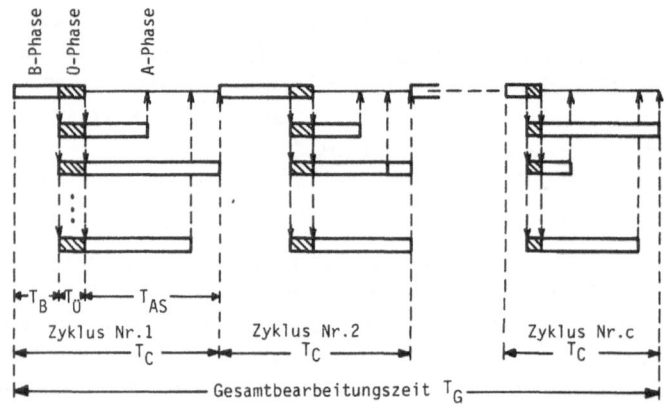

Abb. 10. Gesamtbearbeitungszeit

Die Bestimmung globaler Leistungsmaße, wie zum Beispiel

Durchsatz des Gesamtsystems
Auslastung der einzelnen Prozessoren
mittlere Anzahl gleichzeitig arbeitender A-Prozessoren
mittlere Anzahl wartender Anforderungen oder Teilanforderungen
mittlere Antwortzeit, etc.,

ist nur dann möglich, wenn wir zuerst das mikroskopische Verhalten des Systems untersuchen, insbesondere

Mittelwert, Varianz und Verteilungsfunktion der A-Phase (häufig als Synchronisationszeit bezeichnet), das heißt Zeitintervall zwischen dem Augenblick „alle Teilaufgaben werden gestartet" und dem Zeitpunkt „der letzte parallele Teilablauf ist beendet".

Mittelwert, Varianz und Verteilungsfunktion der Zykluszeit, das heißt der Summe aus B-Phase, $\ddot{U}$-Phase und A-Phase.

Mittelwert, Varianz und Verteilungsfunktion der Gesamtbearbeitungszeit jeder einzelnen Anforderung.

Mikroskopische Analyse. Die Länge der A-Phase (Synchronisationszeit) wird bestimmt durch das Maximum von n Bedienungsphasen T_{A_i}, $i \in \{1, 2, \ldots, n\}$ der A-Prozessoren. Die Verteilungsfunktion ist deshalb gegeben durch das Produkt aller individuellen Verteilungsfunktionen $F_{A_i}(t)$:

$$F_{AS}(t) = P(T_{AS} \leqslant t) = P(T_{A_1} \leqslant t) \cdot P(T_{A_2} \leqslant t) \cdots P(T_{A_n} \leqslant t)$$

$$F_{AS}(t) = \prod_{i=1}^{n} F_{A_i}(t). \tag{5}$$

Da die Zykluszeit gleich der Summe von B-Phase, $\ddot{U}$-Phase und A-Phase ist, ist ihre Verteilungsfunktion durch die Faltung dieser drei Verteilungsfunktionen bestimmt:

$$F_C(t) = F_B(t) * F_{\ddot{U}}(t) * F_{AS}(t). \tag{6}$$

Schließlich ergibt sich, völlig analog, die Verteilungsfunktion der Gesamtbearbeitungszeit G als Faltung der Verteilungsfunktionen für die einzelnen Zyklen:

$$F_G(t) = F_C(t) * F_C(t) * \cdots * F_C(t). \tag{7}$$

Abhängig vom Typ der vorgegebenen Verteilungsfunktionen $F_B(t)$, $F_{\ddot{U}}(t)$ und $F_{A_i}(t)$, $i \in \{1, \ldots, n\}$ ist eine Auswertung dieser Formeln entweder analytisch oder numerisch möglich [7, 14]. Mittelwert $E[T_G]$ und Varianz $\mathrm{VAR}[T_G]$ können entsprechend bestimmt werden.

Globale Leistungsmaße für das gesättigte System. Nimmt man an, daß in der Eingangs-Warteschlange stets eine oder mehrere Anforderungen auf Bedienung warten, so reiht sich eine Gesamtbearbeitungszeit an die andere. Für diesen Extremfall kann man aus der mikroskopischen Analyse eine Vielzahl von globalen Größen ableiten, zum Beispiel:

Auslastung des B-Prozessors

$$Y_B = (E[T_B] + E[T_{\ddot{U}}])/E[T_C].$$

Auslastung der A-Prozessoren

$$Y_{A_i} = (E[T_{\ddot{U}}] + E[T_{A_i}])/E[T_C]; \qquad i \in \{1, 2, \ldots, n\}.$$

Durchsatz des Gesamtsystems

$$D = 1/E[T_G].$$

Globale Leistungsmaße für das ungesättigte System. Die Ankunftsabstände neu eintreffender Anforderungen seien exponentiell verteilt mit dem mittleren Ankunftsabstand a_m. Das heißt: Treffen mehrere Anforderungen statistisch verteilt kurz nacheinander ein, so müssen verschiedene Anforderungen warten. Sind die Ankunftsabstände sehr lang, so ist es möglich, daß unser Multiprozessor-System für einige Zeit unbeschäftigt ist. Dieser zeitlich schwankende Verkehr wird mit dem klassischen $M|G|1$-Warteschlangenmodell [1, 15] erfaßt, in welches unsere Ergebnisse aus der Mikro-Analyse eingesetzt werden:

Mittlere Anzahl von Anforderungen, die in der Eingangswarteschlange warten

$$E[X] = \frac{\left(\dfrac{1}{a_m}\right)^2 E[T_G]^2}{2\left(1 - \dfrac{1}{a_m}E[T_G]\right)} \cdot \left\{1 + \frac{\mathrm{VAR}[T_G]}{E[T_G]^2}\right\}.$$

Mittlere Antwortzeit

$$E[T_R] = \frac{\dfrac{1}{a_m}\cdot E[T_G]^2}{2\left(1 - \dfrac{1}{a_m}E[T_G]\right)} \cdot \left\{1 + \frac{\mathrm{VAR}[T_G]}{E[T_G]^2}\right\} + E[T_G].$$

Auslastung des B-Prozessors

$$Y_B = a_m^{-1}E[T_G]\,(E[T_B] + E[T_U])\,E[T_C]^{-1}.$$

Auslastung der A-Prozessoren

$$Y_{A_i} = a_m^{-1}E[T_G]\,(E[T_{A_i}] + E[T_U])\,E[T_C]^{-1}.$$

Mittlere Anzahl gleichzeitig arbeitender A-Prozessoren während der A-Periode

$$E[I] = \left(\sum_{i=1}^{n} E[T_{A_i}]\right)\Big/ E[T_{AS}].$$

6. Synthese

6.1. Allgemeines

Ziel sämtlicher verkehrstheoretischer Untersuchungen ist es, wirtschaftlich optimale Rechnerstrukturen, Rechnerkonfigurationen und Betriebsarten zu finden. Optimierung komplexer Gesamtsysteme ist aber mit den heute zur Verfügung stehenden mathematischen Hilfsmitteln (und der begrenzten Rechnerleistung) in einem Schritt nicht möglich. Deshalb untersucht und optimiert man Teilsysteme und Teilaspekte und bestimmt das Gesamtoptimum iterativ.

Je nach Umfang des Optimierungsproblems verwendet man verschiedene Verfahren. Wir unterscheiden zwei Gruppen:

Exakte Optimierungsverfahren. Die exakten Methoden der mathematischen Optimierung eignen sich insbesondere für die Untersuchung von Modellen mit nur wenigen Parametern und Variablen. Die Probleme werden als nichtlineare oder ganzzahlige Optimierungsprobleme formuliert [17].

Heuristische Optimierungsverfahren. Bei der Untersuchung komplexer Modelle treten sehr viele Parameter auf: verschiedene Strukturkonzepte, verschieden schnelle Prozessoren, Speicher und Übertragungssysteme, verschiedene Möglichkeiten für den Betriebsablauf, etc. etc. Um den enormen Rechenzeitaufwand der exakten Methoden zu vermeiden, verwendet man häufig Näherungsverfahren, z. B. Gradienten-Verfahren oder Monte-Carlo-Verfahren [17].

6.2. Synthese optimaler Betriebsabläufe bei vorgegebener Programmstruktur

Gegeben sei ein Anwenderprogramm mit Typ-1-Struktur, vergleiche Abb. 6, mit den folgenden Eigenschaften:

die maximale Parallelität beträgt n,

die Verteilungsfunktion der einzelnen, parallel ablauffähigen Teile sei beliebig und einheitlich $F_S(t)$, ihr Mittelwert $E[T_S]$,

jedes Anwenderprogramm bestehe (o.B.d.A.) aus einem Zyklus.

Sind die Übergabephasen $(F_{\ddot{U}}(t), E[T_{\ddot{U}}])$ von B- zu den A-Prozessoren vernachlässigbar kurz gegenüber den Bearbeitungsphasen, so ist die Gesamtbearbeitungszeit $(F_G(t), E[T_G])$ in jedem Fall bei n parallel arbeitenden A-Prozessoren minimal.

Messungen und Laufzeitabschätzungen am EGPA-Pilotprojekt haben jedoch gezeigt, daß der zeitliche Anteil der Übergabephase beträchtlich sein kann und abhängig ist von der Anzahl anzusteuernder A-Prozessoren. Mit anderen Worten, die optimale Anzahl, das heißt jene Anzahl, bei der die Gesamtbearbeitungszeit minimiert wird, ist abhängig vom relativen Übermittlungsaufwand α:

$$\alpha = E[T_0]/E[T_S],$$

wo

$E[T_0]$: mittlere Zeit zur Ansteuerung eines A-Prozessors

$E[T_S]$: mittlere Zeit zur Bearbeitung einer der n Teilaufgaben

Bezeichnet man mit a die Anzahl an einem Anwenderprogramm parallel arbeitenden („aktiven") A-Prozessoren, $1 \leqslant a \leqslant n$, so kann man die Suche nach der günstigen Aufteilung als Optimierungsproblem formulieren:

Minimiere die mittlere Gesamtbearbeitungszeit

$$E[T_G] = E[T_B + T_{\ddot{U}}(\alpha, a) + T_{AS}(a)]$$

mit Berücksichtigung der sich ändernden Bedienungszeit-Verteilungsfunktionen $F_{A_i}(t, a)$ der aktiven A-Prozessoren und deren Einfluß auf die mittlere Synchronisationszeit $E[T_{AS}(a)]$.

Die Nebenbedingung zeigt an, daß — abhängig von a — die aktiven A-Prozessoren eine oder mehrere parallel ablauffähige Teilaufgaben nacheinander bearbeiten. Mittelwerte $E[T_{A_i}(a)]$ und Verteilungsfunktionen $F_{A_i}(t, a)$ ändern sich deshalb und beeinflussen die Synchronisationszeit.

Bei den folgenden numerischen Auswertungen wird angenommen, daß die Gesamtlänge der Übertragungsphase proportional zur Anzahl aktiver A-Prozessoren ist:

$$E[T_{\ddot{U}}(\alpha, a)] = (a - 1) \cdot E[T_0] = (a - 1) \cdot \alpha \cdot E[T_S].$$

6.3. Numerische Ergebnisse

Die Abb. 11 bis 13 zeigen einige typische Beispiele für den Verlauf der Gesamtdurchlaufzeit einzelner Anwenderprogramme.

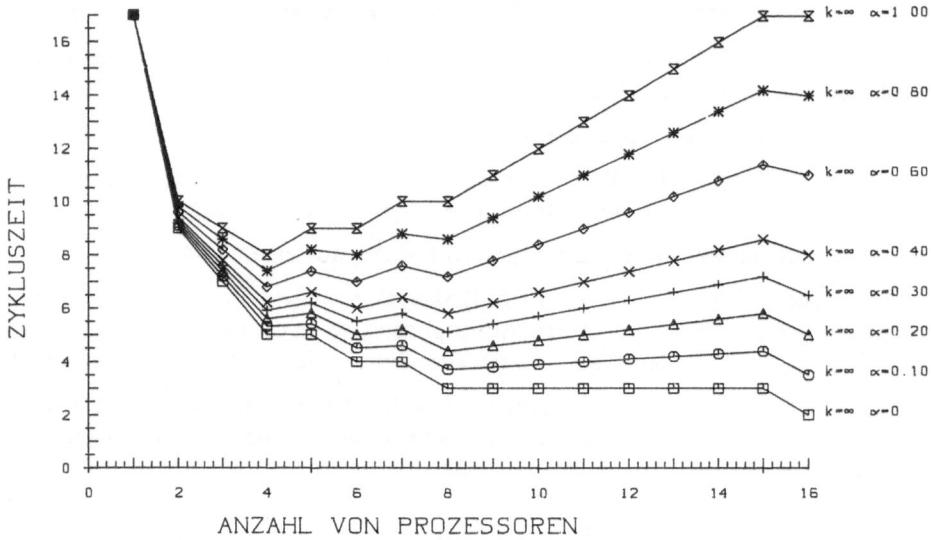

Abb. 11. Konstante Verteilung

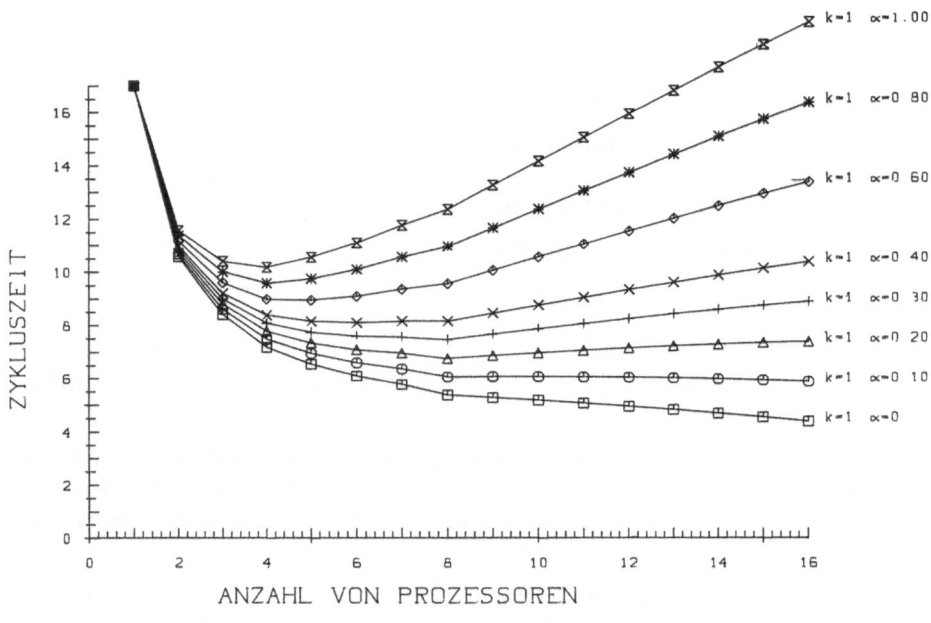

Abb. 12. Exponential-Verteilung

Die Diagramme geben eine Auskunft über

die Abhängigkeit der Gesamtdurchlaufzeit von der Anzahl aktiver Prozessoren,

die starke Verschiebung der Gesamtdurchlaufzeit durch den relativen Übermittlungsaufwand α und

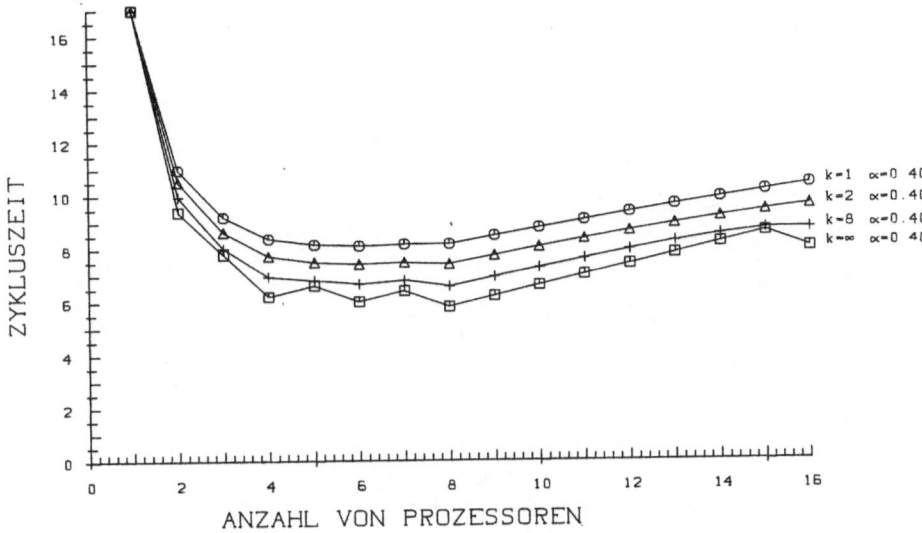

Abb. 13. Erlang-*k*-Verteilung

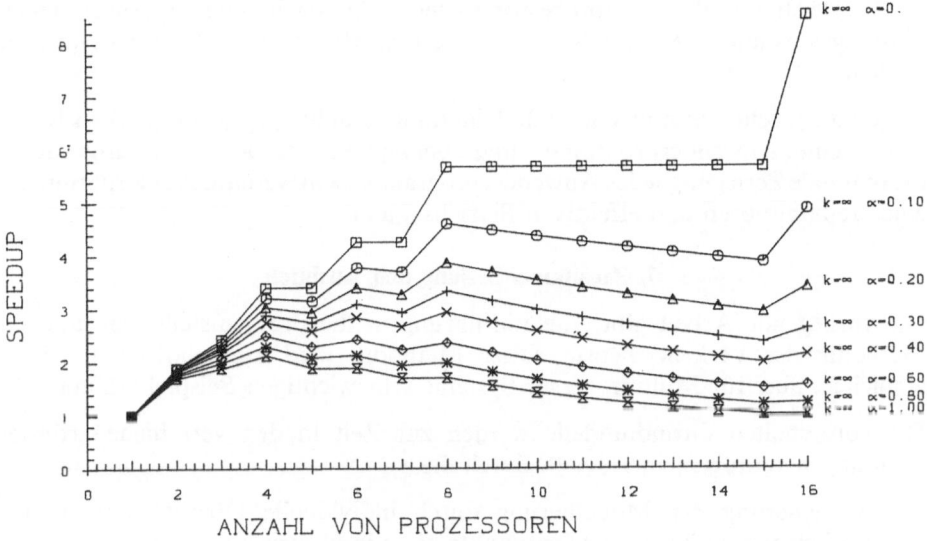

Abb. 14. Konstante Verteilung

die Beeinflussung der Gesamtdurchlaufzeit durch die Verteilungsfunktion der parallel ablauffähigen Teilaufgaben (Exponential-, Erlang-2-, Erlang-8- und konstante Verteilung, $k = \infty$).

Die Abb. 14 und 15 zeigen Beispiele für den Geschwindigkeitsgewinn („Speed-up *S*") eines Mehrprozessor-Systems

$$S = E[T_G(1)]/E[T_G(a)], \qquad a = \{1, 2, \ldots, n\}$$

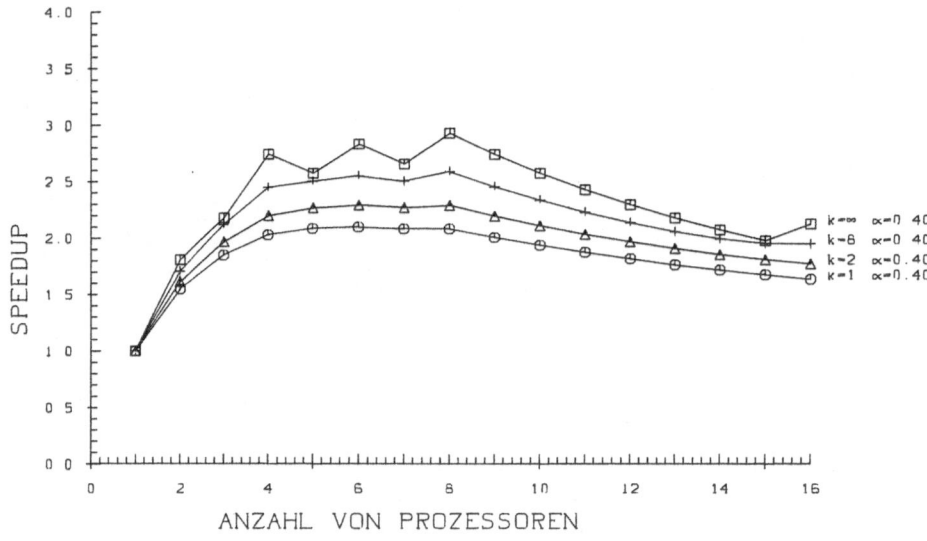

Abb. 15. Erlang-k-Verteilung

im Vergleich mit dem Einprozessor-System; für wachsenden relativen Übermittlungsaufwand zeigen die Kurven den durch Messungen bekannten typischen
Verlauf.

Insgesamt gesehen ermöglichen alle Diagramme, abhängig von typischen Kenn-
größen eines Anwenderprogramms und abhängig von der Rechnerkonfiguration,
die optimale Zerlegung jedes Anwenderprogramms, ein wesentliches Kriterium für
einen reibungslosen und effektiven Betriebsablauf.

7. Zusammenfassung und Ausblick

Die vorliegende Arbeit gibt eine Einführung in die Problemstellungen und die
Methodik der Verkehrstheorie. Diese Methodik wird exemplarisch an einem
einfachen, aber für Multiprozessor-Systeme sehr wichtigen Beispiel erläutert.

Die vorgestellten Grundmodelle werden zur Zeit in den verschiedenartigsten
Richtungen verallgemeinert, z. B. durch die

Verfeinerung der Modellierung durch individuelle Übergabephasen und
zeitlich verschobene Startzeitpunkte für die aktiven A-Prozessoren (Start-
Perioden-Modell),

Verfeinerung der Modellierung durch zusätzliche Rück-Übergabephasen
(Start-Stop-Perioden-Modell),

Berücksichtigung von Speicherkonflikten bei Code- und Datasharing,

Berücksichtigung von Prioritäten bei der Steuerung des Ablaufgeschehens,

Verallgemeinerung der Verteilungsfunktionen für Bedienungs- und Über-
tragungsphasen,

Berücksichtigung der Programm-Struktur realer Anwenderprogramme etc. etc.

Bereits diese Beispiele zeigen, welche Vielzahl wichtiger und interessanter verkehrstheoretischer Fragestellungen noch zu bewältigen ist. Diese Untersuchungen unterstützen den Konstrukteur von Hardware- und Systemsoftware beim Entwurf zukunftsweisender Rechnerkonzepte.

Wir danken Herrn Dipl.-Inf. H. J. Fromm und Herrn Dipl.-Inf. F. Kneißl für die kritische Durchsicht des Manuskripts und wertvolle Anregungen.

Literatur

[1] Cohen, J. W.: The single server queue. Amsterdam-London: North-Holland 1969.

[2] Despain, A. M., Patterson, D.: X-tree, a tree structured multi-processor computer architecture. SIGARCH Newsletter, Computer Architecture News 6, 144–151 (1978).

[3] Frank, H., Frisch, I. T.: Communication, transmission and transportation networks. Reading, Mass.: Addison-Wesley 1971.

[4] Händler, W., Hofmann, F., Schneider, H. J.: A general purpose array with a broad spectrum of applications. Computer Architecture. (Informatik-Fachberichte, Bd. 4) (Händler, W., Hrsg.), S. 311–335. Berlin-Heidelberg-New York: Springer 1975.

[5] Harris, J. A., Smith, D. R.: Hierarchical multiprocessor organisations. Computer Architecture News 5, 41–48 (1977).

[6] Herzog, U., Hoffmann, W.: Synchronization problems in hierarchically organized multiprocessor computer systems. In: Performance of Computer Systems. Proceedings of the 4th International Symposium on Modeling and Performance Evaluation of Computer Systems, Vienna, Austria, February 6–8, 1979 (Arato, M., Butrimenko, A., Gelenbe, E., Hrsg.).

[7] Herzog, U.: Performance characteristics for hierarchically organized multiprocessor computer systems with generally distributed processing times. In: Proceedings of the Ninth International Teletraffic Congress (ITC), October 1979, Torremolinos, Spain, Session 44.

[8] Herzog, U., Hoffmann, W., Kleinöder, W.: Performance modeling and evaluation of hierarchically organized multiprocessor computer systems. Int. Conf. on Parallel Processing, Aug. 21–24, 1979, Bellaire (USA).

[9] Hoffmann, W.: Warteschlangenmodelle für die Parallelverarbeitung. Dissertation, Universität Erlangen-Nürnberg, 1978, Arbeitsberichte des IMMD, Band 11, Nr. 17.

[10] Hoffmann, W.: Queueing models for parallel processing and their application to a hierarchically organized multiprocessing system. 1st European Conf. on Parallel and Distributed Processing, Toulouse, February 14–16, 1979.

[11] Hoffmann, W., Kleinöder, W.: Warteschlangenmodelle für Mehrprozessorsysteme: Maximale Bedienungszeit von l parallel arbeitenden Bedienungsstationen. 9. Jahrestagung der Gl, Bonn (Informatik Fachberichte, Bd. 19), S. 503–514. Berlin-Heidelberg-New York: Springer 1979.

[12] Klar, R.: Hardware-measurements and their application on performance evaluation in a processor-array. Computing, Suppl. 3, pp. 65–88. Wien-New York: Springer 1981.

[13] Kleinöder, W.: Modelling of the communication overhead in a hierarchically organized multiprocessor system. Internal paper, 1979.

[14] Kleinöder, W.: Numerische Auswertung von Funktionen von Verteilungsfunktionen. Programmpaket, 1980.

[15] Kleinrock, L.: Queueing systems, Vol. 1: Theory. J. Wiley 1975.

[16] Kober, R.: Parallel system structures. Siemens Forschungs- und Entwicklungsberichte, 7, Nr. 6 (1978).

[17] Neumann, K.: Operations-Research-Verfahren, Bd. I, II. München-Wien: Carl Hanser 1975.

[18] Schwandt, J.: An approach to use evaluation nets for the performance evaluation of transaction-oriented business computer systems. In: Computer Performance (Chandy, K. M., Reiser, M., Hrsg.). Amsterdam-New York-Oxford: North-Holland 1977.

[19] Shimor, A., Wallach, Y.: A multibus-oriented parallel processor system. IEEE Trans. IECI-25, 137–141 (1978).

[20] Walke, B.: Realzeitrechner-Modelle, Theorie und Anwendung. München-Wien: Oldenbourg-Verlag 1978.

Prof. Dr. U. Herzog
W. Kleinöder
Institut für Mathematische Maschinen
und Datenverarbeitung
Universität Erlangen-Nürnberg
Martensstraße 3
D-8520 Erlangen
Bundesrepublik Deutschland

Computing, Suppl. 3, 65–88 (1981)
© by Springer-Verlag 1981

Hardware Measurements and Their Application on Performance Evaluation in a Processor-Array*

R. Klar, Erlangen

Abstract — Zusammenfassung

Hardware Measurements and Their Application on Performance Evaluation in a Processor-Array. The applicability of hardware measurements to different performance measures is discussed. As an example it is shown that software events, e.g. the process-flow, can be evaluated by means of pure hardware measurements if a good machine architecture supports the system's organization by appropriate hardware.

Hardware-Messungen zur Leistungsbewertung in einem Prozessorfeld. Die Eignung von Hardware-Messungen zur Leistungsbewertung bei verschiedenen Leistungsmaßen wird diskutiert. An einem Beispiel wird gezeigt, daß Software-Ereignisse, hier die Abfolge von Prozessen, mittels reiner Hardware-Messungen bewertet werden können, wenn die Maschinenarchitektur die Systemorganisation durch geeignete Hardware unterstützt.

> ... was man nicht weiß, das eben brauchte man,
> und was man weiß, kann man nicht brauchen.
> Goethe, Faust

1. Introduction

Computers are deterministic automata, the programs they execute are designed in the intention to give well-defined instructions to the hardware, and the data fed into the computer are well-known information. In spite of the fact that as a matter of principle one has full knowledge of the activities in the computer the high complexity of real hardware and software practically makes it impossible to know all machine-states and all state transitions in an operating machine. There especially remain many questions on the flow of activities within the computer which cannot easily be answered. Thus, it is convenient to adopt the fruitful experiences of other engineering disciplines with the method of measuring the characteristics of a system, in assessing the performance of a computer system by measurements.

This paper discusses what problems arise in defining performance and proposes a performance measure which extends Ferrari's performance indices by two additional indices "reliability" and "program development time". Once a practicable performance measure has been defined, there remains the problem of applying it, for instance, in measuring the performance of a given or planned computer system. The role of measurements in the field of performance evaluation, especially that of hardware measurements as one of several evaluation tools is described and some

---

* This work is sponsored by the Bundesminister für Forschung und Technologie.

examples show the historical development of hardware measurements. The last chapter is dedicated to some recent measurements of process-flow in the processor-array EGPA (Erlangen General Purpose Array), which have been done by pure hardware monitoring.

2. The Problem of Defining Performance

The user of a computer system esteems the performance of a computer system if he can solve his problem with a small amount of work and in a short time. He does not primarily ask for details as cpu-throughput or channel-activity but for perceivable characteristics as response time, time to compile, time to find a program error, turnaround-time and run time of the correct program. These characteristics have changing significance in the different phases of the process of solving a problem, see Fig. 1.

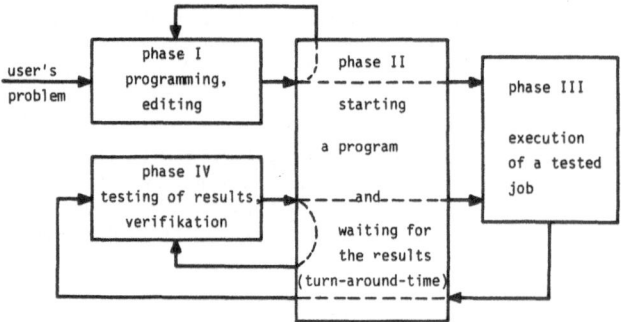

Fig. 1. The process of solving a user-problem as a multiphase process with feedback

In phases I and IV above all other features of the system, one is interested in the quality of debug programs, compilers, editors, in the file-management and, hence, to some extent in the capacity of primary and secondary memory. Summarizing, the computer should support the user instead of frustrating him, it should behave in a "friendly" way. A central role for this and all other work plays the turnaround-time (phase II) which is determined by the organization of the computer center as well as by the features of the operating system and the speed of the processor. It is only the phase III where one particularly needs the classical performance measure, i.e. an excellent processing power of the central processing unit [15], [37]. And even in this phase of intensive computation not only the speed of the processor but also features as data transfer rates or memory organization play an important role in the total performance. Phase IV symbolizes that a program usually needs several runs for testing and debugging before a (hopefully) fault-free version is developed [21][1].

The many different phases of the problem-solving process and the viewpoint of the respective user or evaluator naturally lead to manifold proposals for a definition of performance. Peter Denning describes this difficult situation with the sceptical statement: "We demand good performance but we do not have clear notions what good performance is, or how to tell when it has been achieved" [7]. Though this critical statement should be taken in earnest, it can be said that there exist some

---

[1] A recent paper of R. E. Brooks analyzes also behavioral and psychological techniques to the evaluation of programming languages, i.e. on phases I and IV [44].

practicable proposals for a definition of performance. Ferrari introduces the term "performance index" [12] and defines three index classes:

productivity given in terms of [volume/time]
responsiveness given in terms of [time]
utilization given in terms of [relative activity-time].

In this approach all effective power of the system, as remarked by the user, is inherent in the index class "responsiveness" which, for instance, includes turnaround-time or response-time. This classification of performance measures comprises the assessment of the work within phase III and to some extent in phases I and II but it gives no measure for the "program development time" which is given by the duration and the necessary number of test runs (phase IV), the latter highly depending on the quality of the software support for program-development. Svoboda informally mentions this problem by the question: "How well does the system enable me to do what I want to do?" [42].

A second essential quality of a system which is not included in Ferrari's classification is its reliability which gives a measure for the chance to find the system in operation when it is needed. It seems that in the field of reliability-research one begins to consider again the proposals of Hughes who recommended to use hardware measurements as a means for better system reliability [22]. On the 9th Ann. Symp. on Fault Tolerant Computing (1979) several papers delt with this interdependence of reliability and performance [33], [14], [25]. However, these approaches treat only one aspect, that of the influence of the system's reliability on its performance, and they mostly deal with the performance of multiprocessor systems with fail-soft strategies and changing number of available processors.

In order to include these aspects too, I propose to add two more criteria: "program development time" and "reliability" to Ferrari's "performance indices", see Table 1. Unfortunately, these additional criteria make it more difficult again to define an overall[2] performance measure. A formal approach given by Estrin does not solve this problem neither [9].

Estrin proposes an overall "computer power" P as a weighted (w_i) sum of the performances P_i of all n components which contribute to the total work of the system:

$$\text{computer power } P := \sum_{i=1}^{n} w_i \cdot P_i.$$

Though formally perfect, this formula only defines a meaningful power P, if it is possible to specify all components P_i and their importance w_i.

Analyzing the model of Fig. 2 it would be desirable to specify first the user's demand to the system, i.e. to specify the workload, and to construct systems which satisfy the workload requirements with minimal costs. There are many serious efforts to describe workload [2], [10], [18], but two experiences thwart a workload-definition which remains valid for a long time:

---

[2] The many different aspects of computer performance may be inconvenient if one aims at optimal simplicity, but it is inavoidable that a complex object can only be assessed by a multitude of attributes.

- the workload normally changes with time

- even if the original problem remains unchanged, there exists a feedback between system and user which leads to an adaption of the workload to the system's properties, see dashed line in Fig. 2.

As a consequence of these dynamically changing workloads a straightforward construction of a computer system for a given workload is normally not possible (dedicated computers with constant workload excluded).

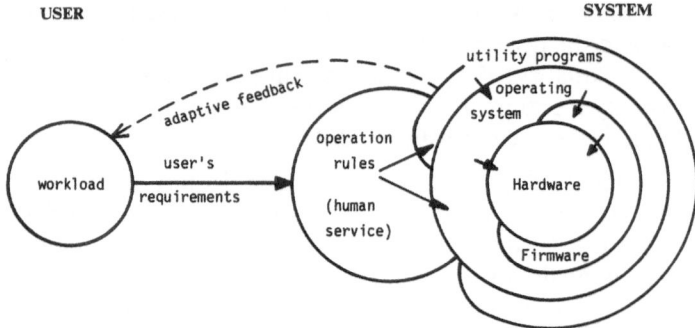

Fig. 2. A user's access to a computer system is a process which goes through a multitude of different levels which all contribute to the total system power [29], [42]

But it seems reasonable to follow Denning's first proposal [7] in dividing the jobs (workload) into K classes wk and to analyze the structural requirements of each class wk ($k = 1, 2, \ldots, K$) separately. Each real workload would be a subset of these classes with weighted elements (weight: gk).

$$\text{workload} := \sum_{k=1}^{K} gk \cdot wk.$$

In natural extension of the concept of a workload which consists of workload-components it is only consequent to define the performance to be achieved by a computer system as consisting of performance components, see Table 1, where Ferrari's performance indices are used as the first three components. Extending Denning's proposal, the desired performance should be definable for each workload-component wk depending on the user's needs (Table 1).

Table 1. *Performance components pci describing different user interests with respect to system performance*

$pc1$	productivity
$pc2$	responsiveness
$pc3$	utilization
$pc4$	program development time
$pc5$	reliability

Summarizing these considerations, we see that there are two kinds of criteria necessary for defining a performance measure for the design of new computers and for the evaluation of existing computers:

wk: workload components (job classes which characterize the workload)

pci: performance components (desired system-characteristics).

The achieved performance of a computer under a given workload is not regarded to be an absolute value of a single performance measure but it is seen as a multitude of relative performances Pi

$$Pi := \sum_{k=1}^{K} gk \times \frac{pci(wk)\,\text{achieved}}{pci(wk)\,\text{desired}}$$

(each for one performance component pci) which indicate to which degree the desired performance has been achieved.

If two computers are to compose, all relevant performance components have to be taken into account with their respective weight. This leads to a total performance P which is relative in a double sense:

the performance Pi of pci is related to the desired performance of the ith component

the importance of the different performance aspects represented by the components pci depends on the respective application. It should be taken into account as a weight-factor "significance of pci".

$$P := \sum_{i}\sum_{k} (\text{significance of } pci) \times gk \times \frac{pci(wk)\,\text{achieved}}{pci(wk)\,\text{desired}}.$$

This definition of a relative performance thwarts all efforts to define a simple performance measure but it has the advantage to show to the user that his first task in performance evaluation is to specify what he wants and that only application-specific measures meet his actual needs.

Example. Let us assume a computer system which has to compute large background jobs with numeric computations (workload $w1$), which has to answer requests from remote terminals within approximately 5 seconds and which has to have a reliability $R(t)$. But development of new programs shall be rare and the utilization of the system shall be of secondary importance, i.e. the significance of $pc3$ and $pc4$ can be assumed to be zero. The remaining performance components $pc1$, $pc2$, $pc5$ represent the desired performance if they are defined as follows:

$pc1(w1, w2)$ desired := a typical benchmark shall be computed in T minutes if n terminals are operating

$pc2(w2)$ desired   := a request shall be answered in at least 5 seconds (since jobs of class $w2$ have higher priority than those of class $w1$, the influence of $w1$ may be disregarded)

*pc*3 desired   := the system shall have a reliability $R(t)$. $R(t)$ is the probability that the system correctly works in the interval $[0, t]$, if it was well operating at time $t = 0$ (the reliability is assumed to depend only on the system's configuration but not on the workload).

3. Performance Evaluation

Once a performance measure has been defined, the problem is to find out whether a computer design (structure) or an actually built computer fulfills the specified requirements. Table 2 resumes the most common techniques for performance evaluation in a similar way as Lucas did 1971 in his survey [30]. While Lucas considers how these techniques may support one of the three purposes

● selection of an existing computer for a given or estimated workload

● projection of experiences with existing computers onto new systems

● monitoring of an existing system with the intention to optimize the hardware configuration or the software,

the resume of Table 2 relates evaluation techniques and performance components.

Timings and mixes serve for prediction, whereas kernels and benchmarks serve for measurement of the productivity of a CPU or a complete system, both without analyzing the structural reasons of a predicted or measured performance. In contrary to this, analytic models, simulation and monitoring use the structures of hardware and software as a necessary prerequisite for understanding the causes of an observed performance.

It is not very surprising that the common evaluation techniques only master the traditional performance components which describe a system which is thought to be reliable and which does not include the human factors represented by the performance components "program development time". While there exist well developed tools for an analysis of systems reliability by analytic models and by simulation, the idea of measuring reliability is really new. It would be an interesting application of benchmarks to study the quality of fail-soft-strategies in a system like EGPA [17] or CM* [13] under forced elimination of one or more processors of the array. Until now the human factors are rarely included in performance evaluation. None of the regarded evaluation techniques is suited for assessing the man-machine interdependence since they only take into account the properties of the machine. Some new attempts to include psychological aspects in performance considerations are restricted to the performance of programmers who had learned in different ways [32][3]. It would be of interest to know the performance, a user can achieve under different computer systems or different strategies of the operating system.

Emphasizing that the desirable role of a computer is that of a "friendly" tool which is easy to handle and which is adapted to the user's desires, the author has to admit that this paper, too, mainly contributes to the classical approaches in measuring what is going on in the central processing unit. But the results of these cpu-measurements support the human user in disclosing the real-time interaction of

---

[3] The recent paper of Brooks [44] is not yet regarded here.

Table 2. *The applicability of the most common evaluation methods for assessing the quality of hardware and software and for assessing the five performance components pci of Table 1. The performance components $p2$ to $p5$ are characterized by* − *(not suited),* + *(suited),* ++ *(well-suited)*

Evaluation method	Conditions for the applicability of the respective evaluation method	Suited for assessing the hardware- and/or software quality	Suited for assessing the performance components pci				
			$pc1$ productivity	$pc2$ respon.	$pc3$ util.	$pc4$ prog. dev. time	$pc5$ reliab.
Timings	Execution time of operations	Hardware	CPU and ALU	−	−	−	−
Mixes	Execution time and work-load-specific frequency of operations	Hardware	CPU and ALU	−	−	−	−
Kernels	Execution time of typical programs	Hardware and hardware support for planned software	CPU, ALU and main memory	−	−	−	−
Models	Assumptions on workload and on the computer (-design) to be evaluated	More suited for hardware than for software	Total system or system moduls	+	++	−	++
Simulation	Execution time and work-load-specific frequency of operations (-design) to be evaluated	Very well suited for hardware and software	Total system or system moduls	+	++	−	++
Benchmarks	Require an existing and well-operating object computer	Total system performance including hardware and software	Total system throughput	+	−	−	+
Hardware-monitoring		Normally only hardware sometimes extension to software	Total system or hardware modules	++	++	−	+
Software-monitoring		Software	Total system or modls	++	+	−	−
Hybrid-monitoring		Hardware and software	Total system or moduls	++	++	−	−

processes, in terms of offering an insight in the dynamic flow of process-activities. A better insight will help the system programmer to find better solutions, thus, there may be an indirect contribution to the performance component "program development time".

4. A Short Review of Hardware Measurements

Since the measurements of process-flow in the processor-array EGPA have been done by hardware, it may be useful to see these measurements in the larger context of the history of hardware-monitoring. Anticipating a comparison of different measurement approaches, I would like to make a critical remark:

In spite of the fact that the first hardware-monitors go back to the early sixties one has to take notice of the frustrating experience that nearly all efforts in designing and using hardware-monitors had and have to begin at a zero-starting-point as if there had not been any previous work on this field.

A first reason for this situation is the disproportion of the small effort which is necessary to design a hardware-monitor and the much higher amount of work needed for definition, execution and evaluation of an experiment which uses a hardware-monitor as a measuring instrument.

A second reason for the recurrent character of many of the published papers is the fact that the experiments and their results are obsolete every time a new computer or a new operating system has been put into service. There arise new questions and new measurement problems with every new object system. Nevertheless, some principles of a hardware measurement reappear nearly unchanged in each experiment:

> definition of events
> detection of events
> recording of events
> recording of elapsed time
> recording of number of events
> evaluation of the recorded results
> interpretation and application of the results.

Only the practical implementation of the last two steps is highly dependent from the measured object-system and the desired results, whereas the first five steps are very similar in all hardware measurements. This is why commercial hardware monitors appeared on the market only a few years after the first monitors had been built by manufacturers and universities for machines like IBM 7090/7094 in 1963 [24], for an IBM /360 time-sharing system in 1967 [39] and for a DEC PDP-7 in 1968 [26].

The different types of hardware measurements which have been executed in the past can be threefold characterized:

a) The first distinguishing features are the information paths between monitor and object computer used for the measurement [27]. Fig. 3 shows in addition to path I which is essential for any hardware measurement the two paths II and III which provide for possibilities surpassing standard hardware measurements. Most of the early hardware monitors were instruments using only path I. They collected the measured data in an own memory and/or displayed them immediately. Typical examples are utilization monitors recording CPU and channel activities [24], [3], [43], [39] or Apple's program monitor which recorded traces of the instruction counter contents of an IBM 7090 [4]. The immediate display of results is favorized in the work of Nonnenmacher [35] and Stang and Southgate [40]. Path II is the prerequisite for influencing hardware measurements by software events occurring in the object computer, i.e. for hybrid measurements. The necessity for influencing the hardware monitor by the software of the object computer has been emphasized by Morgan [34] and by Estrin for the (never built) SNUPER computer [8]. Path III enables the monitor to send results of the measurement back to the object-computer. If the operating system of the object-computer is prepared to use the monitor's data as a decision-aid it can adapt itself to new workload situations etc. which are perceived by the hardware-monitor. This idea of an adaptive operating system proposed by Spies and Klar in 1969 [26] seems to come up again [11]. The idea of feedback from monitor to object is also mentioned by Aschenbrenner who planned a channel interface from the ARGONNE neurotron monitor to an IBM 360 equipment [5].

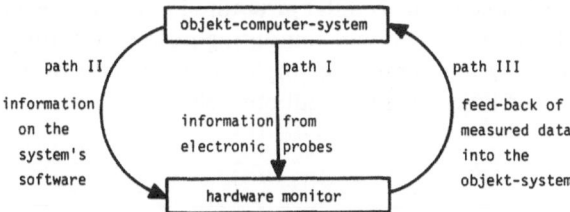

Fig. 3. The three essential information paths between the measured computer and the measuring instrument

b) A second essential property of a measurement is the type of collected data. If only the utilization of the different system components is needed, the counters of the monitor can gather information on all interesting activities over a relatively long observation interval, providing a result of the type "mean". But if one wishes to know the causes of a resulting utilization it is necessary to measure how the different hardware parts and software processes dynamically interact. In this case one needs "dynamic traces" of the interesting activities.

c) The third distinguishing feature has come up with modern computer architecture which deals with multiprocessor systems, processor arrays and computer networks. These computer systems need additional coordination mechanisms and a hardware measurement supporting them will also need additional synchronization features. One example for measurements in a processor-array is the hardware measurement of the coordination in Hydra, the operating system of Carnegie-Mellon University's multi-miniprocessor C.mmp which has been done in 1977 by Marathe and Fuller [31]. The problems arising in monitoring computer networks have been studied by Morgan at the University of Waterloo, Canada, who proposes remote

computer controlled hardware monitors with additional telephone lines to the
controlling computer [34]. The monitors are placed at the nodes of the network.

5. The Integration of a Hardware-Monitor into the EGPA-Pyramid

The Erlangen General Purpose Array EGPA is a "three-dimensional" processor-
array which has the structure of a pyramid, see Fig. 4. The pyramid is instrumented
by a hardware-monitor, called "ZÄHLMONITOR III", see Fig. 5, with all three
information paths I, II and III for hardware measurements, software influences
(hybrid measurements) and result feed-back. The favored measurements are
hardware supported measurements which yield "traces" of software events. The
special problems of parallel processing in the pyramid are overcome by a set of
simultaneously operating comparators.

Once central idea of the EGPA-structure is to concentrate the administrative work
in the top of the pyramid or in the higher levels, e.g. I/O-operations and operating
system functions, while the lower and larger processor-plains have to process user
problems in parallel. Another essential principle of EGPA is to achieve uncon-
ventional computing with conventional hardware in using microprogrammable
processors and linking conventional processors and memories in such a way that
they build up a freely extensible cellular structure [17]. The free extensibility of the
array is a means for achieving higher computing power by adding more processors
and memories to the system without changing the structure of the elementary cells
(see Fig. 4) and their links to the neighbour-cells.

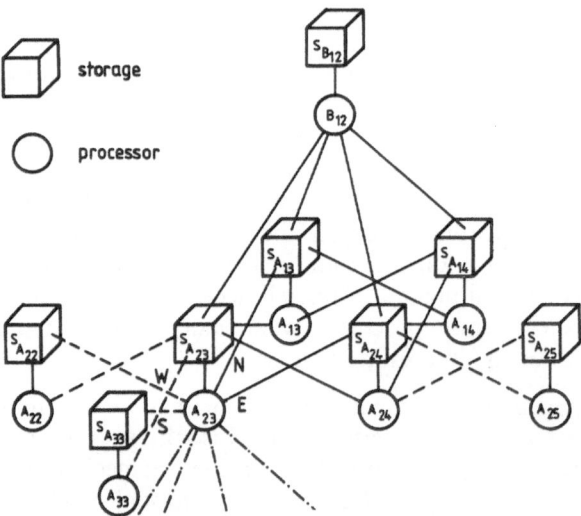

Fig. 4. One elementary pyramid of the EGPA-system. Possible extensions to other elementary pyramids
within the A-array (———) and to a lower level (—·—) indicate that one processor (e.g. A23) is
interconnected to no more than nine memories. Memories have to have only six-ports, since there exists
only one interconnection to a processor in the next higher level

These links interconnect a given processor (e.g. $A23$) with the storages $SA13$, $SA24$, $SA33$, $SA22$ of its "northern", "eastern", "southern" and "western" neighbours and with storages of the four immediately subordinated processors in the next lower level. In each level, all processors at the borders of the array are connected with their "neighbours" at the opposite border to form a toroidal closing of this level. At the moment all experimental studies are done with an elementary pyramid consisting of one B-processor and four A-processors, see Fig. 5.

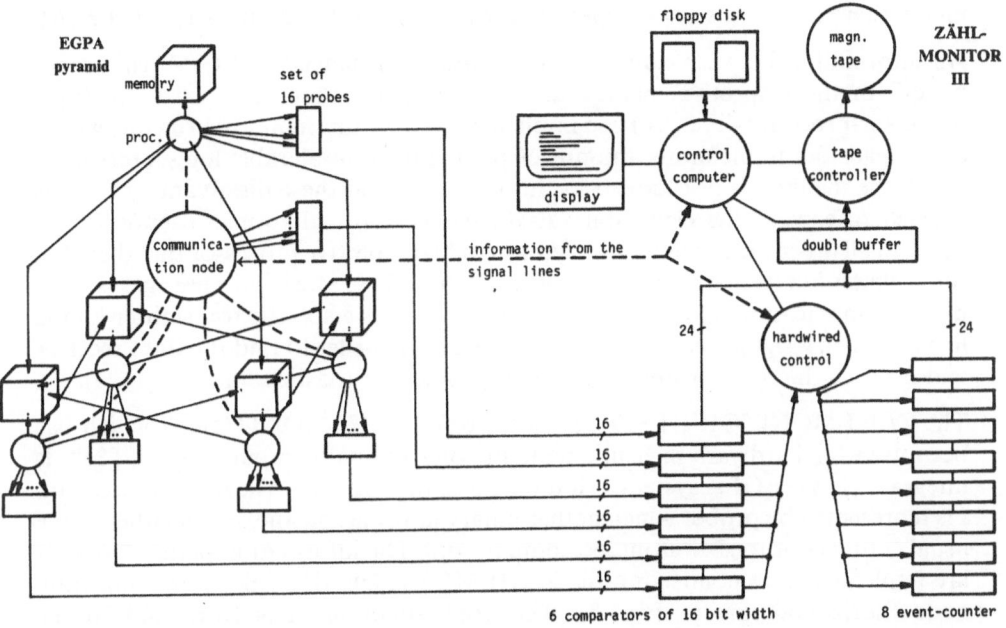

Fig. 5. The hardware monitor ZÄHLMONITOR III is connected to the communication-node of the EGPA-pyramid as if it were a sixth processor (dashed lines). The displayed parts of the figure show the resources used for the measurement of process activities

The internal structure of each processor is normally that of a conventional processor of the Princeton type, operating a word of N bits (called "horizontal" data) in parallel. However, using the postulated microprogrammability, the N-bit-processor can also be regarded as a block of N one-bit-processors operating on N "vertically" stored bit strings of arbitrary length, e.g. m bits. The simultaneous operation on N different bit strings can be done in such a way that it appears to be associative in the sense of an associative processor like STARAN [36]. In spite of this apparent bit-string-processing not N bit strings are accessed from the memory but a sequence of m conventional N-bit-words [16]. This "quasivertical" access allows for utilization of conventional memories.

The processors in the lowest level (A-processors) can operate in three modes as far as their grouping to subarrays is concerned:

1. no grouping; the processors work independently from each other

2. total grouping; all processors operate as a whole on the same instruction but on different data (ILLIAC IV-Mode)

3. partial grouping; the processors of the A-plane are grouped to sub-arrays depending on the problem to be solved. The most intensively studied application of partial grouping is the dataflow-mode.

Combining these three interconnection-modes with the ability of each processor to process data in the classical "horizontal" (H) mode as well as in the "vertical" (V) mode, there are six modes of operation, called $H1$, $H2$, $H3$ and $V1$, $V2$, $V3$ [6].

All information between adjacent processors is exchanged in EGPA via "mail-boxes" in the respective memories. Fig. 4 displays that there exist no direct processor-processor-links. A rigid implementation of this mailbox-principle would either lead to a tremendous amount of polling or to intolerable long intervals in which the mailbox is not looked in. In order to avoid these disadvantages it was decided to expand the elementary EGPA-concept by additional attention-links between all processors which call attention to the respective processor that there lies some "letter" in its mailbox. The coordination of these attention-messages is done by a communication node [20]. The node recognizes a specific transmitter by the line on which a signal arrives, decodes this signal in order to find the right receiver and informs the receiver about the message's sender (dashed lines in Fig. 5).

The ZÄHLMONITOR III [19], a successor of ZÄHLMONITOR II which has been used for hardware measurements in conventional computers [28], [38], is integrated in the EGPA system as if it were a sixth processor. The information path I is represented by probes which gather binary information and lead it either to the usual counters or to six automatic comparators. The information paths II and III are implemented in connecting the ZÄHLMONITOR III to the communication node (horizontal line in Fig. 5). The used attention links from and to the communication node are designed for short messages, e.g., for software controlled start/stop commands to the monitor or short load indicators as page-fault frequency. A second implementation of path II can be achieved in using two of the comparators (which need not to be connected to different processors) for comparing memory addresses with a given address and recording the contents of the memory data register at each address match.

While the path II is positively intended to give ZÄHLMONITOR III the properties of a hybrid monitor [8], [41], [23], it is not planned at the moment to use the path III for constructing an adaptive operating system [26]. But path III shall be a means for influencing software measurements by the hardware monitor, thus making up some sort of "inverse" hybrid monitor.

The recorded data may incidentally be used for utilization statistics, but the main objective is to get insight in the dynamic flow of activities in the pyramid, as will be described later.

The modes of operation in EGPA which implement parallel processing, need tools for synchronizing the different processors working on the same problem.

ZÄHLMONITOR III can simultaneously measure up to six independent bit patterns which may arrive asynchronously. Therefore, the monitor is an appropriate tool for evaluation of the synchronization mechanisms implemented in EGPA. It should be noted that the monitor can record the correct sequence of incoming events if they arrive in a distance of more than 100 ns [20].

6. Measurement of Process-Flow in the EGPA-System

The designer of an operating system can evaluate the effectiveness of the implemented algorithms only if he knows the dynamic behaviour of all activities in the system. However, he risks to get drowned in a deluge of information if he does not restrict himself to a small subset of all activities going on in the system. One approach to choose a reasonable subset of activity characteristics is to regard all activities within an uninterrupted processing phase of a user- or a system-process as *one* activity. Since there is exactly one process (per processor) operating at the same time, it is sufficient to record only the stream of processes without any process internals. This provides a well-defined description which is much more detailed than accounting information, but free from all internal bagatelles of a processes run. Normally, only software measurements can recognize which process is active at a given time. A severe disadvantage of this method is the fact that an evaluation-program would run on the object-system to be measured, thus changing the original process-flow. The drawback of software measurements has been avoided in the measurements of the EGPA-system since the processors which are used in the EGPA-pyramid (AEG-Telefunken 80-60) have an interesting feature which enables the registration of process-flow by pure hardware measurements[4].

6.1. Principles of the Measurement

The scheduler of the operating system MARTOS is assisted by microprogrammed routines and by a hardware-priority-register SYR[12:19] which contains the process-number of the active process [1]. All processes p of a "subsystem", e.g. all programs and support software of a user's job, have to have different process numbers p [5]. Thus, the process-number can immediately be regarded and used as a priority, providing a considerable acceleration of the process of finding that waiting process which has the highest priority when the active process is interrupted or becomes dormant or finished. A hardware measurement recording the flow of process numbers in the priority register results in an exhaustive and precise description of all activities on the process-level.

A sequence S of sequence steps s_i

$$S ::= \text{ordered set of sequence steps } s_i;$$

$$s_i ::= (p_i, tp_i); \qquad i = 1, 2, 3, \ldots$$

[4] The described experiments are promoted by priority-handling hardware and use the advantage of hardware measurements not to disturb the original process-flow. But it should be noted that software measurements would not only suffer from the induced artifacts but also from the need to modify the microprograms which perform the process-activation/-deactivation. A modification of these essential and nontrivial microprograms would be a severe and critical operation.

[5] The allocation of process numbers p is carried through by the operating system MARTOS dynamically and parametrized. The user has only to specify relative priorities according to his intentions.

is the result of the measurements (where $p_i ::=$ number p of the process which has been active in the ith sequence step s_i and tp_i is the duration of the process p in the ith sequential step).

These properties of the object-computers are effectively applicated by respective parts of the hardware-monitor.

A specific feature of ZÄHLMONITOR II and III is the automatic event comparator which looks at a stream of events and selectively records only those bit patterns which are distinct from their predecessors. The measurement using the automatic event comparator is done in the following way: Eight inputs of a 16-bit-comparator are connected via test probes to the priority-register SYR[12:19]. Each time, a load pulse for the priority-registers is observed, the – possibly new – process number in SYR[12:19] is compared with the preceding process number. If the new process number turns out to be different from the preceding one, the present sequence step s_i is finished and step $s_i + 1$ begins. The duration tp_i of the process p which has been active in step s_i and the process number p_i are stored in the buffer memory. A fast hardware controller controls the comparison, the storing of s_i in the buffer memory and the process-change at the same time.

If the first buffer-memory is full, its contents is stored on the tape and incoming results are stored in the second buffer-memory. The data-rate of the incoming results is small enough to guarantee that no information is lost in cause of the tape's speed.

A problem specific to the EGPA-system is the concurrency of processes in the different processors, each of them generating an a priori independent stream of process runs. The correlation between these streams depends on the operating mode and therefore it is of high interest to know this correlation in order to evaluate the implementation of the operating modes. The ZÄHLMONITOR III meets these requirements by a hardwired control unit for all comparators, see Fig. 5, which is fast enough to recognize the correct sequence of arriving process numbers p_i if their times of arrival differ more than 100 ns. The following results stem from the first project phase with single-processor experiments.

6.2. Analysis of Competing Processes: An Example

The ZÄHLMONITOR III has been used to measure the process-flow in a single processor of the EGPA-system. The load chosen for this experiment consisted of either one or two translations of a program of about 1000 lines of SL3-code[6]. We made this choice since the SL3-compiler has some relevancy for the EGPA project and because of reproducibility.

The hardware configuration has been a single processor with either a 256 kB memory or a 512 kB memory. As indicated before, the hardware measurement has been recording the sequence S consisting of process number p_i and duration tp_i of p in the ith step. With off-line evaluation of S, the following dynamic characteristics have been investigated:

---

[6] AEG-Telefunken offer for their computers 80-60 a very interesting higher programming language SL3, based on ALGOL 68 with integrated machine-oriented elements.

typical activity-time tp of a process p
dynamic neighbourhood, e.g. $p_i - 1$ and $p_i + 1$ of the process p_i
dependency of activity-time tp_i from predecessor and successor processes
relative portion of user-, system- and idle-time
contention between two jobs.

The Observed Processes

Using skilful priority allocation to the utility processes led to unequivocal process-number definitions, so that each measured process number exactly characterizes one of the interesting activities. This allocation is given in Table A1 of the appendix. While most system activities are always represented by the same process number, a utility or user activity, e.g. code generation, may have different process numbers for different jobs. This property has been used to distinguish the activities of the two simultaneously started translations; i.e. job A and job B in Table 3 and in Fig. 8.

Results

The four experiments resulted in a total processing time which is highly depending on the available amount of main memory[7]:

single job, 256 kB:	459 sec	per translation
single job, 512 kB:	410 sec	per translation
two jobs, 256 kB:	1208 sec, i.e. 604 sec	per transaction
two jobs, 512 kB:	836 sec, i.e. 418 sec	per translation.

It is obvious that in the case of the smaller main memory it would have been better to load only one job at a time, since simultaneous start of two jobs at a time leads to a competition overhead of about 30%.

The typical activity time tp of a process p and its relative frequency as well as the relative portion of the total processing time consumed by a process p are given in Table A2 of the appendix. All results of Table A2 are evaluated as the mean of the total processing time. Table 3, representing a short summary of Table A2, indicates that a main memory which is too mall will be the essential bottleneck of the system:

The process 16 which handles page faults ("Kachelbefreiung") consumes only a half percent of the total time if enough main memory is available but it needs four and twelve times more if a too small memory forces continuous swapping. This result is also reflected by a significant larger cpu-wait component.

These overall characteristics have been computed off-line from a complete trace of the process-flow in the system, which provides also for information on the transitions between the different processes. Fig. 6 shows the graph of a transition matrix.

---

[7] These results have been measured under a maintenance version (MV10) from late 1978.

Table 3. *Relative frequency and relative portion of the total processing time for the essential classes of activities*

Activity	Process no.	Relative frequency of the resp. processes				Relative portion of total time, consumed by the resp. processes			
		1 job 256 kB	1 job 512 kB	2 jobs 256 kB	2 jobs 512 kB	1 job 256 kB	1 job 512 kB	2 jobs 256 kB	2 jobs 512 kB
Clock and page fault act.	9, 16	2.7	2.2	4.3	2.1	2.0	0.4	6.0	0.5
Interrupt and I/O handling	13, 14, 15	58.5	59.9	57.4	64.6	7.2	8.0	6.4	9.1%
Command decoding	17	0.3	0.2	0.5	0.3	0.5	0.6	0.5	0.6
Loading a "Teilsystem"	19	0.8	0.6	0.7	0.6	0.8	0.9	0.6	0.9
Database handling	30	5.0	5.2	3.6	4.1	1.2	1.4	0.9	1.3
Complication	167, 169, 170, 177, 179, 180	5.0	4.5	8.5	5.1	13.6	15.1	11.2	14.3
Code generation	108, 109, 110, 118, 119, 120	13.3	13.5	10.3	10.3	21	18.1	12.6	17.6
Wait process	255	14.2	13.6	14.6	12.8	58.3	55.5	61.8	55.1%

relative frequency of the processes activity

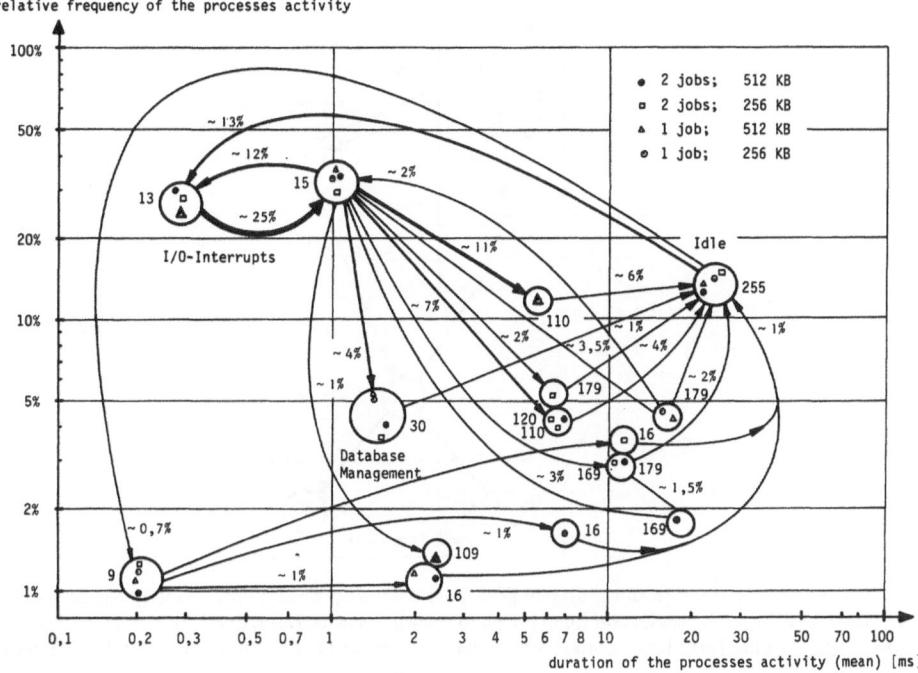

Fig. 6. Transition graph

Each process is plotted in a double logarithmic scale at a point which indicates how long the process has been active and how often it has been activated. The four experiments are marked by (●, □, △, ⊙) and it can be seen that all system processes except process 16 remain nearly unchanged in the four cases, i.e. they take nearly the same point in the two-dimensional duration/frequency space. The process 16, however, does at first sight only change its characteristics as far as duration and frequency are concerned, but not its intercommunication with other processes, see bold lines in Fig. 7.

A more detailed analysis shows that the triangle (9, 16, 255) which normally handles only the real time clock, is also reached from process 15 if a too small memory produces page faults, which are handled by process 16 (see dashed line in Fig. 7).

The history of the two extreme experiments (1 job/512 kB and 2 jobs/256 kB) is plotted in Fig. 8. All thirty seconds the relative activity of the most essential processes has been evaluated, providing a clear picture of what is going on in the system. The single job is finished after 6 minutes and 45 seconds, while the competing two jobs A and B need 20 minutes and 7 seconds.

In the compilation phase (108 − 119) job A has always the higher priority but job B is able to perform an essential part of its compilation in parallel. The code generation phase runs under inverse priorities, in spite of this, the job A having lower priority than job B begins its code generation before job B, see interval X in

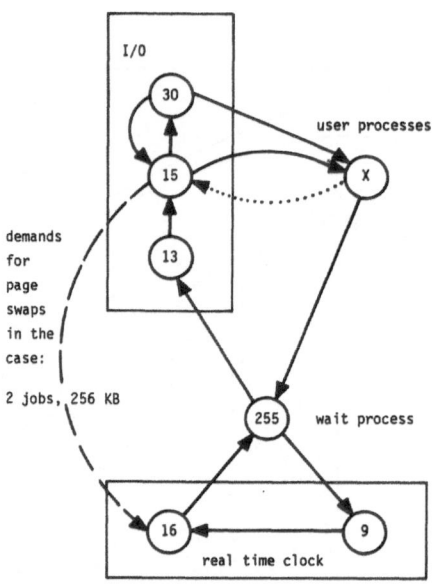

Fig. 7. The main activity flow in the system goes from the wait process to preparing I/O-processes and from there to the user processes and finally back to the wait process (bold lines). I/O requests from user processes (dotted line) are also essential and frequent. The dashed edge from 15 to 16 is only used in case of page swaps

Fig. 8. As soon as job *B* has finished its compilation (process 120), it starts its code generation (process 169) suppressing that of job *A* (process 179). Nevertheless, the job *A* is able to hinder job *B* significantly without taking much advantages of its competition, see interval *Y* in Fig. 8.

Another result of this history of the translation is that the codegenerator seems to have all necessary information in the main memory so that it can perform its work in one intensive phase. A comparison between the single job and the job *A* which performs the last part of its activities also without competitor, shows that the main memory of 256 kB is even too small for one job running at a time. While the single job in a 512 kB memory reaches up to 75% cpu-utilization, job *A* does only reach some 55 percent because of the "small" 256 kB memory.

If the history trace indicates that there might be critical competition situations which should be avoided, the complete trace has to be analyzed. Table A3 of the appendix shows like a magnifying-lens what activities are going on in detail at the beginning of the interval *Y* in the double job run with a 256 kB memory: the beginning of process 169 (job *B*) leads to a suppression of the earlier started process 179 (job *A*).

Conclusion

The level of processes has been shown to be suited for an analysis of the dynamic behaviour of single or competitive jobs under a given operating system and main

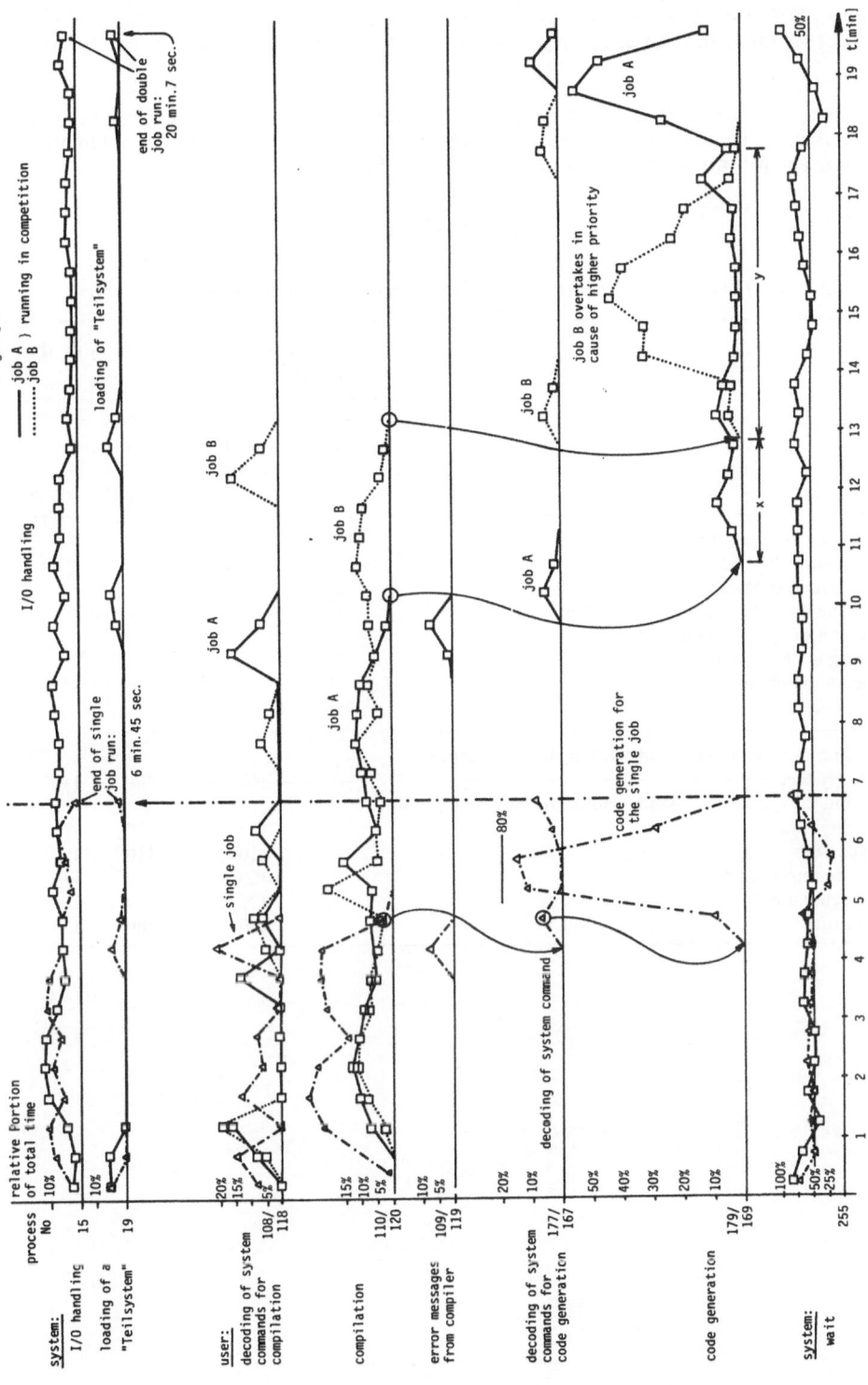

Fig. 8. Flow of process activities in a single processor for two cases: 1. one translation (single job: —·—), 2. two competing translations A and B
(job A: ———, job B: ······)

memory size: the results are detailed enough for receiving a precise insight and the amount of measured data is small enough to be managed without large efforts.

I would like to thank my colleagues U. Hercksen, W. Kleinöder, J. Stelzner, and H. Woitok for their help in preparing, executing and interpreting the measurements and also L. Lange and P. Schapelt for their great care and patience in drawing the figures and typing the manuscript.

7. Appendix

Table A1. *The representation of system- and utility-activities by different process numbers*

Activity	Process number associated with the activity		
	System tasks	Single translation	Two translations
			Job *A* / Job *B*
Clock interrupt handling	9		
Channel interrupt handling	13		
I/O handling evoked by 13	15		
Real-time clock handling and "Kachelbefreiung"	16		
Decoding of system commands	17		
Loading a "Teilsystem"	19		
Database handling	30		
Wait process	255		
Decoding of system commands within the compilation-"Teilsystem"		108	108 / 118
Decoding of system commands within the codegeneration-"Teilsystem"		177	177 / 167
Compilation		110	110 / 120
Error messages from compiler		109	109 / 119
Code generation		179	179 / 169
Optimizing		180	180 / 170

Table A2. *Mean of relative frequencies, of activity times tp and of the relative portion of total elapsed time, computed for the total processing time*

No. p of process	Function of process p	Relative frequency of process p				Activity time tp (mean) [ms]				Relative portion of total time			
		1 job 256 kB	1 job 512 kB	2 jobs 256 kB	2 jobs 512 kB	1 job 256 kB	1 job 512 kB	2 jobs 256 kB	2 jobs 512 kB	1 job 256 kB	1 job 512 kB	2 jobs 256 kB	2 jobs 512 kB
9	Clock interrupt	1.1%	1.1%	1.2%	1%	0.2	0.2	0.2	0.2	0.04%	0.04%	0.04%	0.04%
13	Selch-interrupt by page fault	24.7%	24.6%	27.9%	30.1%	0.3	0.3	0.3	0.3	1.2%	1.3%	1.3%	1.6%
14	IMX-interrupt by page fault	0.1%	0.1%	0.1%	0.1%	0.3	0.3	0.3	0.3	0%	0%	0%	0%
15	I/O-handling evoked by 13/14	33.8%	35.3%	29.4%	34.4%	1.0	1.0	1.0	1.1	6%	6.7%	5.1%	7.5%
16	Handling of *RT*-clock and of "Kachelbefreiung"	1.6%	1.1%	3.1%	1.1%	7.1	1.9	11.6	2.4	2%	0.4%	6%	0.5%
17	Decoding of system commands	0.3%	0.2%	0.5%	0.3%	11.1	15.7	6.2	11.1	0.5%	0.6%	0.5%	0.6%
19	Loading a "Teilsystem"	0.8%	0.6%	0.7%	0.6%	5.6	7.7	5.2	7.2	0.8%	0.9%	0.6%	0.9%
30	Database handling	4.99%	5.2%	3.6%	4.1%	1.4	1.4	1.5	1.6	1.2%	1.4%	0.9%	1.3%
108	Compilation	0.5%	0.3%	0.3%	0.3%	61.7	83.3	32.7	44.5	4.8%	5.3%	1.8%	2.6%
109	Compilation	1.3%	1.3%	0.5%	0.6%	2.4	2.4	2.4	2.4	5.2%	0.6%	0.2%	0.3%
110	Compilation	11.5%	11.9%	3.9%	4.1%	5.5	5.6	6.5	7.0	11%	12.2%	4.2%	5.9%
118	Compilation			0.7%	0.6%			16.0	21.4			1.9%	2.6%
119	Compilation			0.6%	0.6%			2.3	2.4			0.2%	0.3%
120	Compilation			4.3%	4.1%			6.1	7.0			4.3%	5.9%
167	Code generation			0.1%	0.1%			21.8	32.0			0.4%	0.6%
169	Code generation			2.9%	1.8%			10.4	18.1			5%	6.7%
170	Code generation			0.1%	0.1%			4.7	6.4			0.1%	0.1%
177	Code generation	0.2%	0.1%	0.2%	0.1%	37.7	54.1	16.1	21.4	1%	1.2%	0.4%	0.6%
179	Code generation	4.6%	4.2%	5.1%	2.9%	15.8	17.5	6.2	11.5	12.4%	13.7%	5.2%	6.8%
180	Code generation	0.2%	0.2%	0.1%	0.1%	6.6	6.9	5.1	5.9	0.2%	0.2%	0.1%	0.1%
255	Wait-process	14.2%	13.6%	14.6%	12.8%	23.7	22.0	25.6	21.2	58.3%	55.5%	61.8%	55.1%

Table A3. *Complete trace of the starting phase of the code generation of job B (process 169)*

ZEIT (SEC)	KXNR	DAUER (MSEC)	ZEIT (SEC)	KXNR	DAUER (MSEC)	ZEIT (SEC)	KXNR	DAUER (MSEC)
	17	6.106		13	.230		17	11.571
	167	65.459		15	.528	792.4	167	14.618
	170	9.037		13	.252		170	.146
	30	1.392		15	1.275		179	.298
	15	.541		179	.450		255	20.557
	30	2.098		255	40.960		13	.327
	15	1.229		13	.291		167	5.019
	30	.255		15	.789	→	169	4.019
	170	.208		30	14.029		179	.295
	179	.736		15	3.026		255	5.107
791.6	255	41.216		30	.270		9	.198
	13	.291	791.9	255	15.258		16	9.933
	15	.747		13	.378		13	.286
	30	2.304		179	5.794		16	13.594
	15	1.080		255	30.490		169	1.869
	30	.270		9	.198		179	.295
	255	28.237		16	44.288	792.5	255	116.326
	13	.616	792.0	255	84.378		13	.306
	15	.230		13	.291		16	2.552
	179	1.443		15	.997		179	.297
	255	22.554		30	2.002	792.6	255	21.683
	13	.533		15	1.080		13	.321
	15	.528		30	.270		169	1.506
	13	.251	792.1	255	82.458		179	.296
	15	.974		13	.307		255	14.438
	179	1.405		16	2.506		13	.321
791.7	255	33.485		255	17.894		169	1.510
	-13	.291		13	.614		179	.296
	15	.747		15	.230		255	14.438
	30	3.046		179	1.440		13	.321
	15	.541	792.2	255	26.701		169	1.520
	30	2.571		13	.533		179	.296
	15	1.080		15	.528		255	10.291
	30	.270		13	.252		13	.321
	255	16.384		15	1.280		169	2.645
	13	.616		179	2.306		179	.296
	15	.230		255	63.718		255	13.107
	179	1.688		13	.291		13	.321
	255	26.214		15	.789		169	1.538
	13	.533		30	1.803		179	.296
	15	.528		15	.542		255	10.266
	13	.251		30	1.573		13	.321
	15	.974		15	.542		169	1.502
	179	1.419		30	1.208		179	.296
	255	9.446		170	13.107	792.7	255	26.854
	13	.292	792.3	255	23.194		13	.321
791.8	15	.747		13	.325		169	1.507
	30	6.403		179	.469		179	.296
	15	1.080		170	5.774		255	10.291
	30	.270		179	.819		13	.321
	255	15.309		255	46.438		169	1.528
	13	.616		13	.322		179	.296
	15	.230		170	1.138		255	26.854
	179	4.622		167	5.162		13	.321

References

[1] AEG-Telefunken: Prozeßrechner AEG 80-40, 80-60. Befehlshandbuch, Konstanz, Pub. Nr. ESV. 16.26/0977 (1977).
[2] Agrawala, A. K., Mohr, J. M., Bryant, R. M.: An approach to the workload characterization problem. Computer **9**, 18–32 (1976).
[3] Anderson, D. W., et al.: General purpose hardware monitor. IBM Techn. Disclosure Bull. **10**, 1184–1186 (1968).
[4] Apple, C. T.: The program monitor – A device for program performance measurement. ACM 20th Nat. Conference 1965, pp. 66–75.
[5] Aschenbrenner, R. A., et al.: The neurotron monitor system. AFIPS **39**, 31–37 (1971).
[6] Bode, A., Händler, W.: Classification d'architectures parallèles: Introduction de la notion ECS et application au projet EGPA. R.A.I.R.O. Informatique/Computer Science **12**, 317–331 (1978).
[7] Denning, P. J.: Why our approach to performance evaluation is SDRAWKCAB. ACM Performance Evaluation Review **2**, 13–16 (1973).

[8] Estrin, G., et al.: SNUPER-computer, a computer in instrumentation automation. Proc. AFIPS **30**, 645–656 (1967).

[9] Estrin, G., Muntz, R. R., Uzgalis, R. C.: Modeling, measurement and computer power. Proc. AFIPS **40**, 725–738 (1972).

[10] Ferrari, D.: Workload characterization and selection in computer performance measurement. Comp. **5**, 18–24 (1972).

[11] Ferrari, D.: An approach to the design of a learning memory manager. SIGMETRICS/CMG VIII Conf. on Computer Performance, Washington D.C., 1977.

[12] Ferrari, D.: Computer systems performance evaluation. Englewood Cliffs, N.J.: Prentice-Hall 1978.

[13] Fuller, S. H., Ousterhout, J. K., Raskin, L., Rubinfeld, P. I., Sindhu, P. J., Swan, R. J.: Multimicroprocessors: An overview and working example. Proc. IEEE **66**, 216–228 (1978).

[14] Gay, F. A., Ketelsen, M. L.: Performance evaluation for graceful degrading systems. Proc. 9th Int. Symp. on Fault-Tolerant Computing, Madison, 1979, pp. 51–58.

[15] Gibson, J. C.: The Gibson mix. IBM Techn. Rep. 00.2043 (1970).

[16] Händler, W., Klar, R.: Fitting processors to the needs of a general purpose array (EGPA). Proc. of Micro-8, Chicago, 1975, pp. 87–97.

[17] Händler, W., Hofmann, F., Schneider, H. J.: A general purpose array with a broad spectrum of applications. 1st Workshop on Computer Architecture, Erlangen, May 1975 (Informatik-Fachberichte, Vol. 4), pp. 311–334. Berlin-Heidelberg-New York: Springer 1976.

[18] Hellerman, L.: A measure of computational work. IEEE Trans. Comp. **C-21**, 439–446 (1972).

[19] Hercksen, U., Klar, R., Stelzner, J.: Instrumentierung eines Prozessor-Feldes. 9. Jahrestagung der GI, Bonn (Informatik-Fachberichte, Vol. 19), pp. 467–478. Berlin-Heidelberg-New York: Springer 1979.

[20] Hercksen, U., Hessenauer, H., Klar, R., Stelzner, J.: An integrated hardware-monitor for evaluation of process parameters in the processor array EGPA. Internal Report, University Erlangen, 1979.

[21] Huang, J. C.: Program instrumentation and testing. Computer **11**, 25–32 (1978).

[22] Hughes, J.: Performance evaluation techniques and system reliability – A practical approach. ACM/NBS Performance Evaluation Workshop, San Diego, 1973.

[23] Hughes, J., Cronshaw, D.: On using a hardware monitor as an intelligent peripheral. ACM Performance Evaluation Review **2**, 3–19 (1973).

[24] IBM anonym: Throughput evaluations for IBM 7090/7094 data processing systems. Internal Report, 1963.

[25] Iyer, R. K.: On the employment of variance for reliability modelling of fault tolerant systems. Proc. 9th Int. Symp. on Fault-Tolerant Computing, Madison, 1979, pp. 63–66.

[26] Klar, R., Spies, P. P.: Adaptive Betriebsprogramme und ihre Unterstützung durch einen Zählmonitor. In: Betriebsprogrammierung. Vorträge des Kolloquiums des IMMD, Erlangen 1968 (Händler, W., Spies, O., eds.), pp. 151–174. München-Wien: Oldenbourg 1969.

[27] Klar, R.: Messung von Rechneraktivitäten. Arbeitsberichte des IMMD, Erlangen **4**, No. 2 (1971).

[28] Klar, R., Schreiber, H., Widjaja, H. C.: Messungen mit dem Zählmonitor II. Arbeitsberichte des IMMD, Erlangen **8**, No. 9 (1975).

[29] Klar, R.: Digitale Rechenautomaten. Berlin-New York: W. de Gruyter 1975.

[30] Lucas, H. C.: Performance evaluation and monitoring. Computing Surveys **3**, 79–92 (1971).

[31] Marathe, M., Fuller, S.: A study of multiprocessor contention for shared data in C.mmp. SIGMETRICS/CMG VIIIth Conf. on Computer Performance, Washington D.C., 1977.

[32] Mayer, R. E.: A psychology of learning BASIC. Comm. ACM **22**, 589–593 (1979).

[33] Meyer, J. F., Furchtgott, D. G., Wu, L. T.: Performability evaluation of the SIFT computer. Proc. 9th Int. Symp. on Fault-Tolerant Computing, Madison, 1979, pp. 43–50.

[34] Morgan, D. E., Banks, W., Colvin, W., Sutton, D.: A performance measurement system for computer networks. Information Processing **74**, 29–33 (1974).

[35] Nonnenmacher, W.: Das Siemens Datenverarbeitungssystem 3003. Siemens Zeitschrift **38**, 141–152 (1964).

[36] Rudolph, J. A.: A production implementation of an associative array processor STARAN. Proc. AFIPS **41**, 229–241 (1972).

[37] Schmid, E.: Rechenzeitvergleich bei Digitalrechnern. Computing **5**, 163–177 (1970).

[38] Schreiber, H.: Hardware-Messung und Analyse des Ablaufgeschehens in Rechnerkernen. Arbeitsberichte des IMMD, Erlangen 11, No. 7 (1978).
[39] Schulman, F. D.: Hardware measurement device for IBM system /360 time-sharing evaluation. Proc. 22nd Nat. Conf. ACM P-67, 103−109 (1967).
[40] Stang, H., Southgate, P.: Performance evaluation of third-generation computing systems. Datamation 1969, 181−189.
[41] Svoboda, L.: Online system performance measurements with software and hybrid monitors. ACM 4th Symp. on Operating System Principles, Yorktown Heights 1973.
[42] Svoboda, L.: Computer performance measurement and evaluation methods: Analysis and application. New York: Elsevier 1976.
[43] Tesdata: Warum Hardware-Messung? Eine Einführung in die Leistungsmessung an EDV-Anlagen mit Hardware-Monitoren. ONLINE, Zeitschrift für Datenverarbeitung, No. 9, 10 (1974).
[44] Brooks, R. E.: Studying programmer behavior experimentally: The problems of proper methodology. CACM 23, No. 4, 207−213 (1980).

Dr. R. Klar
Institut für Mathematische Maschinen
und Datenverarbeitung (III)
Universität Erlangen-Nürnberg
Martensstrasse 3
D-8520 Erlangen
Federal Republic of Germany

Computing, Suppl. 3, 89 – 104 (1981)

On the Reachability Problem for Persistent Vector Replacement Systems

H. Müller, Erlangen

Abstract – Zusammenfassung

On the Reachability Problem for Persistent Vector Replacement Systems. The reachability problem for persistent vector replacement systems is shown to be decidable by giving an algorithm for constructing a semilinear representation of the reachability set.

Das Erreichbarkeitsproblem für persistente Vektor-Ersetzungs-Systeme. Das Erreichbarkeitsproblem für persistente Vektor-Ersetzungs-Systeme (isomorph zu verallgemeinerten Petri-Netzen) wird als entscheidbar nachgewiesen durch Konstruktion eines Algorithmus, der eine semilineare Darstellung der Erreichbarkeitsmenge liefert.

0. Introduction

Petri nets have turned out to be a useful model for research of fundamental problems of parallel data processing. Some decidability and complexity questions in this area are settled [1, 3]. The fundamental problem of reachability is until now proved decidable only for special classes of Petri nets respectively equivalent models as vector addition systems (VAS) [2, 6]. Sacerdote and Tenney [9] have claimed decidability for the general case but have not as yet provided a rigorous proof. In the known decidable cases semilinearity of the reachability set plays an important part in the proof. Because of the existence of VAS of dimension 6 with a non-semilinear reachability set (see [2]) these methods must fail for higher dimensions. Landweber and Robertson [5] have shown semilinearity of the reachability set for persistent Petri nets, but their proof is not constructive and yields therefore no decision procedure for the reachability problem. In this paper we give as a main result an effective construction for a semilinear representation of the reachability set for any persistent vector replacement system (and thus for persistent Petri nets). This yields decidability of reachability, inclusion and equivalence for persistent vector replacement systems. Contrasting to the last inclusion and equivalence are undecidable for the class of arbitrary VAS (Hack [1]).

The construction is based on reachability trees introduced by Karp and Miller [4]. The efficiency of the construction is bad. Because of the existence of sequences of VAS with finite reachability sets not boundable by primitive recursive functions (see Rackoff [8]) the construction needs time and space not boundable by primitive recursive functions.

1. Notations and Definitions

Let $\mathbb{Z}$ denote the set of integers, $\mathbb{N}$ denote the set of nonnegative integers. Let $\mathbb{Z}^n$ ($\mathbb{N}^n$) denote the set of n-tuples of elements of $\mathbb{Z}$ ($\mathbb{N}$) with the usual componentwise defined extension of operations and relations unless otherwise specified. An important exception is the relation $<$ on $\mathbb{N}^n$. $(x_1, \ldots, x_n) \leqslant (y_1, \ldots, y_n)$ is defined componentwise by $x_i \leqslant y_i$ for $i = 1, \ldots, n$. But $x < y$ by $x \leqslant y$ and $x \neq y$, that is $x_i \leqslant y_i$ for $i = 1, \ldots, n$ and $x_j \neq y_j$ for some j, $1 \leqslant j \leqslant n$. Some simple but important facts about this partial order on $\mathbb{N}^n$ are given in the following lemma.

Lemma 1.1. *a)* $<$ *is a well-founded partial order on* $\mathbb{N}^n$, *that is, all descending chains are finite.*

b) Any set of pairwise incomparable elements of $\mathbb{N}^n$ *is finite.*

c) Any infinite sequence of pairwise different elements has a strictly increasing subsequence.

d) Any set $S \subseteq \mathbb{N}^n$ *has a finite set* $\min(S)$ *of minimal elements.*

Let P be a finite subset of $\mathbb{Z}^n$ and $\alpha | P \to \mathbb{N}$. Using the abbreviation

$$\alpha * P = \sum_{p \in P} \alpha(p) \cdot p,$$

define for $C \subseteq \mathbb{N}^n$

$$\mathscr{L}(C, P) := \{x | (\exists c \in C)(\exists \alpha | P \to \mathbb{N}) x = c + \alpha * P\}.$$

For convenience we write $\mathscr{L}(c, P)$ for $\mathscr{L}(\{c\}, P)$.

S is *linear*, iff $(\exists s \in \mathbb{N})(\exists P \subseteq \mathbb{N}^n)(P$ finite and $S = \mathscr{L}(s, P))$.

A set is *semilinear*, iff it is a finite union of linear sets.

A set S is called *effectively semilinear* iff there is given an algorithm yielding a representation $S = \bigcup \{\mathscr{L}(s, P) | (s, P) \in I\}$ by computing a finite set $I \subseteq \mathbb{N}^n \times$ set of finite subsets of $\mathbb{N}^n$.

Important for decidability problems is the following lemma.

Lemma 1.2. *Membership, inclusion and equality is decidable for effectively semilinear sets.*

Proof. i) Membership: Let be given an effective representation $S = \bigcup \{\mathscr{L}(s, P) | (s, P) \in I\}$, I finite and $x \in \mathbb{N}^n$. To decide $x \in S$ it suffices to decide $x \in \mathscr{L}(s, P)$, for I is finite. This can be done by solving a system of linear equations got from $x = s + \alpha * P$.

ii) Inclusion: It suffices to consider the question $S_1 \subseteq S_2$ with a linear set $S_1 = \mathscr{L}(a, A)$ and $S_2 = \bigcup \{\mathscr{L}(s, P) | (s, P) \in I\}$. Then $S_1 \subseteq S_2$ is expressible by

$$(\forall \alpha \in \mathbb{N}^{|A|}) \bigvee_{(s, P) \in I} (\exists \beta \in \mathbb{N}^{|P|}) a + \alpha * A = s + \beta * P.$$

This last formula can be translated into a formula of the theory of addition (Presburger arithmetic), which is decidable (see e.g. [7]).

iii) Decidability of equality follows directly by

$$S_1 = S_2 \leftrightarrow S_1 \subseteq S_2 \wedge S_2 \subseteq S_1.$$

A *vector replacement scheme* of dimension n is a finite family $W|T \to \mathbb{Z}^n \times \mathbb{Z}^n$ of transitions $W(t) = (u_t, v_t)$ with $u_t \leqslant v_t$.

A *vector replacement system* (VRS) is a pair (W, x) of a vector replacement scheme W and an *initial vector* $x \in \mathbb{N}^n$.

Each transition (u_t, v_t) defines a *transition relation* $\overset{t}{\to}$ on $\mathbb{N}^n$ by

$$x \overset{t}{\to} y \quad \text{iff} \quad y + u_t \geqslant 0 \wedge y = x + v_t.$$

t is *enabled* at x iff $x + u_t \geqslant 0$. These two notions are extended to sequences of transitions in T^* by induction:

$$x \overset{\Lambda}{\to} x \; (x \in \mathbb{N}^n); \; \Lambda \text{ is enabled at } x \text{ for all } x \in \mathbb{N}^n,$$

$$x \overset{\delta t}{\to} y \quad \text{iff} \quad \exists z (x \overset{\delta}{\to} z \wedge z \overset{t}{\to} y) \; (\delta \in T^*, t \in T),$$

$$\delta t \text{ is enabled at } x \text{ iff } \exists z (x \overset{\delta}{\to} z \wedge t \text{ is enabled at } z).$$

A set or a sequence A of elements of T^* is called *enabled* at x iff every element of A is enabled at x. The set $L_W(x) := \{\delta | \delta \text{ is enabled at } x\}$ of all finite transition sequences enabled at x is called the (non-terminal) *language* of (W, x). The *reachability set* of (W, x) is the set $R_W(x) := \{y | (\exists \delta \in T^*) x \overset{\delta}{\to} y\}$. We extend this notion allowing a set M of initial vectors by setting

$$R_W(M) := \{y | (\exists x \in M) y \in R_W(x)\} = \bigcup_{x \in M} R_W(x) (M \subseteq \mathbb{N}^n).$$

If W is known from the context, we omit the subscript W. Directly from these definitions we have:

Lemma 1.3.

a) $\qquad\qquad M_1 \subseteq M_2 \to R(M_1) \subseteq R(M_2)$

and

b) $\qquad\qquad R(M_1 \cup M_2) = R(M_1) \cup R(M_2) \qquad (M_1, M_2 \subseteq \mathbb{N}^n).$

For simplicity let $T = \{1, \ldots, k\}$.

For $\delta \in T^*$ the *folding (Parikh-mapping)* of δ is a k-dimensional vector $\text{fold}(\delta) = (f_1, \ldots, f_k) \in \mathbb{N}^k$ whose ith component f_i is the number of occurrences of i in the sequence δ. Sequences $\delta, \tau \in T^*$ with $\text{fold}(\delta) = \text{fold}(\tau)$ are called *folding-equivalent*.

For $\delta = t_1 \cdots t_{|\delta|} \in T^*$ the *displacement* is $\text{dis}(\delta) = \text{dis}(t_1 \cdots t_{|\delta|}) = \sum_{j=1}^{|\delta|} v_{t_j}$.

Folding and displacement are monoid homomorphisms and are combined to get the *extended Parikh mapping* $\text{EPK}|T^* \to \mathbb{N}^{k+n}$ by $\text{EPK}(\delta) = (\text{fold}(\delta), \text{dis}(\delta))$.

Easily proven is

Lemma 1.4. $\mathrm{fold}(\delta) = \mathrm{fold}(\tau)$ *implies* $\mathrm{dis}(\delta) = \mathrm{dis}(\tau)$.

Next let us introduce the *difference operation on* T^* by

$$\delta \doteq \Lambda := \delta,$$

$$\delta \doteq t := \textbf{if } t \textit{ in } \delta \textbf{ then } \textit{result of deleting the first} \\ \textit{occurrence of } t \textit{ in } \delta \textbf{ else } \delta,$$

$$\delta \doteq (\tau t) := (\delta \doteq \tau) \doteq t \qquad (\delta, \tau \in T^*, t \in T).$$

Some intuitively obvious properties of the difference operation are given.

Lemma 1.5. *For all* $u, v, w \in T^*$

a) $u \doteq vw = u \doteq wv,$

b) $\mathrm{fold}(v) = \mathrm{fold}(w)$ *implies* $u \doteq v = u \doteq w,$

c) $\mathrm{fold}(u) \leqslant \mathrm{fold}(v)$ *implies* $\mathrm{fold}(v) = \mathrm{fold}(u(v \doteq u)).$

The proofs are simple exercises on induction.

A vector replacement system (W, x) is *persistent* iff

$$(\forall y \in R_W(x))(\forall t_1, t_2 \in T) \ (t_1 \text{ enabled at } y \text{ and } t_1 \neq t_2 \text{ and} \\ t_2 \text{ enabled at } y \text{ implies } t_1 t_2 \text{ enabled at } y).$$

The persistency criterion for Petri nets given by Starke [10] based on work of Landweber and Robertson [4] is easily transferred to the following persistency criterion for VRS.

Lemma 1.6 (Persistency criterion). *The* VRS (W, x) *is persistent iff for every* $y \in R_W(x)$ *and for every pair* δ, τ *of finite transition sequences enabled at* y *the sequence* $\delta(\tau \doteq \delta)$ *is enabled at* y.

Short: $\delta, \tau \in L_W(y) \to \delta(\tau \doteq \delta) \in L_W(y)$.

$\delta \in T^*$ is called a *period* at $x \in \mathbb{N}^n$ iff δ is enabled at x and $\mathrm{dis}(\delta) > 0$. Persistency guarantees transmission of periods at x to vectors y reachable from x in the following sense.

Lemma 1.7. *Let* (W, x_0) *be a persistent* VRS *and* p *a period at* $x \in R_W(x_0)$. *Then for any* $y \in R_W(x)$ *a period* p' *at* y *can be constructed effectively which is folding equivalent to* p.

Proof. Let $x \xrightarrow{\delta} y$. We do induction on $|\delta|$.

i) $\delta = \Lambda$: Trivial, because of $y = x$ and $p' = p$.

ii) $\delta = t \in T$: If p does not contain t then we have $p \doteq t = p$ and the persistency criterion implies $p' = p$ is enabled at y. If p does contain t there exists a partition $p = p_1 t p_2 \wedge \textit{not } t \textit{ in } p_1$ such that by the persistency criterion $p \doteq t = p_1 p_2$ is enabled at y. Because of $\mathrm{fold}(t p_1 p_2) = \mathrm{fold}(p)$ Lemma 1.4 gives $\mathrm{dis}(t p_1 p_2) = \mathrm{dis}(p) > 0$. Therefore exists x' with $x \xrightarrow{t p_1 p_2} x' > x$ and by monotony t is enabled at x'. Therefore $p' = p_1 p_2 t$ is enabled at y and $\mathrm{fold}(p_1 p_2 t) = \mathrm{fold}(p)$.

iii) $\delta = \delta' t$: by the induction hypothesis let $x \xrightarrow{\delta'} y'$ and p' be a period at y' with $\mathrm{fold}(p') = \mathrm{fold}(p)$. Use ii) at y' instead of x.

We extend the operation $*$ by

$$\alpha * A := \sum_{i=1}^{m} \alpha_i \, \mathrm{dis}(\delta_i) \text{ for } \alpha \in \mathbb{N}^m \text{ and } A = \langle \delta_1, \ldots, \delta_m \rangle,$$

a sequence with $\delta_i \in T^*$ ($i = 1, \ldots, m$) and abbreviate $\mathscr{L}(x, \{\mathrm{dis}(\delta_i) | i = 1, \ldots, m\})$ by $\mathscr{L}(x, A)$.

Lemma 1.8. *Let (W, x) be any (not necessarily persistent) VRS. For any sequence $A = \langle p_1, \ldots, p_m \rangle$ of periods at x holds $\mathscr{L}(x, A) \subseteq R_w(x)$.*

Proof by Induction on $m = |A|$. If $A = \langle \, \rangle$ (the empty sequence) then we have $\mathscr{L}(x, A) = \{x\} \subseteq R_W(x)$ trivially. For $|A| \neq 0$ and any $y \in \mathscr{L}(x, A)$ we have $y = x + \alpha * A = x + \sum_{i=1}^{m-1} \alpha_i \, \mathrm{dis}(p_i) + \alpha_m \, \mathrm{dis}(p_m)$ for some $\alpha \in \mathbb{N}^m$. For $\alpha_m = 0$ by induction hypothesis $y \in R_W(x)$. For $\alpha_m \neq 0$ the qualities of a period and monotony of the transition relation ensure the existence of a path

$$x \xrightarrow{p} x_1 \xrightarrow{p} x_2 \cdots \xrightarrow{p} x_{\alpha_m} = x' \text{ with } x < x_1 < x_2 \cdots < x_{\alpha_m}.$$

Because of $x < x'$ $A' := \langle p_1, \ldots, p_{m-1} \rangle$ is a sequence of periods at x'. $y \in \mathscr{L}(x', A')$ and the induction hypothesis give $y \in R_W(x')$ and $y \in R_W(x)$.

For the following let $A = \langle \delta_1, \ldots, \delta_m \rangle$ be a finite sequence of elements $\delta_i \in T^*$. A is called *reduced* (relative to EPK) iff *not* $\exists i, j (i < j$ *and* $\mathrm{EPK}(\delta_i) \leqslant \mathrm{EPK}(\delta_j))$.

2. Results and Proof Outline for the Main Theorem

2.1 Main Theorem. *For any persistent vector replacement system (W, x_0) the reachability set is effectively semilinear.*

Outline of Proof. For linear sets $\mathscr{L}(x, A)$ of initial vectors (where A is a reduced sequence of periods at x) we construct a *set reachability tree* $\mathrm{SRT}(x, A)$ by modification of the well-known Karp/Miller-reachability tree. The tree construction gives a partial representation of the reachability set (compare (4.15), (4.16)):

(2.2) $R_W(\mathscr{L}(x, A)) = \mathscr{L}(C, A) \cup \bigcup \{R_W(\mathscr{L}(x(\xi), A'(\xi))) | \xi \text{ jump origin}\}.$

C is a finite set and each jump origin ξ is a vertex of the constructed tree leading to a longer sequence of periods $A'(\xi)$ (given by Algorithm 4.11). $A'(\xi)$ may be not reduced. Iterating (2.2) directly leads in some cases to infinite computations. By a reduction procedure (Theorem 3.3) — for which persistency is essential — we can return to reduced sequences of periods:

(2.3) $R_W(\mathscr{L}(x(\xi), A'(\xi))) = \bigcup \{R_W(\mathscr{L}(y, B)) | (y, B) \in I_\xi\}$ with

I_ξ finite *and* for any $(y, B) \in I_\xi$: B is a reduced sequence

of periods at y.

Combining (2.2) and (2.3) we get (Theorem 4.14) for some finite sets C and I:

(2.4) $R_W(\mathcal{L}(x, A)) = \mathcal{L}(C, A) \cup \bigcup \{R_W(\mathcal{L}(y, B))|(y, b) \in I\}$ and

      for any $(y, B) \in I$: B is a reduced sequence of periods at y.

Starting with $R_W(x_0) = R_W(\mathcal{L}(x_0, \text{empty sequence}))$ and using (2.4) iteratively we can construct a *jump tree* (Algorithm (5.2)), which is finite because no infinite reduced sequence of periods can exist and which gives the desired representation of $R_W(x_0)$. Sections 3, 4, 5 give details of the reduction, the set reachability tree and the jump tree respectively.

By Lemma 1.2 the main theorem implies:

Corollary 2.5. *The reachability problem for persistent vector replacement systems is decidable.*

Corollary 2.6. *Inclusion respectively equality of the reachability sets of persistent vector replacement systems is decidable.*

3. Reduction of Periods

3.1 Reduction Lemma. *Let $A = \langle p_1, \ldots, p_m \rangle$ be a sequence of periods at $x \in R_W(x_0)$ and (W, x_0) a persistent VRS. If p_i, p_j are periods with $\text{EPK}(p_i) < \text{EPK}(p_j)$ and*

$$A' := \langle p_1, \ldots, p_{j-1}, p_j \doteq p_i, p_{j+1}, \ldots, p_m \rangle =: A\begin{bmatrix} p_j \\ p_j \doteq p_i \end{bmatrix}$$

then A' is a sequence of periods at $x + \text{dis}(p_i)$ and the following equation holds

$$R_W(\mathcal{L}(x, A)) = R_W(\mathcal{L}(x, A - p_j)) \cup R_W(\mathcal{L}(x + \text{dis}(p_i), A')).$$

Proof. Because of $x + \text{dis}(p_i) > x$ all p are periods at $x + \text{dis}(p_i)$. By the persistency criterion $p_i(p_j \doteq p_i)$ is enabled at x and therefore $p_j \doteq p_i$ is enabled at $x + \text{dis}(p_i)$. By $\text{dis}(p_i) < \text{dis}(p_j)$, Lemma 1.4 and Lemma 1.5c) we get $\text{dis}(p_j \doteq p_i) > 0$. This proves $p_j \doteq p_i$ to be a period at $x + \text{dis}(p_i)$.

i) Inclusion from left to right: This follows with Lemma 1.3 from

(3.2) $\mathcal{L}(x, A) \subseteq \mathcal{L}(x, A - p_j) \cup \mathcal{L}(x + \text{dis}(p_i), A').$

To show (3.2) let $y \in \mathcal{L}(x, A)$ with $y = x + \alpha * A$, $\leqslant \alpha \in \mathbb{N}^m$. For $\alpha_j = 0$ we have $y \in \mathcal{L}(x, A - p_j)$. For $\alpha_j \neq 0$ $\text{EPK}(p_i) < \text{EPK}(p_j)$ implies $\text{fold}(p_i) \leqslant \text{fold}(p_j)$. Lemma 1.4 excludes equality, therefore $\text{fold}(p_i) < \text{fold}(p_j)$ and $\text{dis}(p_i) < \text{dis}(p_j)$. Lemma 1.5c) gives $\text{fold}(p_j) = \text{fold}(p_i(p_j \doteq p_i))$, and with Lemma 1.4 $\text{dis}(p_j) = \text{dis}(p_i(p_j \doteq p_i)) = \text{dis}(p_i) + \text{dis}(p_j \doteq p_i)$. Therefore we have

$$y = x + \text{dis}(p_i) + \sum\{\alpha_\mu \cdot \text{dis}(p_\mu)|\mu \in \{1, \ldots, m\}\backslash\{i,j\}\}$$
$$+ (\alpha_i - 1 + \alpha_j)\text{dis}(p_i) + \alpha_j \text{dis}(p_j \doteq p_i)$$
$$\in \mathcal{L}(x + \text{dis}(p_i), A').$$

ii) Inclusion from right to left: $\mathcal{L}(x, A - p_j) \subseteq \mathcal{L}(x, A)$ implies together with Lemma 1.3a)

$$R_W(\mathcal{L}(x, A - p_j)) \subseteq R_W(\mathcal{L}(x, A)).$$

It remains to show $R_W(\mathscr{L}(x + \mathrm{dis}(p_i), A')) \subseteq R_W(\mathscr{L}(x, A))$. Let

$$y \in R_W(\mathscr{L}(x + \mathrm{dis}(p_i), A')).$$

Then there exist $x', x'' \in \mathbb{N}^n$, $\delta \in T^*$ and $\alpha \in \mathbb{N}^m$ with

$$x' \overset{\delta}{\to} y \quad \text{and}$$

$$x'' = x + \mathrm{dis}(p_i) + \sum \{\alpha_\mu \, \mathrm{dis}(p_\mu) | \mu \in \{1, \ldots, m\} \setminus \{j\}\} \quad \text{and}$$

$$x' = x'' + \alpha_j \, \mathrm{dis}(p_j \doteq p_i).$$

$x'' \in \mathscr{L}(x + \mathrm{dis}(p_i), A)$ implies by Lemma 1.8 $x'' \in R_W(x + \mathrm{dis}(p_i))$ and also $x'' \in R_W(x)$. By Lemma 1.7 we get a period p'_j at x'' folding equivalent to $p_j \doteq p_i$. The path $x'' \overset{p_j'^{\alpha_j}}{\to} x' \overset{\delta}{\to} y$ shows $y \in R_W(x'') \subseteq R_W(\mathscr{L}(x, A))$.

3.3 Reduction Theorem. *Let (W, x) be a persistent* VRS, *A a finite sequence of periods at x and A_{red} the reduced initial segment of A of maximal length. There is effectively constructible a finite set M of pairs (y, B) with*

a) B is a reduced sequence of periods at y leaving A_{red} as initial segment and

b) $R_W(\mathscr{L}(x, A)) = \bigcup \{R_W(\mathscr{L}(y, B)) | (y, B) \in M\}$.

Proof. We give an algorithm that constructs a tree labelled by pairs $(x(\eta), A(\eta))$ where for any vertex η $A(\eta)$ is a sequence of periods at $x(\eta)$ having A_{red} as an initial segment.

3.4 Algorithm for the Reduction Tree.

> **Input:** W, x, A;
> create root; $x(\text{root}) := x$; $A(\text{root}) := A$;
> **while** $\exists \eta$ **not** reduced $A(\eta)$ **do**
> > choose η with $A(\eta) = \langle p_1, \ldots, p_m \rangle$ **not** reduced **and**
> > $\mathrm{EPK}(p_i) \leqslant \mathrm{EPK}(p_j)$;
> > **if** $\mathrm{EPK}(p_i) = \mathrm{EPK}(p_j)$ **then** construct a son labelled $(x, A - p_j)$
> > **else** construct two sons labelled $(x, A - p_j)$ resp.
> > $$\left(x + \mathrm{dis}(p_i), A \begin{bmatrix} p_j \\ p_j \doteq p_i \end{bmatrix} \right)$$
>
> **fi**
>
> > > **od**

This algorithm and the resulting tree have the following properties:

(3.5) $A(\eta)$ is a sequence of periods at $x(\eta)$ having A_{red} as an initial segment.

Proof. Follows directly by tree induction from Lemma 3.1.

(3.6) The Algorithm 3.4 terminates with a finite tree.

Proof. To each vertex associate the vector $(|A(\eta)|, \sum_{p \in A(\eta)} \mathrm{EPK}(p)) \in \mathbb{N}^{1+k+n}$. This vector decreases by passing from a vertex to his sons. By Lemma 1.1 (wellfoundedness) every path in the tree must have finite length.

(3.7) $R_W(\mathscr{L}(x, A)) = \bigcup \{R_W(\mathscr{L}(x(\eta), A(\eta)))|\eta \text{ leaf of the reduction tree}\}.$

Proof by repeated application of the reduction lemma.

4. The Set Reachability Tree

In this section we give an algorithm which leads to a partial computation of the reachability set (again in the form of a tree) for a linear set of initial vectors. The computation is stopped when new periods occur. In other words $R_W(\mathscr{L}(x, A))$ is reduced to a finite family of sets of the form $R_W(\mathscr{L}(y, B))$ with a bigger period sequence B.

4.1 Algorithm for the Set Reachability Tree SRT(x, A).

Input: a VRS(W, x), a reduced sequence $A = \langle p_1, \ldots, p_m \rangle$ of periods at x; create root; $x(\text{root}) := x$; type(root) := unfinished; $A(\text{root}) := A$;

> **while** $\exists \eta$ type(η) = unfinished **do**
> > choose η with type(η) = unfinished;
> > **if** $\exists \xi$ (ξ ancestor of η and $x(\xi) \leqslant x(\eta)$)
> > > **then if** $\exists \xi$ (ξ ancestor of η and $x(\eta) \in \mathscr{L}(x(\xi), A)$)
> > > > **then** type$(\eta) :=$ unessential leaf
> > > > **else** type$(\eta) :=$ jump leaf **fi**
> > > **else for each** $t \in T$ **do**
> > > > **for each** $\alpha \in \min\{\alpha|\alpha \in \mathbb{N}^m \text{ and } x(\eta) + \alpha * A + u_t \geqslant 0\}$ **do**
> > > > > construct a son (η, t, α) of η;
> > > > > mark the edge from η to (η, t, α) with (t, α);
> > > > > $x(\eta, t, \alpha) := x(\eta) + \alpha * A + v_t$;
> > > > > $A(\eta, t, \alpha) :=$ sequence of periods at $x(\eta, t, \alpha)$
> > > > > > transmitted by Lemma 1.7 from $A(\eta)$;
> > > > > type$(\eta, t, \alpha) :=$ unfinished   **od od**;
> > > > **if** η has no son **then** type$(\eta) :=$ terminal leaf
> > > > > **else** type$(\eta) :=$ finished **fi**
> > **fi od**

output the constructed tree, called SRT(x, A).

In the following we prove some properties of Algorithm 4.1, especially termination and properties of the result SRT(x, A). First we show how to compute the finite set $MM := \min M$ for

$$M = \{\alpha|\alpha \in \mathbb{N}^m \text{ and } x(\eta) + \alpha * A + u_t \geqslant 0\}$$

for given $x(\eta)$, $A = \langle p_1, \ldots, p_m \rangle$, u_t. Let $\Pi_i(x)$ be the ith component of $x \in \mathbb{N}^m$.

4.2 Algorithm for MM.

For $i = 1$ **to** m **do** $w_i := \mathrm{dis}(p_i)$ **od**;

if $x + u_t \geqslant 0$ **then** $MM := \{\mathbf{0}\}$
   else $S := \{i | \Pi_i(x + u_t) < 0\}$;
       for each $s \in S$ **do** $\tilde{A}_s := \{w | \exists i \ (1 \leqslant i \leqslant m \ \wedge \ w = w_i \ \wedge \ \Pi_s(w) > 0\}$ **od**;
       if $(\exists s \in S) \tilde{A}_s = \emptyset$ **then** $MM := \emptyset$
          else for each $s \in S$ **do**
              for each $w \in \tilde{A}_s$ **do**
              $\beta_{s,w} := \min\{\beta | \Pi_s(x + \beta w + u_t) \geqslant 0\}$ **od od**;
              for $i = 1$ **to** n **do**
              $\beta_i := \max\{\beta_{s,w_i} | w_i \in \tilde{A}_s\}$ **od**;
              $MM := \min\{\alpha | \alpha \in \mathbb{N}^n \ \wedge \ \alpha \leqslant \beta \ \wedge \ x + \alpha * A + u_t \geqslant 0\}$
     fi
fi

Proof of Correctness. If $x + u_t \geqslant 0$ then clearly $\mathbf{0} \in \mathbb{N}^m$ is the only minimal element of M. Let now **not** $x + u_t \geqslant 0$. There exist negative components of $x + u_t$. The indices of these components are collected in the finite nonempty set S.

The displacements of periods with negative s-component are collected in $\tilde{A}_s$. If $\tilde{A}_s$ is empty for some $s \in S$ then M must be empty and hence $MM = \emptyset$ too. For the remaining case we compute an upper bound for MM. To show that β is indeed an upper bound, suppose $\alpha \in MM \ \wedge \ \exists i \ \Pi_i(\alpha) > \Pi_i(\beta)$. Let $\alpha' := (\alpha_1, \ldots, \alpha_{i-1}, \beta_i, \alpha_{i+1}, \ldots, \alpha_m)$. We show $\alpha' \in M$ and therefore $\alpha' < \alpha$ by discussing the following cases.

For $\mu \neq S$ we have

$$\Pi_\mu(x + \alpha' * A + u_t) \geqslant \Pi_\mu(x + u_t) \geqslant 0.$$

For $\mu \in S$ and $w_i \notin \tilde{A}_s$ we have $\Pi_\mu(w_i) = 0$ and

$$\Pi_\mu(x + \alpha' * A + u_t) = \Pi_\mu(x + \alpha * A + u_t) \geqslant 0.$$

For $\mu \in S$ and $w_i \in \tilde{A}_s$ we have

$$\Pi_\mu(x + \alpha' * A + u_t) \geqslant \Pi_\mu(x + \beta_i w_i + u_t) \geqslant \Pi_\mu(x + \beta_{\mu,w_i} w_i + u_t) \geqslant 0.$$

(4.3) Any vertex in the tree $\text{SRT}(x, A)$ and in any intermediate tree has only a finite set of sons which are effectively constructed by Algorithm 4.2.

(4.4) If $\langle (t_1, \alpha^{(1)}), \ldots, (t_r, \alpha^{(r)}) \rangle$ is the sequence of edge markings for path from the root to η, then

$$x + \left(\sum_{\rho=1}^{r} \alpha^{(\rho)} \right) * A \xrightarrow{t_1 \ldots t_r} x(\eta) = x + \sum_{\rho=1}^{r} \alpha^{(\rho)} * A + \text{dis}(t_1 \cdots t_r).$$

Proof by Induction on r. For $r = 1$ direct from definition of Algorithm 4.1. For $r \neq 1$ let η' be the father of η and by induction hypothesis

$$x + \sum_{\rho=1}^{r-1} \alpha^{(\rho)} * A \xrightarrow{t_1 \ldots t_{r-1}} x(\eta') = x + \sum_{\rho=1}^{r-1} \alpha^{(\rho)} * A + \text{dis}(t_1 \cdots t_{r-1}).$$

By Algorithm 4.1 we know

$$x(\eta') + \alpha^{(r)} * A \xrightarrow{t_r} x(\eta) = x(\eta') + \alpha^{(r)} * A + v_t.$$

Monotony and $\alpha^{(r)} * A \geqslant 0$ give the desired result.

(4.5) The conditions

(4.5.1) $\exists \xi (\xi$ ancestor of η **and** $x(\xi) \leqslant x(\eta))$ and

(4.5.2) $\exists \xi (\xi$ ancestor of η **and** $x(\xi) \in \mathscr{L}(x(\xi), A))$

are decidable.

Proof. The set of ancestors is finite. For $x(\eta) \in \mathscr{L}(x(\xi), A))$ use Lemma 1.2.

(4.6) The Algorithm 4.1 terminates with a finite tree $\mathrm{SRT}(x, A)$.

Proof. Suppose Algorithm 4.1 does not terminate. Then the constructed tree is infinite and by König's lemma has an infinite path $\langle \eta_i | i \in \mathbb{N} \rangle$ with pairwise different $x(\eta_i)$-values. By Lemma 1.1c) there exist indices j_1, j_2 with $j_1 < j_2$ and $x(\eta_{i_{j_1}}) < x(\eta_{i_{j_2}})$. This contradicts the negation of (4.5.1) which is necessary for non-termination.

(4.7) For any vertex η with $\mathrm{type}(\eta) = $ terminal leaf
$$R_W(\mathscr{L}(x(\eta), A)) = \mathscr{L}(x(\eta), A).$$

Proof. For terminal leaves the above defined set M is empty. Therefore for any $y \in \mathscr{L}(x(\eta), A)$ no transition is enabled.

(4.8) For any vertex η with $\mathrm{type}(\eta) = $ finished:
$$R_W(\mathscr{L}(x(\eta), A)) = \mathscr{L}(x(\eta), A) \cup \bigcup_{\eta' \text{ son of } \eta} R_W(\mathscr{L}(x(\eta'), A)).$$

Proof. i) Let $y \in R_W(\mathscr{L}(x(\eta), A))$ and $\alpha \in \mathbb{N}^m$, $\delta \in T^*$ such that

$$x' := x(\eta) + \alpha * A \overset{\delta}{\to} y.$$

Case 1 $\delta = \Lambda$. Then $y = x' \in \mathscr{L}(x(\eta), A)$.

Case 2 $\delta = t\delta'$. t is enabled at x'. Thus $x(\eta) + \alpha * A + u_t \geqslant 0$. There exists a minimal $\beta \leqslant \alpha$ with $x(\eta) + \beta * A + u_t \geqslant 0$. Therefore η has a son $\eta' := (\eta, t, \beta)$ with $x(\eta') = x(\eta) + \beta * A + v_t$ and $x'' := x(\eta) + \alpha * A + v_t \in \mathscr{L}(x(\eta'), A)$.

$$x'' \overset{\delta'}{\to} y \text{ shows } y \in R_W(\mathscr{L}(x(\eta'), A)).$$

ii) By Lemma 1.8 we have $\mathscr{L}(x(\eta), A) \subseteq R_W(\mathscr{L}(x(\eta), A))$. Let now $y \in R_W(\mathscr{L}(x(\eta'), A))$ for some son $\eta' = (\eta, t, \alpha)$ of η. Then there exist δ, x' and $\beta \in \mathbb{N}^m$ with

$$x' = x(\eta') + \beta * A \overset{\delta}{\to} y.$$

By $x(\eta') = x(\eta) + \alpha * A + v_t$ we get

$$x(\eta) + (\alpha + \beta) * A \overset{t\delta}{\to} y.$$

Thus $y \in R_W(\mathscr{L}(x(\eta), A))$.

(4.9) For any vertex η:

type(η) = unessential leaf $\leftrightarrow$ $\exists\xi(\xi$ ancestor of $\eta \wedge x(\eta) \in \mathscr{L}(x(\xi), A))$

and

type(η) = jump leaf $\qquad \leftrightarrow (\exists\xi(\xi$ ancestor of $\eta \wedge x(\xi) < x(\eta))$

$\qquad\qquad$ **and** $\forall\xi(\xi$ ancestor of $\eta \to x(\eta) \notin \mathscr{L}(x(\xi), A)))$.

Proof by inspection of Algorithm 4.1.

For describing new periods some further terminology is needed. We call a pair (ξ, η) of vertices a *jump* in SRT(x, A) iff type (η) = jump leaf $\wedge \xi$ ancestor of $\eta \wedge x(\xi) < x(\eta)$. If (ξ, η) is a jump, ξ is called a *jump origin*. ξ is called a *minimal jump origin* if ξ is a jump origin and on the path from the root to ξ there is no other jump origin.

The preceding properties of SRT(x, A) are true for arbitrary VRS. For the following we have to restrict on persistent VRS.

Lemma 4.10. *If (W, x) is persistent, then for any vertex η $A(\eta)$ is a sequence of periods at $x(\eta)$ folding equivalent to A.*

Proof by Tree Induction. $A(\text{root}) = A$ is trivial. By Lemma 1.7 the property is transmitted to successors.

For any jump origin ξ we construct a new (not necessarily reduced) sequence of periods $A'(\xi)$ at $x(\xi)$ having a strict initial segment folding equivalent to A.

4.11 Algorithm for $A'(\xi)$.

Input SRT(x, A), ξ jump origin;
let jump$(\xi) = \{(\xi, \eta_1), \ldots, (\xi, \eta_e)\}$ be the set of jumps originating at ξ;
for any $(\xi, \eta) \in$ jump(ξ) **do**
let $\langle (t_1, \alpha^{(1)}), \ldots, (t_{n(\xi,\eta)}, \alpha^{(n(\xi,\eta))}) \rangle$ be the sequence of edge markings on the path from ξ to η in SRT(x, A) and let be p_i' an element of $A(\xi)$ folding equivalent to p_i $(i = 1, \ldots, m)$;

$$\alpha := \sum_{i=1}^{n(\xi,\eta)} \alpha^{(i)};$$

$$p(\xi, \eta) := p_1'^{\alpha_1} \cdots p_m'^{\alpha_m} t_1 \cdots t_{n(\xi,\eta)} \ \textbf{od};$$

$A'(\xi) := A(\xi)\langle p(\xi, \eta_1), \ldots, p(\xi, \eta_e)\rangle$.

(4.12) The resulting sequence $A'(\xi)$ is a sequence of periods at $x(\xi)$ having a strict initial segment folding equivalent to A with

(4.13) $\qquad\qquad R_W(\mathscr{L}(x(\xi), A)) = R_W(\mathscr{L}(x(\xi), A'(\xi)))$.

Proof. By (4.10) $A(\xi)$ is folding equivalent to A. Therefore $A'(\xi)$ has the asserted initial segment. By (4.4) and because p_i' is period (hence enabled) at $x(\xi) + \text{dis}(p_1'^{\alpha_1} \cdots p_{i-1}'^{\alpha_i} p_i^\nu)$ we get

$$x(\xi) \stackrel{p(\xi,\eta)}{\to} x(\eta)$$

and

$$\mathrm{dis}(p(\xi,\eta)) = x(\eta) - x(\xi) > 0.$$

This proves $p(\xi,\eta)$ as a period at $x(\xi)$. By (4.12) we get

$$\mathcal{L}(x(\xi), A) \subseteq \mathcal{L}(x(\xi), A'(\xi))$$

and with Lemma 1.3

$$R_W(\mathcal{L}(x(\xi), A)) \subseteq R_W(\mathcal{L}(x(\xi), A'(\xi))).$$

To prove the opposite inclusion let $y \in R_W(\mathcal{L}(x(\xi), A'(\xi)))$. Then there exist x', $\alpha \in \mathbb{N}^m$, $\beta \in \mathbb{N}^e$, $\delta \in T^*$ with

$$x' = x(\xi) + \alpha * A + \beta * \langle p(\xi,\eta_1), \ldots, p(\xi,\eta_e)\rangle \overset{\delta}{\to} y.$$

$p(\xi,\eta_i)$ is period at $x(\xi) + \alpha * A$ and therefore $p(\xi,\eta_1)^{\beta_1} \cdots p(\xi,\eta_e)^{\beta_e}$ is enabled at $x(\xi) + \alpha * A$. Thus $y \in R_W(\mathcal{L}(x(\xi), A))$.

The constructions in this section are summarized in Theorem 4.14.

Theorem 4.14. *Given a persistent n-dimensional* VRS(W, x_0), *a vector* $x \in R_W(x_0)$ *and a reduced sequence* A_x *of periods at* x *there are effectively constructible a finite set* $C_x \subseteq \mathbb{N}^n$ *and a finite set* I_x *of pairs* (y, B) *with*

i) $y \in \mathbb{N}^n$,

ii) *B is a reduced sequence of periods at* y *with a strict initial segment folding equivalent to* A_x *and*

iii) $R_W(\mathcal{L}(x, A_x)) = \mathcal{L}(C_x, A_x) \cup \bigcup \{R_W(\mathcal{L}(y, B))|(y, B) \in I_x\}.$

Proof. By Algorithm 4.1 we construct the set reachability tree SRT(x, A_x). Let $C_x := \{x(\eta)|\mathrm{type}(\eta) \in \{\text{finished, terminal leaf}\} \wedge \textbf{not } \exists\xi(\xi \text{ ancestor of } \eta \wedge \xi \text{ jump origin})\}.$

By iterated application of (4.8) we get

(4.15) $R_W(\mathcal{L}(x, A_x)) = \bigcup \{\mathcal{L}(x(\eta), A_x)|\mathrm{type}(\eta) \in \{\text{finished, term. leaf}\} \wedge$

   $\textbf{not } \exists\xi(\xi \text{ ancestor of } \eta \wedge \xi \text{ jump origin})\}$

   $\cup \bigcup \{R_W(\mathcal{L}(x(\xi), A_x))|\xi \text{ jump origin}\}$

   $\cup \bigcup \{R_W(\mathcal{L}(x(\eta), A_x))|\mathrm{type}(\eta) = \text{unessential leaf} \wedge$

   $\textbf{not } \exists\xi(\xi \text{ ancestor of } \eta \wedge \xi \text{ jump origin})\}.$

We show that the third term on the right side of (4.15) is dispensable:

(4.16) $R_W(\mathcal{L}(x, A_x)) = \bigcup \{\mathcal{L}(x(\eta), A_x)|\mathrm{type}(\eta) \in \{\text{finished, term. leaf}\} \wedge$

   $\textbf{not } \exists\xi(\xi \text{ ancestor of } \eta \wedge \xi \text{ jump origin})\}$

   $\cup \bigcup \{R_W(\mathcal{L}(x(\xi), A_x))|\xi \text{ jump origin}\}.$

Proof. i) Inclusion from right to left by weakening (4.15).

ii) Inclusion from left to right: Let $y \in R_W(\mathcal{L}(x, A_x))$. Then there exist $\beta \in \mathbb{N}^{|A_x|}$ and $\delta \in T^*$ of minimal length such that $x + \beta * A_x \overset{\delta}{\to} y$. By the minimality of δ there is no p' folding equivalent to some p in A_x such that $\delta = \delta_1 p' \delta_2$ for some $\delta_1, \delta_2 \in T^*$ (otherwise we get $x + \beta * A_x + \text{dis}(p) \overset{\delta_1 \delta_2}{\to} y)$ is enabled at $x + \beta * A_x$. Therefore exists a path pf in $\text{SRT}(x, A_x)$ from the root to some η with edge marking $(t_1, \alpha^{(1)}), \ldots, (t_r, \alpha^{(r)})$ satisfying

(a) pf contains no jump origin with possible exception of η,

(b) $t_1 \cdots t_r$ is an initial segment of δ,

(c) if η is no jump origin, then $y \in \mathcal{L}(x(\eta), A_x) \wedge$
type$(\eta) \in \{\text{finished, terminal leaf}\} \wedge$
not $\exists \xi (\xi$ ancestor of $\eta \wedge \xi$ jump origin),

(d) if η is a jump origin, then $y \in R_W(\mathcal{L}(x(\eta), A_x))$.

This path can be constructed by the following algorithm.

4.17 Algorithm for *pf*.

    Input $\delta = t_1 \cdots t_s \in T^*$, $\text{SRT}(x, A_x)$ $\{x + \beta * A_x \overset{\delta}{\to} y\}$

    $\eta_0 :=$ root; $i := 0$; $\delta_1 := \Lambda$; $\delta_2 := \delta$;

    while not η_i jump origin $\wedge$ $\delta_2 \neq \Lambda$ **do**

    $\{t_{i+1}$ enabled at $x + \beta * A_x + \text{dis}(\delta_1) \wedge$ type$(\eta_i) = $ finished $\wedge$

$$\delta = \delta_1 \delta_2 \wedge \delta_1 = t_1 \cdots t_i \wedge \sum_{j=1}^{i} \alpha^{(i)} \leqslant \beta\}$$

    $\delta_1 := \delta_1 t_{i+1}$; $\delta_2 := \text{tail}(\delta_2)$; $i := i + 1$;

    choose $\alpha^{(i)} \in \min\{\beta' | x(\eta_{i-1}) + \beta' * A + u_{t_i} \geqslant 0\}$;

    $\eta_i := (\eta_{i-1}, t_i, \alpha^{(i)})$ **od.**

Algorithm 4.17 terminates with a path pf obviously satisfying (a), (b) and $i < r \to \eta_i$ is no jump origin. If the last vertex η_r is no jump origin then by the while condition $\delta_2 = \Lambda$ yields $y \in \mathcal{L}(x(\eta_r), A_x)$. In case η_r is a jump origin $y \in R_W(\mathcal{L}(x(\eta_r), A_x))$ follows. The loop invariant is easily verified. For "type$(\eta_i) = $ finished" is needed the minimality of δ.

(c) respectively (d) yield

$$y \in \bigcup \{\mathcal{L}(x(\eta), A_x) | \text{type}(\eta) \in \{\text{finished, term. leaf}\} \wedge$$

$$\textbf{not } \exists \xi (\xi \text{ ancestor of } \eta \wedge \xi \text{ jump origin})\}$$

$$\cup \bigcup \{R_W(x(\eta), A_x)) | \eta \text{ jump origin}\}.$$

This proves (4.16).

Combining (4.12) with the Reduction Theorem 3.3 we get for any jump origin ξ a finite set $M(\xi)$ with

$$(4.18) \qquad R_W(\mathscr{L}(x(\xi), A_x)) = R_W(\mathscr{L}(x(\xi), A'(\xi)))$$
$$= \bigcup \{R_W(\mathscr{L}(y, B)) | (y, B) \in M(\xi)\}$$

and

(4.19) $(y, B) \in M(\xi) \to B$ is a reduced sequence of periods at y having a strict initial segment folding equivalent to A_x.

(4.16) and (4.18) together yield i), ii), iii) in Theorem 4.14, if we define

$$I_x := \bigcup \{M(\xi) | \xi \text{ jump origin in } \mathrm{SRT}(x, A_x)\}.$$

5. Jump Tree and Proof of the Main Theorem

5.1 Main Theorem. *For a persistent vector replacement system* (W, x_0) *the reachability set is an effectively semilinear set.*

Proof. We give an algorithm for constructing a further tree, called *jump tree*, which yields a finite I of pairs (x, B) satisfying

i) $x \in \mathbb{N}^n \wedge B$ finite subset of $\mathbb{N}^n$ and

ii) $R_W(x_0) = \bigcup \{\mathscr{L}(x, B) | (x, B) \in I\}$.

5.2 Algorithm for the Jump Tree.

> **Input** persistent $\mathrm{VRS}(W, x_0)$ of dimension n
> create root; $x(\text{root}) := x_0$;
> $\qquad\qquad C(\text{root}) := C_{x_0} \{\text{computed in } (4.14)\}$;
> $\qquad\qquad A(\text{root}) := \emptyset$;
> $\qquad\qquad I(\text{root}) := I_{x_0} \{\text{computed in } (4.14)\}$;
> **while** $\exists \eta\, I(\eta) \neq \emptyset$ **do**
> $\qquad$ **for each** $(y, B) \in I(\eta)$ **do**
> $\qquad$ construct a son $\eta' = (\eta, y, B)$ of η;
> $\qquad$ $x(\eta') := y$; $C(\eta') := C_y$;
> $\qquad$ $A(\eta') := B$; $I(\eta') := I_y$ $\qquad\qquad$ **od od**.

Properties of Algorithm 5.2 and the constructed tree:

(5.3) For any vertex η: $A(\eta)$ is a reduced sequence of periods at $x(\eta)$.

Proof. Trivial for the root. For any other vertex η', son of η, $(x(\eta'), A(\eta')) = (y, B) \in I(\eta) = I_{x(\eta)}$ we get (5.3) by Theorem 4.14ii).

(5.4) ξ ancestor of $\eta \to A(\eta)$ contains a strict initial segment folding equivalent to $A(\xi)$.

Proof. Follows by induction on the length of the path from ξ to η from Theorem 4.14ii).

(5.5) Algorithm 5.2 terminates with a finite tree.

Proof. Suppose 5.2 does not terminate. Because $I(\eta)$ is finite for any vertex η, any vertex has only finitely many sons and Königs infinity lemma would yield an infinite path $\langle \eta_i | i \in \mathbb{N} \rangle$. Let $A(\eta_i) = \langle p_1^{(i)}, \dots, p_{n_i}^{(i)} \rangle$ and define

$$w_i := \text{EPK}(p_i^{(i)}) \text{ for } i \neq 0.$$

Because of (5.4) we have $n_i \geqslant i$ and $(\forall j \leqslant n_i)\text{EPK}(p_j^{(i)}) = w_j$. Because any $A(\eta_i)$ is reduced, we get

$$w_i \neq w_j \quad \text{if} \quad i \neq j.$$

By Lemma 1.1c) there must be indices i, j with $i < j \wedge w_i < w_j$. $A(\eta_j)$ reduced yields a contradiction.

(5.6) For any vertex η:

$$R_W(\mathcal{L}(x(\eta), A(\eta))) = \mathcal{L}(C(\eta), A(\eta)) \cup \bigcup \{R_W(\mathcal{L}(x(\eta'), A(\eta')))|\eta' \text{ son of } \eta\}.$$

Proof follows directly from Theorem 4.14iii). By iterated application of (5.6) we get

(5.7) $R_W(x_0) = \bigcup \{\mathcal{L}(C(\eta), A(\eta))|\eta \text{ vertex in the jump tree}\}.$

To get the main theorem let $I := \{(x(\eta), A(\eta))|\eta \text{ vertex in the jump tree}\}.$

Addendum (April 17, 1980). E. Mayr has announced another proof of the main theorem (to appear in TCS) and a proof for decidability of the reachability problem for general VRS (personal communication).

Appendix on correction (September 8, 1980). Minor changes of the given algorithms lead to a decision procedure for persistence of arbitrary VRS. Decidability of persistence was independently proved by Ernst Mayr, TU Munich, and Jan Grabowski, Humboldt-Universität Berlin, too.

The given algorithms correctly remain, if the assumption of persistence is weakened to the conjunction of two properties which guarantee the inheritance of periods (as in Lemma 1.7) and a reducibility analog to the Reduction Lemma 3.1. This gives effectively semilinear reachability sets for a broader class of VRS.

References

[1] Hack, M.: The equality problem for vector addition systems is undecidable. Theor. Computer Sci. **2**, 77−96 (1976).

[2] Hopcroft, J., Pansiot, J.-J.: On the reachability problem for 5-dimensional vector addition systems. Theor. Computer Science **8**, 135−159 (1979).

[3] Jones, N. D., Landweber, L. H., Lien, Y. E.: Complexity of some problems in Petri nets. Theor. Computer Science **4**, 277−299 (1977).

[4] Karp, R. M., Miller, R. E.: Parallel program schemata. J. Comput. System Sci. **3**, 147−195 (1969).

[5] Landweber, L. H., Robertson, E. L.: Properties of conflict-free and persistent Petri nets. J. Ass. Computing Machinery **25**, 352−364 (1978).

[6] van Leeuwen, J.: A partial solution to the reachability problem for vector addition systems. 6th Ann. ACM Symp. on the Theory of Computing, pp. 303−309 (1974).

[7] Machtey, M., Young, P.: An introduction to the general theory of algorithms. New York: North-Holland 1978.

[8] Rackoff, C.: The covering and boundedness problems for vector addition systems. Theor. Comp. Sci. **6**, 223−231 (1978).

[9] Sacerdote, G. S., Tenney, R. L.: The decidability of the reachability problem for vector addition systems. 9th Ann. ACM Symp. on Theory of Computing, pp. 61–77 (1977).

[10] Starke, H. P.: Semilinearity and Petri nets. Fundamentals of Computation Theory 79 (Budach, L., ed.), pp. 423–429. Berlin: Akademie-Verlag 1979.

Prof. Dr. H. Müller
Institut für Mathematische Maschinen
und Datenverarbeitung (III)
Universität Erlangen-Nürnberg
Martensstrasse 3
D-8520 Erlangen
Federal Republic of Germany

Computing, Suppl. 3, 105 – 124 (1981)
© by Springer-Verlag 1981

Application of Graph Rewriting to Optimization and Parallelization of Programs

M. Nagl, Koblenz

Abstract – Zusammenfassung

Application of Graph Rewriting to Optimization and Parallelization of Programs. Classical automatic optimization is starting with linearized intermediate code and builds up graph-like data structures (flow graph, DAGs, data flow analysis data). Most of the information which was already known by the upper part of the compiler now has to be detected again. We start with a graph-like intermediate code in which all structural information of the source is still present. Optimization is then carried out by graph manipulations. This is sketched by some examples, namely local common subexpression elimination, motion of loop invariant computations, and induction variable elimination. The usual way in parallelization is also to build up graph-like information (data graph) from flattened code. Here, the parallelization of linear programs and microparallelization within expressions are regarded, starting again with a graph-like intermediate code. There are a lot of further tasks in the context of reliable software generation which can be efficiently performed on high-level intermediate code.

Anwendung von Graphersetzungen auf Optimierung und Parallelisierung von Programmen. Bei der automatischen Optimierung von Programmen beginnt man meist mit linearisiertem Zwischencode und baut daraus, zum Teil durch aufwendige Algorithmen, graphähnliche Datenstrukturen auf. Der größte Teil der so aufgefundenen Information war dem oberen Teil des Compilers bereits bekannt, diese Information wurde aber nicht an den Zwischencode weitergegeben. Wir gehen dagegen gleich von einem graphähnlichen Zwischencode aus, der die Strukturinformation des betreffenden Quellprogramms noch vollständig enthält. Optimierungen werden dann durch Graphmanipulationen auf diesem Zwischencode durchgeführt. Wir betrachten diese Vorgehensweise an zwei Beispielen, nämlich der Elimination (lokaler) gemeinsamer Teilausdrücke und der Optimierung von Schleifen. Bei der Parallelisierung von Programmen baut man sich ebenfalls einen Graphen (Datengraphen) aus Quell- oder Zwischencode auf. Wir gehen auch hier wieder von graphähnlichem Zwischencode aus. Aus diesem Bereich betrachten wir die Parallelisierung von linearen Programmen und von Ausdrücken. Optimierung und Parallelisierung sind nur zwei Aufgaben aus dem Bereich der Erzeugung zuverlässiger und effizienter Software, die sich auf graphähnlichem Zwischencode gut durchführen lassen.

1. Optimization of Programs

Optimization of programs can be carried out on fairly different levels. First, there is *problem-dependent* optimization on *source code level* as proposed in [Kn74] and investigated in [Ba79] and [Lo76]. In this case the knowledge of the programmer about the program he has written is introduced and, therefore, the result of this optimization can be an order of magnitude higher efficient than the other optimization techniques regarded below. A practical proceeding e.g. is to start with a structured, elucid, and well-documented version of a program and to modify it in a man-machine dialog by documenting all optimizing transformations.

The most common optimization technique, however, is *automatic, machine-independent* optimization carried out by an optimizing compiler. Usually, after lexical analysis and after context free as well as context sensitive syntax analysis *intermediate code* is generated. In most cases this code has triple or quadruple form, in some cases tree-like[1] or graph-like form. This kind of optimization is named automatic, as it is independent of the semantics of the underlying program and machine-independent, inasmuch as special features of the target machine are ignored[2]. The aim of this optimization is a semantically equivalent program improved corresponding to run-time or space. This is the level we are mainly dealing with.

The compiler now assigns addresses to user-defined data and compiler-defined data and generates code of assembler or direct loader level. Then some *postoptimization* techniques take place, as peephole optimization (elimination of unnecessary Loads and Stores and multiple Jumps) or replacement of long instructions by short ones whenever it is possible etc.

Automatic optimization is usually started by determining the *basic blocks*[3] of intermediate code, i.e. the sequences of instructions where control flow paths cannot split or glue. Then the *flow graph* is constructed the nodes of which are the basic blocks and some data flow analysis algorithms are carried out which are prerequisite for *standard optimization techniques* like code motion, induction variable elimination, code hoisting, constant folding, elimination of common subexpressions, and copy propagation, which are listed here in an order in which they can be carried out in practice (cf. [AU77]). According to the 90 percent rule, saying, that a program stays 90 percent of its time in 10 percent of its code, namely in its loops, it is especially profitable to concentrate on loop optimization in a first approximation.

In automatic optimization one distinguishes between *local* optimization within basic blocks, *global* optimization regarding all basic blocks of a (sub)program, and *interprocedural* optimization taking into account different procedures and modules.

Automatic optimization is *conservative* in the sense that it does in no case change the semantics of the program. One tries to come close to an optimal program without working unduly hard. However, we rather miss some optimizations than do change the program, whenever there is a possibility that a transformation might alter what the program does.

Compilers usually flatten intermediate code representing it with triples, quadruples, or stack-machine instructions, i.e. they transform to a rather low level. Data flow analysis and optimization usually is carried out on this level. Flattening looses information which is hard to recover. As at least some of this information is needed again for optimization, we usually have to reconstruct a graph-form intermediate code from a flattened one. A standard example for this detour is the detection of loops after having forgotten what the compiler knew at the moment most

---

[1] Sometimes linearized, e.g. in Polish prefix notation.
[2] However, the optimization is driven by the global architecture of the target machine, e.g. if it is a stack machine, if it is a multiprocessor machine etc.
[3] Basic blocks have nothing to do with blocks in the ALGOL sense.

of them have been generated from explicit loops at source level. We avoid this roundabout way by regarding *graph-like intermediate code* and assuming that the compiler directly generates intermediate code of this form. We call this intermediate code for a program its *program graph*. Finally, another argument for a high level intermediate code is that it is hard to make sensible use of a rich instruction set or of multiple registers of the target machine in code generation if the intermediate code is too low.

On the other hand, intermediate code must be lower than source code. For example, subscript calculation of array elements, which is an important task of any optimizing compiler, cannot be optimized on source level as the programmer usually has no access and should have no access to the function assigning addresses. This, however, in no ways implies that information should only be provided at low level or that this information can best be preserved by low level analysis ignoring the knowledge of high level analysis.

2. Parallelization of Programs

There are *different levels* of parallel or asynchronous programming. First, one could formulate an algorithm using the conventional sequential constructs together with a **fork** and **join** construct opening or closing a parallel section of a program, i.e. a list of statements potentially executable in parallel. Programs of this kind are easy to grasp as we can follow the flow of control. We can formalize these programs as graphs of a special class, namely as series-parallel transport networks. This type of parallelism or asynchronism is too restricted for some problems, e.g. for those arising in the implementation of an operating system. Therefore, synchronization mechanisms have been introduced e.g. in ALGOL 68 or PL/1[4]. Finally, the highest level to formulate parallelism is to program in an abstract or virtual configuration of processors appropriate for the problem at hand. Each processor executes some part of program in parallel with others, the result can be made accessible to others e.g. by access rights to common or private memory or by data transfers. Thus, data and messages can be sent from one component of the configuration to another one using defined channels and, furthermore, synchronization tools are available. Finally, one could consider configurations of elementary structures of different types or even configurations which are changing dynamically.

Another problem is to *allocate* a parallel program using one of the above cited mechanisms. There one distinguishes between a priori or static allocation on one hand and dynamic allocation on the other. The latter is especially important if the available physical multiprocessor configuration has many components, as the allocation is changing whenever one component breaks down. Even static allocation is a very hard problem, if the mechanism the programmer is programming in (the virtual configuration) and the actual physical configuration differ considerably in size or structure, i.e. the mapping from logical to physical structure is complex. Here, a demanding task arises for compiler writers. They have to implement this mapping if they implement a programming language within which it is possible to program in virtual configurations.

---

[4] These mechanisms can be specified in an elucid manner by graph grammars too (cf. [Na79]).

To formulate algorithms with parallel constructs demands a new way of thinking. Some people argue that this kind of programming is beyond human capability. Reasons for that are that usually large problems, i.e. which are handling a large quantity of information of complex character, are tackled by parallel programming because they can hardly be executed on conventional hardware and, furthermore, that human beings, due to their development history, are inclined to think sequentially. Moreover, programming in a virtual multiprocessor configuration demands a lot of architectural knowledge, i.e. demands a new type of programmer. Because of these reasons it makes sense to look for algorithms which *automatically synthesize* parallel programs. This is especially evident, if one takes into consideration, that there already exists a vast store of sequential programs for a variety of problems. It would neither be feasible nor reasonable to throw these tools away. Some people even say that this synthesis problem is governing the success of multiprocessor systems (as e.g. EGPA [HHS76]) in computational practice. We are going to demonstrate that this automatic parallelization of sequential programs can again be carried out successfully on high-level intermediate code.

Finally, in the same way as in optimization one could regard parallelization on source code level in a man-machine dialog. Here again, the programmer introduces his knowledge of the actual problem and the system may support this process by proving that the transformations are correct or may itself suggest some transformations.

3. Graph Grammars as a Tool for Abstract Implementation

Directed graphs with labelled nodes and edges are a widely accepted formalism to describe structures of different fields in an elucid and precise way: Substructures correspond to nodes, which are labelled to indicate which substructure they represent, whereas directed and labelled edges express different relations between substructures or the decomposition into further ones. In many applications the structures are altered, yielding a change of the graphs describing them, which can be traced back to different formal rewriting mechanisms.

Manipulations of graphs have been studied in *graph grammar theory* (for an overview see [CER79] and [Na79]). However, the grammatical aspect is only important in some applications. All applications, however, can directly adopt the formalizations of different graph rewriting mechanisms contained in graph grammars. A variety of those mechanisms was developed leading to different types of grammars.

A local manipulation is *sequential* rewriting where a subgraph is replaced by another one while the rest of the host remains unchanged. The embedding of the inserted graph into the host is specified by the so-called embedding transformation. This yields the introduction of a graph production consisting of two graphs, namely the left and right-hand side, and the embedding transformation, which is nothing else than an algorithmic specification of the embedding of the right-hand side depending of the embedding of the left-hand side. A global kind of graph rewriting is *parallel* rewriting, where the host is partitioned into subgraphs corresponding to left-hand sides of productions. The result of a derivation step then is a parallel replacement of all left-hand sides by right-hand sides which are connected appropriately (which can be specified also by the productions). A combination of both derivation mechanisms is *mixed* rewriting where more than one subgraph is replaced but, on the other hand, a part of the host remains unchanged.

The programming of graph modifications within the above concepts can be managed by the exchange of left-hand by right-hand sides, and by embedding and connection transformations respectively. Besides these basic concepts *programmed* and *two-level* graph grammars have been introduced where in the first case we regard complex rewriting steps driven by the run through a flow diagram each elementary operation of which is a sequential, parallel, or mixed rewriting step or, in the second case, the productions to be applied have themselves been derived by applying graph productions.

As stated above, in most application fields only the graph manipulations induced by different rewriting mechanisms are of interest, i.e. in these applications graph rewriting is used as a specification tool to *implement* different applications on an *abstract level*. There is a two-fold abstraction: one in data as we are not interested at this level how a graph is represented in a computer and one in rewriting mechanisms, as we neglect that complex graph rewriting steps have to be decomposed in a real implementation. However, this abstract implementation assumes concrete form if an implementation of the above concepts is available (cf. [BNW78]).

The aim of this paper is to combine optimization, parallelization, and graph rewriting, which is possible by assuming intermediate code in program graph form. Optimization and parallelization leads to transformations of the program graph and that is the point where graph rewriting comes in, namely as abstract implementation of these transformations. There are already three papers, namely [FKZ76], [Ul73], and [Wi79] which combine optimization and graph rewriting. In the first two papers, however, graph grammars are only used for data flow analysis or for the definition of reducible programs in which data flow analysis is easy. In both papers graph rewriting is not used for optimization itself. In [Wi79] trees are used as compiler intermediate code. Two-level tree rewriting with applicability conditions based on attribute and transformational grammars is applied to code motion and constant folding.

We can only give some examples for the application of graph rewriting methods to optimization and parallelization here which, of course, can be improved and extended. The ideas presented may lead to another philosophy in implementing optimizing compilers. At least they give another (more easy?) view of some optimization and parallelization techniques and introduce a uniform notation in which both can be presented.

Let us make some technical remarks corresponding to graphs and graph rewriting we use in the following. As rewriting mechanisms we only need programmed sequential steps. The control diagrams[5], which in most cases are rather simple,

---

[5] The flow diagram driving a complex manipulation step we call control diagram.

consist of nodes drawn as hexagons[6] which indicate the application of a production. If the production was applicable we leave this node along a Y-exit, otherwise along an N-exit. If we indicate more than one production within a node of a control diagram as e.g. in Fig. 10a then we mean application of all productions named there. Embedding transformations are only specified informally here. However, they are not imprecise. The reader who wants to have them formalized may consult [Na79]. Corresponding to embedding transformations we make the following agreement: Whenever a similar node denotation occurs within the left and right-hand side of a graph rule then both nodes behave equally corresponding to embedding transformation, e.g. in Fig. 2b node 1 and 1' of the right-hand side get exactly the same embedding as node 1 of the left-hand side had. Productions are extended by positive and negative application conditions abbreviated as pos.ac and neg.ac as shown e.g. in Fig. 2b. The first means that any occurrence of the left-hand side of a production must be extendable by the graph given in the pos.ac, the latter means that the neg.ac must not occur in the neighbourhood of the actual left-hand side. If pos.ac or neg.ac parts are separated by "or" then we demand that any of the specifications of the pos.ac but none of those of neg.ac is to be found[7].

Corresponding to the graphical representation of program graphs we lay down: Node denotations are only used where necessary, namely in productions to specify embedding transformations. We use integers for node denotations. All other symbols refer to node labels, the node denotation is only implicitly introduced by drawing a certain label at different locations. In Fig. 1b, for example, no node denotation occurs, the upmost node here has two labels, namely "+" and "PROD". Nodes sometimes are drawn as circles (cf. Fig. 2b). The edge labels of the program graph do not appear in its graphical representation. Control flow edges are drawn as ⟶, labels corresponding to the order of operands within operations are omitted as no misunderstandings will arise. An edge of the form ⟶ is used as an edge either of type ⟶ or ⟶, the latter connecting operands with their operator. The programming language we use is a fantasy notation similar to PASCAL.

4. Elimination of Local Common Subexpressions

Basic block optimization is usually carried out after having optimized loops. Two optimization techniques are relevant: local common subexpression elimination (opposite to global common subexpression elimination which is not restricted to basic blocks) and copy propagation. The common strategy is the following (cf. [AU77]). From a flattened intermediate code we reconstruct a directed acyclic graph, in short DAG. This DAG eliminates common subexpressions and unnecessary copies in that way that each common subexpression and each class of copies having the same value is represented only as a single node within this graph[8]. In machine code generation from a DAG code is only generated once for a common

---

[6] Such a node is a combination of a decision and a statement.

[7] It should be mentioned that we could have denoted the graph transformation steps needed in the following by programs of an appropriate programming language for graph problems as e.g. GRAPL [Na80].

[8] Here again we mostly detect those unnecessary copies which are inserted by the intermediate code generator. Thus, we again repair a damage caused by switching too early to machine-like level.

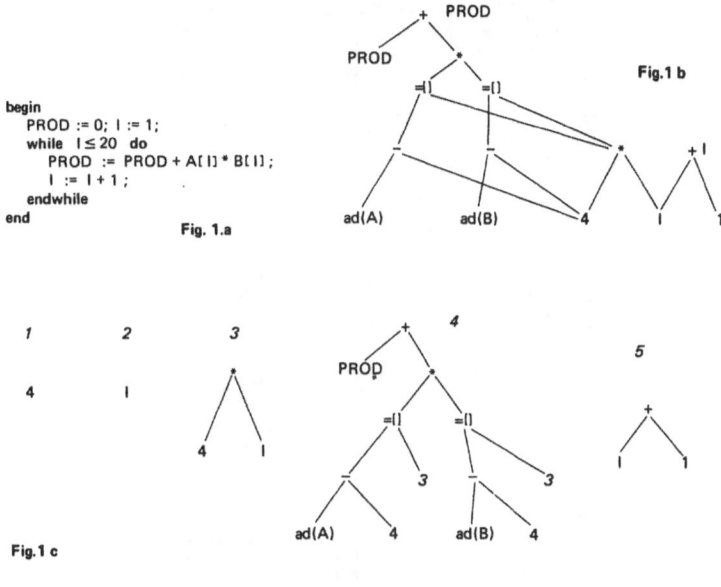

Fig. 1a−c

subexpression and unnecessary copies are eliminated. If a common subexpression has occurred, this DAG is no longer a tree: It is a tree-like structure with additional edges between subtrees (to so-called shared nodes). This DAG is then partitioned into a sequence of trees such that a tree representing a common subexpression must be available when its value is needed, i.e. in the sequence of trees it is before any tree needing its value[9]. For this sequence of trees then optimal machine code is generated, optimal with respect to instruction sequence length and, thus, here also with respect to run-time. Fig. 1 shows this proceeding: In part a) a small program is given calculating the scalar product of two vectors, in part b) the DAG for the body of the loop assuming a 4-Byte target machine, while part c) shows a sequence of trees covering this DAG.

According to the pleading we made in the introductory sections, we start with a high level intermediate code, namely the program graph, in which expressions and assignments are represented as trees. Therefore, the graph construction from a flattened intermediate code is unnecessary. However, within a DAG local common subexpressions are eliminated too. It would cause no problems to describe the transformation of tree-like intermediate code to DAG representation by graph rewriting: We have to glue identical subtrees repeatedly, giving the result the sum of the embedding edges of each of its constituents[10]. But as the DAG is partitioned

---

[9] The information that a single node is occurring in the sequence of trees (e.g. trees 1 and 2 of Fig. 1c) is valuable for the code generator. It might, if possible, generate code such that the values of these nodes are kept in registers.

[10] Furthermore, we have to carry out some simple technical graph transformations.

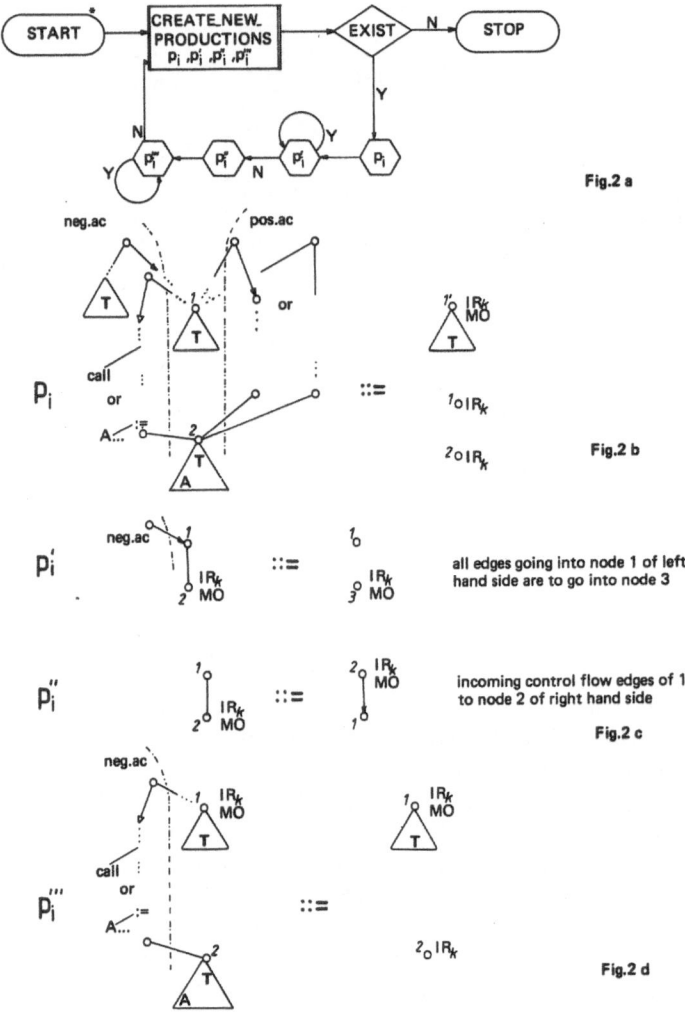

Fig.2 a

Fig.2 b

Fig.2 c

Fig.2 d

Fig. 2a – d

into trees again before code generation, we try to perform these transformations directly on tree-like structured intermediate code.

The central idea of our proceeding on graph-like intermediate code is the following: Whenever two subtrees occur (in directly or indirectly subsequent statements or in the same statement) which have identical structure, i.e. which represent a common subexpression, they are glued together. The remaining single subtree is placed on the path of control just before the statement which contained the first occurrence of this common subexpression. Furthermore, the root of this subtree is additionally labelled with *MO* standing for *m*ultiple *o*ccurrence[11] and a temporary name IR_k

---

[11] Which is a valuable information for the code generator to keep this intermediate result in a register, if possible.

(for *i*ntermediate *r*esult number k). The two subtree occurrences now are represented by single nodes both having the new temporary name as labels. This manipulation is carried out by applying production p_i of Fig. 2b once, p_i' as often as possible, and p_i'' again once, the letter T in p_i indicating that both trees of the left-hand side and the one of the right-hand side have the same structure. When applying production p_i we are sure that the subtree at node 1 is one of the upmost ones, as the negative application condition allows no higher occurrence. The left part of the positive application condition expresses that the tree with root 1 is higher with respect to control flow, the right part that both are contained in the same statement. Please note, that an edge of form —— stands for left of right descendant[12], one of the form —→ for an edge either of form —— or —→. Finally —→ ··· stands for an arbitrary path starting with a —→ edge. When p_i is applied the subtrees with node 1 and 2 are substituted by single nodes 1 and 2 labelled with IR_k. Furthermore, subtree with node 1 is still at its location. By applying p_i' repeatedly and p_i'' once this subtree is hoisted up to control flow level. Now we know that the common subexpression is in upmost position or, saying it the other way, all other occurrences are below this subtree. By applying p_i''' as often as possible all these occurrences are eliminated.

The description up to now was simplified in the sense that between both trees no redefinition of any part of the second tree is allowed. This means that no redefinition of the simple variables (i.e. of leaves of the second tree) is allowed, but also, that no redefinition of *any* array element or *any* location corresponding to a pointer variable or a dereferenced pointer variable or *any* procedure call may occur. This is because the redefinition of $A[I]$ for example, may also be a redefinition of $A[J]$ if $I = J$, or, that we do not know where a pointer is pointing to, or which side effects a procedure call might have[13]. In these cases the second tree, although having the same static structure, may represent another value. All these cases are covered by the negative application condition of productions p_i and p_i'''. If we would have direct define-use information in the sense that there is always an edge of a certain label pointing from the definition (not the declaration) to all corresponding applied occurrences (uses) than we would be able to express these negative application conditions of p_i and p_i''' by positive application conditions: We must demand that all define-use edges ending in corresponding nodes of both trees have a common source[14].

The productions p_i and p_i''' are not productions in the usual sense, they rather represent an infinite class of productions inasmuch as all T-triangles may be replaced by an arbitrary tree. However, for all occurrences of T-triangles the same concrete tree has to be substituted. Thus, we have a two-level production system here. Even if we restrict the trees to be substituted in depth as we know the maximal depth of trees of the program graph then a finite but even large number of possible

---

[12] Or one of the n descendants if we use n-ary operators.

[13] Of course, one can refine this method by investigating in which parts of an array an array element may ly, or to which data structures or parts of it a pointer might point to, or which side effects a procedure call might have. Going the above simple way only misses chances but causes not errors.

[14] In this case by generating these define-use edges one could again apply the brute force method of above. Whenever a redefinition of an array element occurs this is regarded as redefinition of all array elements. Analogously, we proceed with pointer occurrences and procedure calls.

substituents results. However, it is not necessary to determine all possible substituents a priori and, consequently, all forms the schemes p_i and p_i''' can actually have. Contrary, we can restrict ourselves to those subtrees which actually have been detected as occurring at least twice in the program graph of the basic clock we are considering. Therefore, we are generating an actual production fitting to the scheme of p_i, or p_i''' only after having detected multiple subtree occurrence. The box CREATE_NEW_PRODUCTIONS might indicate this procedure. Furthermore, implementation techniques based on hashing which are used in DAG construction to detect subDAGs quickly (cf. [AU77]) can be adopted here to find out multiple subtree occurrences rapidly. This might also be part of CREATE_NEW_PRODUCTIONS.

The programmed rewriting step does not fix the order in which subtrees of the basic block are inspected. This is also left open for the routine CREATE_NEW_PRODUCTIONS. However, we demand that any actual implementation starts with trees of depth 1 (the depth being the maximum number of edges on a path from the root to a leaf) and proceeds to greater depths without having missed an applicable subtree of less order. Then, the result of this extraction process is unique in the sense that we get the same structure for all statements within the basic block, irrespective of the order in which productions are applied.

If we do so we might have hoisted subtrees which only occur as parts of further subtrees which are also hoisted. Thus, as indicated in Fig. 3a, we have no occurrence of IR_k and IR_{k+1} in the following but only those of IR_{k+2}. Thus, it would be more elucid and advantageous for code generation to melt the common subtrees again as indicated in Fig. 3b. However, we could also avoid to hoist a common subtree if all occurrences of this subtree are part of a greater common subtree. This again can be checked by CREATE_NEW_PRODUCTIONS before generating an actual production.

The modified program graph corresponding to the DAG of Fig. 1b or to the sequence of trees of Fig. 1c is drawn in Fig. 4. Here, the common subexpression $I * 4$ has been hoisted. The attentive reader may have recognized that the program

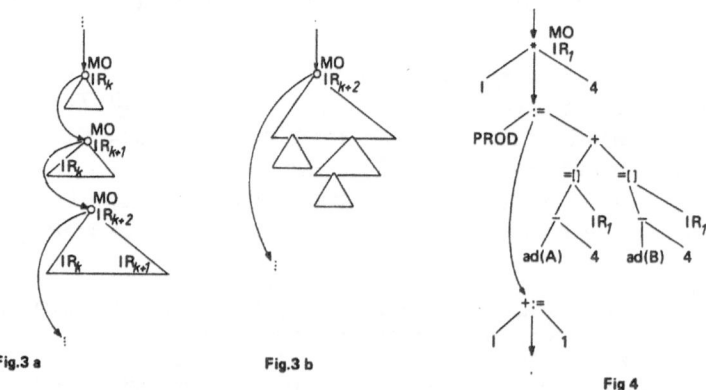

Fig.3 a   Fig.3 b   Fig 4

Figs. 3 and 4

graph of Fig. 4 is not optimal as *ad*(*A*)-4 and *ad*(*B*)-4 are evaluated repeatedly although being loop invariant. This, however, is no longer common subexpression elimination and leads us over to the next section.

5. Motion of Loop Invariant Computations and Induction Variable Elimination

To detect loop invariant computations means to detect expressions all operands of which are constant when control flow is within the loop. This refers to all basic blocks occurring within the loop body. In classical optimization the procedure is as follows (cf. [AU77]):

(1) One has to detect the loops. This problem can be solved efficiently for reducible flow graphs[15] using e.g. an algorithm which generates a spanning tree in a depth first manner. Again, this problem is due to flattening: The compiler knows when a loop occurs and it should pass this information to intermediate code[16]. In a loop there is a basic block, called header, which dominates all basic blocks of the loop, i.e. any control path meeting the loop must have gone through the header before. We create a new basic block, called pre-header, into which all loop-constant computations are to be shifted. Fig. 5 describes this transformation which, of course, is nothing else than a simple sequential rewriting step.

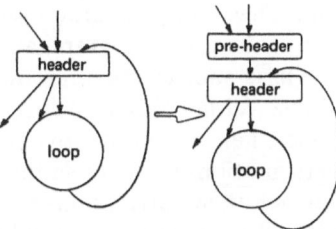

Fig. 5

(2) Assuming use-define-chaining information we then can determine all those quadruple statements the right side of which has only operands defined outside the loop (including constants). Of course, detection of one loop invariant computation may lead to detection of further ones. Finally, we come out with computations representing those parts of expressions of the source program which are loop invariant.

(3) We move constant quadruple statements to the pre-header if they fulfil some very strong requirements: (i) Either the block containing the constant statement dominates all exits of the loop or the left side of this assignment is not used outside (is dead). As most loops are **while-** or **do-**loops the first part of this requirement

---

[15] In reducible flow graphs forwards jumps into the loop body are forbidden. In [U73] a simple graph grammar is given generating all reducible flow graphs. Well-structured programs, of course, have the property of reducibility.

[16] As the programming language we have in mind has exits, but no gotos, a programmer cannot build up loops which are not directly visible as such at source code level.

can hardly be met, as there is always a control path missing the loop body and passing the loop only by its header. (ii) An assignment can only be moved to the pre-header if there is no other assignment to the same name within the loop. (iii) An assignment $A := \dots$ can only be moved to the pre-header if there is no use of A which is reached by any definition other than the statement to be moved. Putting all together, we get that we can only move statements $A := \dots$ where A is dead outside, there is no other assignment to A in the loop and there is no use of A which can refer to another definition of A outside.

It is clear that all these requirements are fulfilled by the temporaries the compiler has generated for those parts of expressions of the source program which are constant within the loop. We claim these are most of the loop invariant computations we can find. So, going the classical way to detect these loop invariant computations is again a detour.

Then, in common optimization, the invariant quadruple statements are moved to the pre-header in the order they are detected. This pre-header is again a basic block. So, local optimization as described in the last section can be applied. In this way a lot of the (nonlocal) common subexpression elimination for loops can be performed, namely for all the constant common subexpressions[17].

We are going another more direct way: We find out those loop invariant subexpressions which in the common proceeding are assigned to a temporary by checking the program graph. These loop invariant subexpressions can also be found by looking for subtrees of the program graph all leaves of which have their definition outside the loop. These subtrees then are moved outside the loop by graph manipulating operations. Within this transformation we try to eliminate common subexpressions at once, i.e. we do not move them all up over the loop in order to apply then the transformations sketched in the last section[18]. If we find a complete tree to be moved, which then corresponds to a source code assignment, then this could have been hoisted by the programmer if he would have inspected his program carefully[19].

We demonstrate loop optimization techniques by regarding a small source program as shown in Fig. 6. It is the body of a merge-sort routine which merges two sorted arrays A, B of length N each to one array C of length $2 * N$. The notation used here for alternatives in the **case**-construct is very elucid but on the other hand implies that pieces of code occur multiply, e.g. $A[I] > B[J]$ and $A[I] \leqslant B[J]$, the latter being equivalent to **not** $(A[I] > B[J])$. Therefore, we start with a program graph where this **case**-construct is transformed into an **if-then-else** cascade as outlined in Fig. 7. This transformation (which is more on source code level and, therefore, could be an operation of the man-machine interaction mentioned above) can again be described simply as a program graph transformation using a single sequential graph rewriting step.

---

[17] The same holds true for copy propagation.

[18] It is clear that there are further common subexpressions which are depending on non-invariant computations. Those lying within one basic block of the loop body can be eliminated applying the transformations of the last section.

[19] Of course, some of the motions the programmer could have also done on source level by splitting assignments into invariant and loop depending parts, which, however, decreases readability.

```
I, J, K := 1 ;
while K≤2 * N do
   casebool
      I>N or else A[I]>B[J]:
         C[K]  := B[J] ;
         J := J + 1 ;
      J>N or else A[I]≤B[J]:
         C[K]  := A[I] ;
         I := I + 1
   endcase
   K := K + 1
endwhile
```

Fig. 6

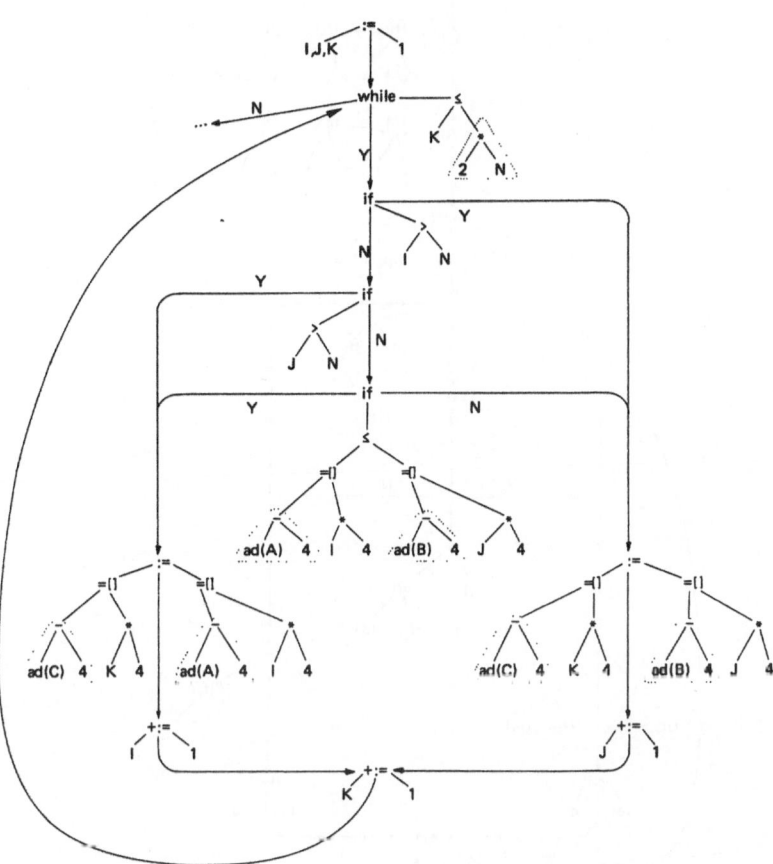

Fig. 7

In our case we get seven occurrences of subtrees corresponding to loop-invariant temporaries which should be moved up over the while-node. These subtrees are encircled by dotted lines in Fig. 7. A subtree is recognized as loop-invariant if all its leaves are loop-invariant. This could be detected by investigating define-use information. However, before we move up a subtree we look for further

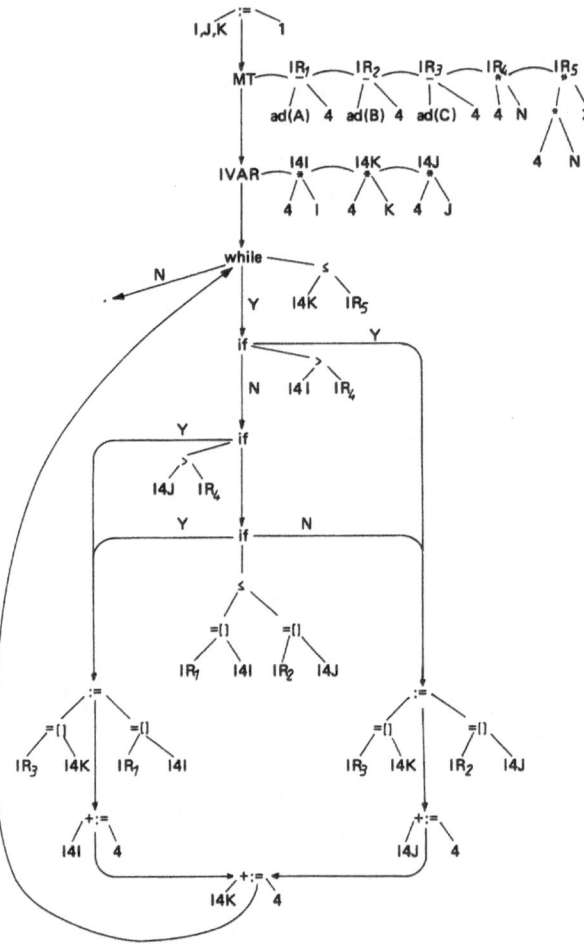

Figs. 8a and b

Fig. 9

occurrences of this subtree. All occurrences are replaced by single nodes having the same label. Thus, e.g. we replace all occurrences of subtrees corresponding to ad(*A*)-4 by a node labelled IR_1 and hang the subtree corresponding to ad(*A*)-4 on a node above of the while-node which is labelled with *MT* for *moved temporary* as outlined in Fig. 9. As this transformation is rather analogous to the elimination of common subexpressions we do not explicate the programmed rewriting step here. Indeed, the transformation needed here is even simpler than that of the last section.

Another very important optimization technique for loops is *induction variable elimination*. A basic induction variable is a variable (either user or compiler defined) occurring only in assignments of the form $L := L + CE$ within loops, where CE is a constant or a constant expression or a loop invariant expression. As loop invariant expressions have already been moved up we have only to look for variables occurring in subtrees of the form of Fig. 8a. In our example, I, J, K are basic induction variables. Nonbasic induction variables are those corresponding to subtrees of form of Fig. 8b with CE_1, CE_2 as above and IV being an already detected induction variable (please note that these subtrees often occur in simplified versions if the linear function is of the form $IV + CE_2$ or $CE_1 * IV$). In our example we have six occurrences of nonbasic induction variables, namely two for each of the expressions $I*4$, $J*4$, $K*4$. These induction variables can again be melted and moved up, if we insert after all basic induction variables corresponding linear progressions $I4I+ := 4$, $I4J+ := 4$ and $I4K+ := 4$, if $I4I$, $I4J$ and $I4K$ are the labels of nodes which are left behind for the subtrees moved. This melting and moving up can again be described using a programmed graph rewriting step analogously to the two cases we have already regarded. As in our case the basic induction variables are only needed within the nonbasic induction variables we can erase the arithmetic progressions of the basic induction variables. We can even replace all occurrences of basic induction variables by other induction variables. The result of these transformations is shown in Fig. 9. Please note that replacing basic by nonbasic induction variables can induce insertion of loop-invariant computations which therefore can again be moved out of the loop as it is the case with the tree with root label IR_5. Comparing Fig. 7 and Fig. 9 it can directly be seen that loop computation is less complicated and loop initialization grew more complicated. However, the latter is only executed once. If we furthermore assume constant folding optimization then the three subtrees with root labels $I4I$, $I4J$, $I4K$ of Fig. 9 could be replaced by the multiple assignment $I4I$, $I4J$, $I4K := 4$ and the multiple assignment I, J, $K := 1$ could be erased.

6. Parallelization of Linear Programs and Expressions

The usual procedure in doing parallelization of linear programs, i.e. of basic blocks, is to determine the data graph[20] from where all independent statements can be seen. Independent statements are those potentially parallelizable. The data graph contains nothing else than direct define-use information. Then, those statements st_1, st_2 can be parallelized which fulfil the following data flow conditions (*),

(*) $\text{In}(st_1) \cap \text{Out}(st_2) = \emptyset$, $\text{Out}(st_1) \cap \text{In}(st_2) = \emptyset$, $\text{Out}(st_1) \cap \text{Out}(st_2) = \emptyset$

where $\text{In}(st_i)$, $\text{Out}(st_i)$ are all the variables which are input of statement st_i or

---

[20] Which should not be interchanged with the flow graph in optimization. A data graph here expresses sequential dependence of a control path through a flow diagram or program scheme. In a linear program any control path is equal to the (static) flow diagram. An edge between st and st' is drawn, whenever st defines a variable used in st'.

which are changed by st_i (cf. e.g. [Ko76]). In the following, we describe this procedure assuming statements within the basic blocks to be simple assignment statements using basic-type variables, i.e. assignments to one basic variable or Read-/Write-statements with length one of parameter list. A variable within a Read-statement is redefined, i.e. treated as if it were the left side of an assignment, whereas an occurrence within a Write-statement is only a use of this variable. So, at all places of definitions or uses of a variable in the following a Read- or Write-statement could be substituted respectively.

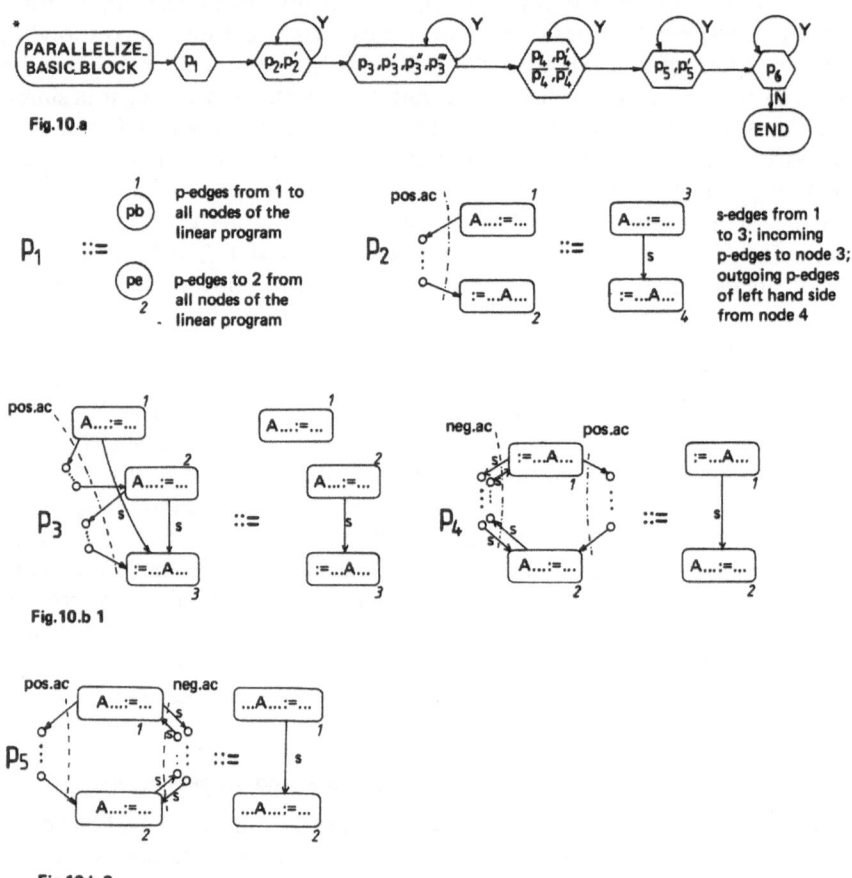

Fig.10.a

P_1

P_2

P_3

Fig.10.b 1

P_5

Fig.10.b 2

Figs. 10a and b

The generation of the data graph and a parallel fork-join-version for a given linear program is the result of a programmed rewriting step PARALLELIZE_BASIC_BLOCK of Fig. 10. The first production p_1 adds a new start node which becomes a fork and a new end node which becomes a join[21]. This is done, as the first and the

---

[21] As to be seen by Fig. 10 we do not regard assignments and expressions as trees as in the above examples, we rather take them as node lables for the reason of simplicity.

last node of the linear program might be executable with other statements in parallel. Between both the parallelized linear program is placed at the end of our transformation procedure. At the beginning we assume all statements to be executable in parallel which is expressed by p-edges (for parallel) generated by production p_1. Note that p_1 has an empty left-hand side, i.e. it only inserts two nodes. The second production inserts direct define-use information between two nodes which ly behind each other (which is expressed by the application condition) and where the second node contains a use of a variable defined by the first. Those statements have to be sequentialized and, therefore, s-edges are inserted. An analogous form has production p_2' which covers the case that the second node is a direct successor of the first one with respect to control flow. Please note that p_2 and p_2' also deal with the case that definition and use corresponds to an arbitrary array element or to a pointer occurrence. All these cases are immediately sequentialized which is a brute force but a safe method[22]. Furthermore, p_2, p_2' erase p-edges ending in node 2 and p-edges originating from node 1 of the left-hand side. Production p_3 erases an s-edge, if there is a later definition in the linear program which is used in the statement corresponding to node 3. As above p_3' covers the case that there is a direct control flow edge between node 1 and 2 and a path between 2 and 3, and analogously p_3'' and p_3''' cover the remaining possibilities of direct connection[23]. At this point of execution of control diagram of Fig. 10a we have exactly generated what is called data graph in parallelization literature if we only regard the s-edges. The following production p_4 tests the first case of the above application condition (∗). Production $\bar{p}_4$ has an analogous form, the definition and use just being interchanged. Independence of both statements is expressed by the negative application condition: There is no s-path in neither direction between the two nodes. The two remaining productions p_4' and $\bar{p}_4'$ cover the cases that node 2 is a direct successor to node 1 with respect to control flow. Please note that application of $\bar{p}_4$, $\bar{p}_4'$ is necessary only because we have deleted s-edges corresponding to a nonactual definition in production p_3, thus making this nonactual definition independent from a following use. However, otherwise we would not have got the data graph after application of productions $p_3, \ldots, p_3'''$. Production p_5 corresponds to the last data flow condition of (∗), p_5' is again the modification due to node 2 being a direct ⟶-successor of node 1. Finally, the last production p_6 erases the original control flow edge thus leaving back p- and s-edges expressing that different statements can be executed in parallel or must be executed sequentially.

The parallelization procedure we have described does in general not yield the maximal parallel version of a basic block. It can be shown that data flow conditions (∗) could be eliminated, i.e. for any linear program with independent operations (which can be taken from the data graph) which do not fulfil conditions (∗), we can

---

[22] So, again ANY$[I]$: = ... and ... : = ... ANY$[J]$... are treated as if ANY$[J]$ were a use of ANY$[I]$ which, of course, is only true for $I = J$. The same rough method is applied for pointers. However, here we assume that our programming language has no data overlapping construct like EQUIVALENCE or COMMON in FORTRAN and that we have no pointers to pointers.

[23] Of course, productions p_3, p_3', p_3'', p_3''' could have been integrated as negative application conditions into productions p_2, p_2'.

give a transformation into an equivalent linear one in which independence of statements implies (∗) (cf. [Ko76]). Then, all sequentialization due to conditions (∗) could be eliminated.

Parallelization could be extended to acyclic sequential programs consisting of sequencing of statements, **if**-statements and **case**-statements and even to cyclic sequential programs which, furthermore, contain different kinds of loops. However, complicated algorithms result and the state of the art is that then only unstructured data can be used. The method described above suggests a rough but practical procedure for arbitrary and therefore also cyclic programs: Restrict parallelization to basic blocks by applying the transformation described above. Clearly, a lot of potential parallelism cannot be detected with this method. We only get local parallelism between statements of basic blocks while the control flow contained in the data flow graph remains unchanged, So, parallelism from interchange of independent statements of different basic blocks, or from interchange of statements belonging to different repetitions of a cycle is not discovered by this method (cf. e.g. [Ku77]).

We furthermore could refine the above method corresponding to array elements and occurrences of pointers: If, for example, we had a redefinition of any array element we have sequentialized all uses and all definitions of any array element occurring later in the original program. The same thing happened in the case of a pointer occurrence. By this proceeding we surely are always on the safe side. In [AU77] the reader can find some algorithms also applicable here, restricting that part of an array in which a redefinition can occur or that part of a data structure an actual pointer might point to. Then, sequentialization must be enforced only for those parts, and all uses and redefinitions not contained in these parts can be left for parallel execution.

The usual procedure in parallelization of expressions, which is sometimes called *microparallelization*, is to generate a tree-like data structure from intermediate code in which subexpressions parallely executable can easily be seen (for a survey of different methods cf. [Ko76]). For example, in Fig. 11 all operations with the same

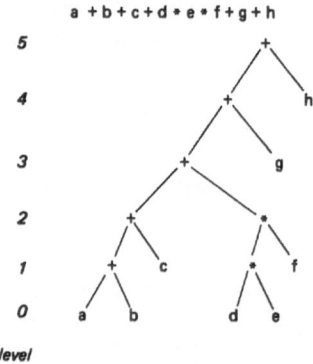

a + b + c + d ∗ e ∗ f + g + h

Fig. 11

level can be parallelized[24]. To generate a tree is not necessary in our case as our intermediate code already has graph form, containing expressions as subtrees[25]. Fig. 11 shows the abstract syntax tree corresponding to the expression $a + b + c + d*i*f + g + h$ which is natural inasmuch as it reflects the execution order from left to right and precedence of operators. Thus, this tree is the result of a parser using a conventional grammar for expressions. However, from the parallelization point of view this tree is in no ways optimal. Making use of the associativity and commutativity of operators one could transform this tree into another one which is broader and less high. This tree then gives more possibilities for parallelization. In other words, we are looking for a balanced version of this tree where the difference in length of all paths ending at leaves is as small as possible. Algorithms doing this work can be adopted from binary search trees and can also be formulated by graph rewriting. However, as operators can occur which are different in precedence or have different numbers of operands, and as function calls can occur within expressions one has to be very careful with these tree transformations.

Putting local parallelization and microparallelization together one can execute subexpressions of those statements in parallel, which themselves can be executed in parallel. This leads to a high degree of parallelism if this degree is reasonable with respect to the number of available processors.

7. Conclusion

In this paper we have shown that the decision for a high level intermediate code of programs is helpful with respect to optimization and parallelization of programs. We have only regarded the automatic modes of optimization and parallelization here, i.e. the tasks a compiler would have to do. Optimization or parallelization on source code level demands a dialog system as in this mode the programmer introduces his knowledge of the actual program. This is not the only reason for a dialog system. There are a lot of further tasks arising in program development which can also be carried out efficiently on a high level intermediate code in an interactive way: Incremental compilation, error detection and program monitoring, verification, handling of large application systems implemented as module plexes etc. Integrating all these tasks results in a dialog system for the development of reliable software as outlined in [Na80].

Thus, the problems sketched in this paper are only a small part of a wide spectrum of problems of that level. The advantage of the approach taken in this paper is not only to save effort in implementation but is also a unification and elucidation of these problems resulting from the program graph as common data structure and abstraction level.

---

[24] Trivially, multiple assignments can be carried out in parallel too.
[25] Thus, with the high-level intermediate code the problem could be regarded as being solved without having done anything. The rest is the scheduling problem, i.e. to determine that degree of parallelization at any point of execution due to available hardware and to generate code for the multiprocessor configuration. This problem, however, is not regarded in this paper.

References

[AU77]   Aho, A. V., Ullman, J. D.: Principles of compiler design. Reading, Mass.: Addison-Wesley 1977.

[Ba79]   Bauer, F. L., et al.: Program development by transformation, Section III of program construction (Bauer, F. L., ed.). Lect. Notes Comp. Sci. **69**, 235 – 492 (1979).

[BNW78]   Brendel, W., Nagl, M., Weber, D.: Implementation of sequential and parallel graph rewriting systems. Applied Computer Science **8**, 79 – 106 (1978).

[CER79]   Claus, V., Ehrig, H., Rosen, B. K. (eds.): Graph grammars and their application to computer science and biology. (Lect. Notes in Comp. Sci., Vol. 79.) Berlin-Heidelberg-New York: Springer 1979.

[FKZ79]   Farrow, R., Kennedy, K., Zucconi, L.: Graph grammars and global program data flow analysis. Techn. Rep., Dpt. Math. Sci., Rice University, Texas.

[HHS76]   Händler, W., Hofmann, F., Schneider, H. J.: A general purpose array with a broad spectrum of applications. (Informatik-Fachberichte, Vol. 4), pp. 311 – 335. Berlin-Heidelberg-New York: Springer 1976.

[Kn74]   Knuth, D.: Structured programming with goto statements. Computing Surveys **8**, 261 – 301 (1974).

[Ko76]   Kotov, V. E.: Theory of parallel programming I, Survey of practical aspects. In: Advances in Information Systems Sciences (Ton, J. T., ed.), Vol. 6, pp. 1 – 55. New York: Plenum Press 1976.

[Ku77]   Kuck, D. J.: A survey of parallel machine organization and programming. Computing Surveys **9**, 29 – 59 (1977).

[Lo76]   Loveman, D. E.: Program improvement by source to source transformation. Proc. 3rd ACM POPL Symp. 140 – 152 (1976).

[Na79]   Nagl, M.: Graph-Grammatiken: Theorie, Anwendungen, Implementierung. Wiesbaden: Vieweg 1979.

[Na80]   Nagl, M.: An incremental compiler as component of a system for software generation. Proc. 6th GI Conference on Programming Languages and Program Development. (Informatik-Fachberichte, Vol. 25), pp. 29 – 44. Berlin-Heidelberg-New York: Springer 1980.

[Na80]   Nagl, M.: GRAPL – A programming language for handling dynamic problems on graphs. In: Discrete Structures and Algorithms (Pape, U., ed.), pp. 25 – 45. München: Carl Hanser Verlag 1980.

[Nr76]   Naring'yani, A. S.: Theory of parallel programming II, Survey of formal models, as [Ko76] pp. 57 – 113.

[Ro77]   Rosen, B. K.: High level data flow analysis. Comm. ACM **20**, 712 – 724 (1977).

[Ro79]   Rosen, B. K.: Data flow analysis for procedural languages. Journ. ACM **26**, 322 – 344 (1979).

[Sn75]   Schneider, H. J.: Syntax-directed description of incremental compilers. (Lect. Notes Comp. Sci., Vol. 26), pp. 192 – 201. Berlin-Heidelberg-New York: Springer 1975.

[Ul73]   Ullman, J. D.: Fast algorithms for the elimination of common subexpressions. Acta Informatica **2**, 191 – 213 (1973).

[Wi79]   Wilhelm, R.: Computation and use of data flow information in optimizing compilers. Acta Informatica **12**, 209 – 225 (1979).

[Wu75]   Wulf, W., et al.: The Design of an Optimizing Compiler. New York: American Elsevier 1975.

[ZB74]   Zelkowitz, M. V., Bail, W. G.: Optimization of structured programs. Software Pract. & Exp. **4**, 51 – 57 (1974).

Prof. Dr. M. Nagl
Seminar für Informatik
EWH Koblenz
Rheinau 3 – 4
D-5400 Koblenz
Federal Republic of Germany

Computing, Suppl. 3, 125—139 (1981)

CAD und Kollaterale

G. Nees, Erlangen

Zusammenfassung — Abstract

CAD und Kollaterale. Zusammenhänge zwischen Computer Aided Design und Paralleloperationen im Sinn von Bündeln kollateral ablaufender Prozesse werden untersucht. CAD-methodologische Ansätze, die Verknüpfungsmöglichkeiten mit dem Parallelrechnen erkennen lassen, werden danach unterschieden, ob sie Simulation verwenden oder nicht. Behandelt werden die Designtheorien von Goldstein und Miller sowie von Radhakrishna Murty, Radju, Bashmakov. Das bekannte Dreiblockbeispiel wird im Rahmen der Goldstein-Millerschen sowie der Raulefschen Theorie betrachtet. Die Simulatoren von Rieger und Grinberg, ferner von Hendrix werden mit dem Kausalbegriff in Verbindung gebracht. Kollateralität tritt auch im Zusammenhang mit Bearbeitungsautomaten auf. Ein interaktiver Ansatz des Verfassers steht am Schluß der Arbeit.

CAD and Collaterals. Relations between Computer Aided Design and parallel operations in the sense of bundles of collaterally running (concurrent) processes are investigated. CAD-methodological approaches can be classified by the use they make of simulation. The design theories both of Goldstein and Miller and of Radhakrishna Murty, Raju, Bashmakov are considered. It is discussed how the theories of Goldstein and Miller as well as of Raulefs are handling the well-known three blocks example. The role of the concept of causality in the simulators of Hendrix and that of Rieger and Grinberg is hinted at. Collaterality is important in connection with object manipulation automata. At the end of the paper the author's interactive approach to collaterality in CAD is presented.

1. Einleitung

Zwei Problemkreise unbezweifelbarer Wichtigkeit sollen in diesem Aufsatz miteinander in Verbindung gebracht werden: Computer Aided Design auf der einen Seite, auf der anderen Paralleloperieren, das heißt die geplante und/oder programmierte Steuerung von synchronisierten Bündeln kollateral ablaufender Prozesse.

CAD ist ein vager Begriff, der CAD-Bereich ein mittlerer Raum, der „oben" (in Richtung größerer Abstraktheit) mit den Informatikanwendungen in der Forschung verschmilzt, „unten" (in Richtung größerer Konkretheit) mit CAM, das heißt Computer Aided Manufacturing (zum Grundsätzlichen siehe Klapp (1977), zur Bedeutsamkeit der Integration der drei Gebiete siehe Wilhelms (1971)). In Nees (1978) wurde eine Klassifikation von CAD-Problemen auf die Weise versucht, daß jedem Problem ein CAD-System (eine Hard/Firm/Software-Implementierung) zugeordnet wurde, das sich dann als Einzelprogramm oder Insel- oder Terminalsystem darstellt. CAD-Anwendungen wurden danach unterschieden, ob sie der Entwicklung technischer Gegebenheiten oder der Abwicklung technischer Abläufe dienen (zum letzteren Fall siehe z. B. Howein (1975)). Schließlich wurde der Begriff „CAD für CAD" eingeführt, um die Weiterentwicklung der CAD-Methodologie abzuschätzen.

Obgleich es möglich wäre, auch hier diesem Faden zu folgen, soll der Herausforderung durch Vagheit begegnet und zunächst eine Taxonomie der rechnergestützten Aktivitäten (angelehnt an Nees (1980)) versucht werden, die gleich als Backus-Normalform angeschrieben wird:

/1.1 Rechnergestützte^Aktivität =
   .2 CAD^eines CA-Designobjekt(s)/CA-Manufacturing
/2   CA-Designobjekt = Prozeß/Ding/Fluß/Text/Bild
/3   Prozeß = (Dialog^bei/Vorgang^bei) Verfahren
/4.1 Verfahren =
   .2 Analyse/Synthese/Steuerung/Überwachung/Abwicklung
/5   Ding = Bauteil/Gerät/Anlage/CAD-System
/6   Fluß = Transport^von Substanz
/7   Substanz = Energie/Information/stoffliches^Gut
/8   Text = Tabelle/Ausdruck
/9   Bild = Diagramm/stetiges^Bild.

Dieser Begriffsbaum ist zweifellos nicht ganz konsistent in sich, inkonsistent mit anderen Fachsprachen, lückenhaft, nicht verzweigt genug, andererseits stellenweise sehr redundant. (Unter /8 versteckt sich Software-Engineering.) Er muß im Augenblick genügen! Unter einem CA-Designobjekt wird nach /1.2 eindeutig das faßliche Ziel eines CA-Designs oder CAD-Vorgangs verstanden (gewisse Fachsprachen gleiten zwischen „Design" als „Gestalten" und „Gestalt" hin und her). Bemerkenswert ist aber, daß eine der Allgemeinheit von /2...9 entsprechende Theorie wenigstens skizziert worden ist, die man als CA-Designtheorie deuten kann. Gemeint ist die „Linguistic theory of design" von Goldstein und Miller (Miller et al., 1976a, b, c, 1977), sie wird in Abschnitt 2 genauer betrachtet. Diese Theorie ist deshalb besonders interessant, weil sie in Analogie zum strukturierten Programmieren eine bemerkenswerte Strukturierung des Designprozesses vorschlägt.

Auch der Begriff der Kollateralität leidet unter Allgemeinheit. Zunächst kann man nicht umhin, Kollateralität sowohl im Designprozeß als auch im Designobjekt zu berücksichtigen, zumal sich letztere oft im Designprozeß spiegelt. Kollateralität im Objekt gibt es selbstverständlich nicht nur dann, wenn dieses Rechner enthält (zu einem wichtigen Fall solcher Art siehe Ernst (1978). Zwei ineinandergreifend rotierende Zahnräder bilden Kollateralen. In bezug auf alle Instanzen von Kollateralität leuchtet jedoch ein, daß CAD effektives Parallelrechnen dringend erfordert. Wurde Computer Aided Design doch am Anfang der sechziger Jahre in der Hoffnung konzipiert, die Kreativität des Designers durch zügigen Mensch-Rechner-Dialog anzuregen und in Gang zu halten (Sutherland, 1963). Dies ist mangels Rechenleistung bei vielen CAD-Vorgängen, z. B. der Realzeitsimulation bestimmter Klassen technischer Anordnungen, bis heute Wunschtraum geblieben.

Einige wenige, jedoch sehr allgemeine CAD-methodologisch relevante Ansätze, die Verknüpfungsmöglichkeiten mit der Technologie des Parallelrechnens versprechen, werden in den folgenden Abschnitten behandelt. Die Ansätze unterscheiden sich auch darin, ob sie auf Simulation des Designobjekts zielen oder nicht. Ist M parameterabhängiges Modell eines Objekts S, so kann man S bekanntlich mindestens prinzipiell mit Hilfe der Anweisung

/10.1 while $M(p_1, \ldots, p_n)$ not optimized do
   .2 begin simulate S; change $p_1, \ldots, p_n$ accordingly end

entwerfen. Der Hendrix-Simulator (Abschnitt 3) ist im Hinblick auf Kollateralität in S geschrieben, ebenso der von Rieger und Grinberg (Abschnitt 4). Ein in der CAD/CAM-Überschneidung angesiedeltes Problem, das dem gleichen Schema folgt, ist der Entwurf der Steuerungen von Robotern mit mechanischen Effektoren. Hier helfen Roboterprogrammiersprachen mit speziellen cobegin...coend-Konstrukten (Abschnitt 5). Alle Entwurfsprozesse dieser Art bieten naturgemäß Ansatzflächen zum Parallelisieren innerhalb des Schemas /10 selbst.

Das Roboterbeispiel führt auf einen Kreis von Problemen, der ebenfalls die Interaktion zwischen Designvorgang und Designobjekt betrifft. Es handelt sich um die Frage, wie das Objekt zusammengesetzt wird, ob es – durch besondere Gestaltung seiner Teile, oder gar Selbstorganisation – seine Montage unterstützt. Man betrachte dazu Abb. 1. Der „Wunschbrunnen" (Miller et al., a.a.O.) kann auf dreifache Weise zusammengesetzt werden. Erstens kann Abb. 1 eine Zeichnung oder ein ebenes Drahtmodell darstellen. Dann ist der Wunschbrunnen z. B. aus acht Strecken kombinierbar. Man kann das Objekt aber auch in drei – ebene oder räumliche – Blöcke zerlegen, die man aufeinandersetzt. Die eleganteste Methode bestünde darin, die Blöcke A, B, C sich in richtiger Weise selbst aufeinander setzen

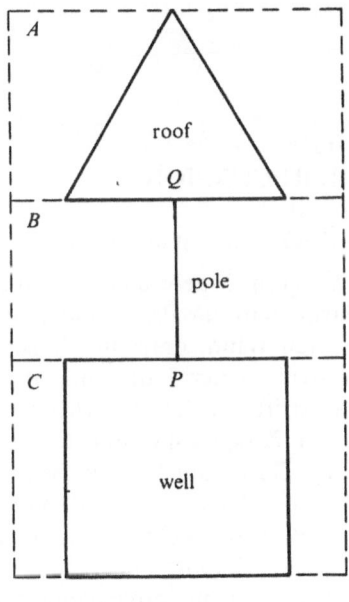

Der Wunschbrunnen

Goldstein/Miller-Modell:

$M_1 \leftrightarrow$ triangle(roof) $\wedge$
horizontal(bottom(side(roof)))

$M_{1,2} \leftrightarrow$
above(roof,pole) $\wedge$
connected(pole,roof,at(Q)) $\wedge$
$Q = $ middle(bottom(side(roof))) $\wedge$
$Q = $ upper(endpoint(pole))

$M_2 \leftrightarrow$ line(pole)

$M_{2,3} \leftrightarrow$
above(pole,well) $\wedge$
connected(well,pole,at(P)) $\wedge$
$P = $ middle(upper(side(well))) $\wedge$
$P = $ lower(endpoint(pole))

$M_3 \leftrightarrow$ square(well) $\wedge$
horizontal(upper(side(well)))

Blockwelt-Modell:

on(A, B) $\wedge$ on(B, C)

Abb. 1

zu lassen. Das ist der Weg, den Raulefs in einem Beispiel zu seiner äußerst weitreichenden Theorie und Praxis des Rechnens, dem Agentenparadigma, verfolgt (Böhm, 1977). Abschnitt 6 ist dem Agentenmodell gewidmet.

Während das Modell von Raulefs über CAD hinausgeht, schlägt Radhakrishna Murty et al. (1978) eine sehr ausführliche, auf CAD abgestimmte deklarative Objektbehandlung vor, in die andere Rechenmodelle, z. B. Agenten, eingehängt werden können (Abschnitt 7). Abschnitt 8 schließlich erwähnt einen Ansatz des Verfassers, der die dialogische Mithilfe des Entwerfers bei der Parallelorganisation von Designprozessen voraussetzt.

2. Die linguistische Designtheorie von Goldstein und Miller

Die Autoren benutzen die Abkürzung SPADE für ihre Problemlösungstheorie und -Praxis. Die Designobjekte sollen zunächst Programme sein, doch zeigt die Lektüre der Goldstein/Millerschen Arbeiten, daß die vorgeschlagene Problemstrukturierung auf Objekte allgemeinerer Art anwendbar ist, insbesondere dann, wenn man die Teile-Konjunktion „PARALLEL" in der von Miller et al. (1977) angegebenen „Problemlösungsgrammatik" nutzt:

/1   PLAN = IDENTIFY/DECOMPOSE/REFORMULATE
/2   IDENTIFY = PRIMITIVE/DEFINED
/3   DEFINED = „call user subprocedure" & PLAN
/4   DECOMPOSE = CONJUNCTION/REPETITION
/5   CONJUNCTION = SEQUENTIAL/PARALLEL
/6.1 SEQUENTIAL = (SETUP/EMPTY)
  .2 + (MAINSTEP + (INTERFACE/EMPTY))* + (CLEANUP/EMPTY)
/7   PARALLEL = (PLAN)*
/8   SETUP = PLAN
/9   MAINSTEP = PLAN
/10 INTERFACE = PLAN
/11 CLEANUP = PLAN
/12 REPETITION = ROUND/RECURSION
/13 ROUND = ITERATION-PLAN/TAIL-RECURSION
/14 ITERATION-PLAN = „repeat step" + SEQ
/15 TAIL-RECURSION = „stop step" + SEQ + „recursion step".

Hier ist „/" als „oder", „ + " als geordnete, „&" als nichtgeordnete Konjunktion zu lesen. Die linguistische Parallele besteht darin, daß ein Problemlösungs-PLAN einen gemäß der Grammatik /1 . . . 15 gebauten Baum darstellt, dessen Blätter Baukastenteile, also z. B. im Fall eines zu konstruierenden Programms Prozeduren aus einer Bibliothek, sind (siehe /3). Dies trifft im CAD/CAM-Bereich auf Programme für Fertigungsmaschinen (z. B. für Zerspanung) und Montageautomaten (Roboter, siehe Abschnitt 5) zu. Ist das Designobjekt kein Programm, so müssen vor allem die Zeilen /12 . . . 15 anders gestaltet werden. Ansatzpunkt für die Schaffung von Kollateralen im Designprozeß bietet Zeile /7, dann aber die Eigenschaft, daß bei der Aufstellung des Lösungsbaums der „/"-Operator im Backtracking-Verfahren abgearbeitet wird. Hier müssen Implementierungen für Multiprocessing-Umgebungen versuchen, kollaterale Prozesse (z. B. Agenten, siehe Abschnitt 6) zu erzeugen.

Es folgen einige Erläuterungen zu den Begriffen in /1 ... 15, soweit sie nicht als selbsterklärend angenommen werden können: IDENTIFY erkennt einen Plan als in der Bibliothek schon vorhanden. Versagt DECOMPOSE, so muß REFORMU-LATE auf den Ansatz angewandt werden. Im Programmfall entspricht „;" (in Pascal-Schreibweise) dem CONJUNCTION-Operator. REPETITION wird gewählt, wenn logisch konjunktive Forderungen im Modellansatz durch (finite) Allquantifikation gegeben sind. SETUP in /6.1 ist ein Anfangsschritt, dagegen bedeutet CLEANUP Aufräumungsoperationen (z. B. Dateischließungen, „undoings", das heißt Rückgängigmachungen). INTERFACE bezeichnet Verknüpfungen von Teilen des Designobjekts, z. B. den Verbindungspunkt zwischen roof und pole beim Wunschbrunnen in Abb. 1. SEQ schließlich ist ein Sequentialisierungsoperator im Zusammenhang mit dem Problem der Elimination von Verknüpfungen („non-linearities") zwischen Designobjektteilen.

Als Zerteiler für die Problemlösungsgrammatik wird ein ATN (Augmented Transition Network; Woods, 1970) verwendet. ATNs sind Zustandsübergangsgraphen, bei denen jede Kante (eventuell rekursiver) Aufruf eines weiteren ATN sein kann. Eingabedatum für das ATN ist ein Modellansatz, z. B. in Prädikatenschreibweise, wie dies in Abb. 1 für den Wunschbrunnen ausgeführt ist. Das ATN benutzt Speicherregister, vor allem:

/16 M: Modell (Problemspezifikation)
/17 S: (in Arbeit befindliche) Lösung
/18.1 CAVEATS: Liste von Warnungen im Hinblick auf den
   .2   weiteren Problemlösungsprozeß
/19   ADVICE: Liste von Empfehlungen
/20   GOALS: Menge von Teilzielen, deren Lösung ansteht
/21 G: Momentan angestrebtes Teilziel.

Das ATN ist in die komfortable SPADE-Software eingebettet, die den Gang (die Pfadfindung) durch die Grammatik im Dialog mit dem menschlichen Problemlöser steuert. Dabei spielen weitere Hilfsoperationen eine Rolle, z. B. ein Hilfs-ATN für das „rationale" Debugging, das heißt die Elimination von Fehlern, die sich in einem früheren Abschnitt des Entwurfsprozesses durch mangelnde Problemkenntnis eingeschlichen haben.

3. Der Hendrix-Simulator

Hendrix geht von der Beobachtung aus, daß alle Prozeß-Simulatoren, die einen konstanten diskreten Zeitschritt voraussetzen, gerade die Ereignisse verfehlen oder mindestens verfälschen können, die zwischen Simulationszeitpunkten beginnen oder enden. Deshalb bestimmen beim Hendrix-Simulator die verschiedenen, durch eine Simulation zusammengefaßten Vorgänge selbst den Fortschritt der Modellzeit. Auf diese Weise können stetige Abläufe und diskrete Ereignisse mit der gleichen Simulationstechnik behandelt werden. Das LISP-Quellprogramm des Hendrix-Simulators ist veröffentlicht (Lowrance et al., 1975; siehe auch Hendrix, 1973). Also könnte der Hendrix-Simulator in neue LISP-Design-Programme des allgemeinen Schemas 1/10 eingepaßt werden.

Der Hendrix-Simulation liegt ein Weltmodell zugrunde, das die Werte aller Simulationsparameter enthält, die boolesche oder physikalische Größen darstellen. Jeder an der Simulation beteiligte Teilvorgang (Prozeß) wird durch eine als Scenario bezeichnete Prozedur beschrieben, die jedenfalls die Initiationsbedingungen des Prozesses, Aktivierungsinstruktionen, sowie zu eliminierende oder neu zu schaffende Initialeffekte beschreibt. Zum Scenario gehören ferner ein Zeitintervall, beginnend mit der Initiations-, endend mit der Unterbrechungszeit. Z. B. enthält das Scenario für die Erzeugung der Stellung UP eines Schalters S durch einen Roboter R unter anderem die folgenden Bestandteile:

/1.1 Initiationsbedingungen:
.2 R is of type ROBOT and S is of type SWITCH
.3 and position of switch S is DOWN
.4 and R has been instructed to SWITCHUP S
/2.1 Zu eliminierende Initialeffekte:
.2 position of switch S is DOWN
.3 and R has been instructed to SWITCHUP S
/3.1 Neu zu schaffender Initialeffekt:
.2 position of switch S is UP.

Außerdem kann das Scenario Fortsetzungsbedingungen, insbesondere jedoch zeitabhängige Gleichungen, einschließen, die graduell verlaufende Vorgänge beschreiben.

Der Hendrix-Simulator bedient sich einer Liste von Steuerblöcken, wobei ein neuer Steuerblock immer dann erzeugt wird, wenn die Initiationsbedingungen eines Scenarios erfüllt sind. In den Steuerblock wird die Unterbrechungszeit des Scenarios aufgenommen. Da jeder Steuerblock genau einen Prozeß bestimmt, kann die äußerste Simulationsschleife folgendermaßen formuliert werden, wobei tm die Modellzeit ist:

```
/4.1    while Liste der Steuerblöcke nicht leer do
  .2    begin Finde den Steuerblock mit der
  .3          frühesten Unterbrechungszeit tu ⩾ tm;
  .4          if Es gibt einen Prozeß, für dessen
  .5              Initiationszeit ti gilt tm ⩽ ti < tu
  .6          then begin Finde einen solchen Prozeß, dessen
  .7                  ti am kleinsten ist;
  .9                  tm := ti; initiiere den Prozeß
  .9              end
/4.10   else begin tm := tu;
  .11          unterbreche den laufenden Prozeß
  .12          end
  .13 end.
```

Dieses einfache Simulationsschema garantiert die lückenlose Überdeckung der Modellzeit.

Ein Rezensent hat bemerkt, daß der Hendrix-Simulator nicht nur als Werkzeug benutzt, sondern zur Diskussion operationaler Modelle des Kausalbegriffs herangezogen werden kann (Gaines, 1975). Hier kann die Simulationsphilosophie nach Hendrix dazu beitragen, den Begriff der Kollateralität in CAD-Systemen zu klären.

4. Der Simulator von Rieger und Grinberg

Dieser Simulator, der ebenfalls in LISP geschrieben ist, hat einen deutlich linguistischen (oder „semantischen") Touch, wenn auch in anderer Weise, als die in Abschnitt 2 betrachtete Designtheorie (Rieger et al., 1977, S. 4). Rieger und Grinberg nehmen unmittelbar auf das CAD-Problem Bezug, wenn sie von ihrer Theorie sagen, daß sie als Basis interaktiver Designsysteme dienen könne, ja sie wagen die Vermutung, vollständig automatische „mechanisms invention" sei im Bereich der Möglichkeiten. Die Verfasser knüpfen im gleichen Zusammenhang einen Faden zum Definitionsproblem des Kausalbegriffs, wenn sie ihren Ansatz zu einer Dezimalklassifikation von Ursache-Wirkungs-Zusammenhängen heranziehen wollen (a.a.O., S. 2). Der erwähnte Ansatz beruht nun auf genau zehn verschiedenen Typen des Kausalnexus sowie vier Kategorien von Ereignissen. Ein zu simulierender Mechanismus ist dann als Graph darstellbar, dessen Knoten Ereignisse und dessen Kanten Kausalzusammenhänge sind (Kausalgraph). Ereignisse sind Aktionen oder Tendenzen oder Zustände oder Zustandswechsel, während die zehn Kausalzusammenhangsarten folgendermaßen gekennzeichnet werden können, wenn SG1, SG2,... simultane globale kausale Rahmenbedingungen, S, S1,... Zustände, SC, SC1,... Zustandswechsel bezeichnen, schließlich A eine Aktion, T eine Tendenz ist (die Verfasser benutzen graphische Symbole an Stelle von Ausdrücken).

/1.1 if SG1 and SG2 and ... and SGn then A/T (A bzw. T)
  .2 causes S/SC to sustain continuous-causally
/2.1 if SG1 and SG2 and ... and SGn then A/T
  .2 causes S/SC to sustain one-shot-causally.

Hier muß A (bzw. T) bei der stetigen Kausierung (continuous causal effect) während des ganzen Vorgangs einwirken, bei der Einzelwirkung (one-shot causal effect) nur momentan, um die Erhaltung des Zustands S bzw. die Änderung SC zu sichern.

/3 S causes A/T by continuous enablement
/4 S causes A/T by one-shot enablement.

In diesen Fällen muß ein Zustand stetig oder momentan eintreten, um eine Aktion bzw. Tendenz zu ermöglichen.

/5.1 if SG1 and SG2 and ... and SGn then S1/SC1 indirectly
  .2 produces S2/SC2 by continuous state coupling
/6.1 if SG1 and SG2 and ... and SGn then S1/SC1 indirectly
  .2 produces S2/SC2 by one-shot state coupling.

Bei /5 ist die fortgesetzte Existenz von S2 (bzw. SC2) an die von S1 (bzw. SC1) gebunden, während bei /6, nach einer anfänglichen Ankopplung, S2 (bzw. SC2) von S1 (bzw. SC1) unabhängig wird.

9*

/7.1 if SG1 and SG2 and ... and SGn then S1/SC1
  .2 is only paraphrases-syntactically different
  .3 from S2/SC2.

Dieser Zusammenhang dient beim Zusammenbau von Mechanismen zur Kopplung von „semantisch äquivalenten" Zuständen oder Zustandswechseln. Als
Beispiel nennen Rieger und Grinberg den als „Photonen existent" deklarierten
Ausgangswert eines Bausteins, der äquivalent ist mit dem Eingangswert „Licht
präsent" eines zweiten Bausteins.

/8.1 if SG1 and SG2 and ... and SGn then
  .2 S1/SC1 and S2/SC2 are mutually exclusive
/9.1 SC1 and SC2 and ... and SCn represent the
  .2 culminations of multiple causal sources for
  .3 a net state change SC
/10 SC reaches a threshold S.

Die Verfasser erwähnen weitere Kausalbindungen, die Motivation und Inten-
tionalität menschlicher Aktoren modellieren sollen, führen dies a.a.O. jedoch nicht
aus. Sie empfehlen Kausalgraphen übrigens auch als deklarative Programmiersprache. Dies wäre eine Sprache für parallele Vorgänge. Ausdrücklich wird in dem
Aufsatz auf Prozesse Bezug genommen, die von „parallel laufenden" physikalischen Gesetzen regiert werden (a.a.O., S. 12, 23).

Die Simulationsstrategie sieht zwei Schritte vor: Der Kausalgraph wird in eine
Population autonomer Recheneinheiten (derzeit jeweils innerhalb eines LISP-
Rahmens realisiert) umgesetzt. Jede der Einheiten rechnet „spontan", wenn sie im
Sinn des Modells kausal dazu angestoßen wird. Dieser Simulationsphilosophie
gegenüber erscheint die Simulation nach Hendrix (siehe Abschnitt 3) zwar als
begrifflich allgemeiner, jedoch dynamisch starrer. Auf jeden Fall dürfte der Rieger-
Grinberg-Ansatz leichter auf Hardwarekonfigurationen umstellbar sein, die ent-
sprechende Populationen aktivierbarer Prozessoren einschließen.

5. Bearbeitungsautomaten

Unter einem Bearbeitungsautomat soll in starker Verallgemeinerung eine Maschine verstanden werden, bei der eine Anzahl von Meßgliedern und Werkzeugen an
einem oder mehreren Werkstücken angreifen. Dabei können die Werkstücke (z. B.
durch Verformung oder Spanabhebung) verändert, oder in einem Montageprozeß
auch zusammengesetzt werden. Das Problem des Reparatur- und Montageautomaten und seiner Programmierung ist besonders intensiv in Stanford, Ca., studiert
worden. Zu erwähnen ist der ältere, sehr umfangreiche Bericht von Nilsson (1975).
Mit der symbolischen Programmierung von Manipulatoren befaßt sich Grossman
et al. (1978).

Entwurf und Programmierung von Objektmanipulatoren stellen ein schwieriges
CAD-Problem dar, bei dem kollaterale Vorgänge behandelt werden müssen, wenn
mehrere Objektmanipulatoren im (Rahmen des) Bearbeitungsautomaten
zusammenarbeiten. Hat man bei Kollateralität in einem Computer allein zeitliche
Abläufe zu synchronisieren, so handelt es sich jetzt zusätzlich um räumliche

Koordination, um die Vermeidung von Lage- und Bewegungskonflikten. Dabei ist zu bedenken, daß der einzelne Manipulator nicht nur bis zu sechs Freiheitsgrade besitzt, sondern mit (mindestens) einem diskret oder stetig krümmbaren Finger ausgestattet sein kann. Schon bei zwei koordinierten Manipulatoren („Händen") stellt sich die interessante Frage, ob man deren Steuerung auf zwei kooperierende Prozessoren verteilt oder nicht. Beim Entwurfsproblem stößt man aus diesem Grund auf den schon in der Einleitung erwähnten Sachverhalt, daß Kollateralität im Designobjekt auf Kollateralität im Designprozeß abgebildet werden muß, denn in diesem tauchen die zwei „Hände" wieder als Design-Unterobjekte auf, verteilt z. B. auf verschiedene Prozesse während der Simulation mit einem der in den vorhergehenden Abschnitten erläuterten Verfahren.

In Grossman et al. (1978) wird über die Sprache AL zur Manipulatorsteuerung berichtet. Al sieht für die Synchronisation von Ereignissen in cobegin... coend-Blöcken zwei Anweisungen

/1 SIGNAL event⌃variable, WAIT event⌃variable

vor. Es ist jedoch auch möglich, Zeitbedingungen mit Hilfe markierter Anweisungen einzuhalten, z. B. durch

/2 PREREQUISITE OF label⌃1 IS label⌃2.

Unterschieden wird außerdem zwischen schwacher und starker Synchronisation der Führung von Manipulatoren. Im allgemeinen Bewegungskommando

/3.1 MOVE object⌃frame TO goal⌃frame, via⌃clauses,
  .2 on⌃condition⌃clauses, with⌃requirement⌃clauses

kann nämlich im Fall von zwei Manipulatoren jeder Parameter durch ein Parameterpaar ersetzt werden:

/4 MOVE (object⌃frame⌃1:object⌃frame⌃2) TO...

wodurch eine schwach synchronisierte Doppeltrajektorie für die beiden Manipulatoren entsteht. In /4 bedeuten frames Koordinatensysteme, während via⌃clauses den Verlauf der Trajektorien festlegen, on⌃condition⌃clauses Bedingungen setzen, unter denen die Bewegungen zustandekommen, schließlich with⌃requirement⌃ clauses z. B. Bewegungsgeschwindigkeiten einstellen. Starke Synchronisation ist notwendig, wenn eine Trajektorie starr an die andere gebunden werden muß (man denke an das Versetzen eines schweren Topfes mit den zwei Händen). In diesem Fall muß eine durch die Anweisung

/5 COORDINATING frame⌃equation

einführbare numerische Gleichung für die starre Kooperation sorgen.

6. Die Sprache CSSA und das Problem der Selbstorganisation

Das von P. Raulefs und seinen Mitarbeitern entwickelte Agentenparadigma ist wahrscheinlich geeignet, einen allgemeinen algorithmischen Rahmen für Prozesse mit kollateralen Teilprozessen auch im CAD-Bereich zu liefern. Modelle des Agentenparadigmas genügen folgenden Bedingungen (Fischer et al., 1980, wo weitere Literatur angegeben ist; siehe dort auch Einzelheiten, da wir vereinfachen müssen): Alle Berechnungen werden von Agenten durchgeführt, die in sich sequentielle, jedoch kollateral (concurrent) arbeitende Aktionen sind. Dabei gibt es keinen globalen Speicher, vielmehr rechnet jeder Agent mit lokalen Daten, sendet jedoch anderen Agenten Nachrichten (messages) zu. Systeme von Agenten („Agentengesellschaften") bilden insofern dynamische Netzwerke, als sowohl die Agenten (die Knoten des Netzes) kreiert und wieder vernichtet, als auch die Verbindungen zwischen ihnen aufgenommen und wieder abgebrochen werden können. Eine der wichtigsten Eigenschaften von CSSA, der Sprache für die Programmierung von Agentengesellschaften, ist jedoch die Steuerungsabstraktion (control abstraction), die sich zu Daten- und Funktionalabstraktion als „dritter Sprachfreiheitsgrad" gesellt. Steuerungsabstraktion erlaubt die Modellierung von Modi des simultanen und des Mehrprozessorrechnens und vermeidet deren starre Vorwegnahme in Sprachen.

Jeder Agent besteht aus einer oder mehreren Clusters von Operationsfähigkeiten (operation-capabilities), die durch Nachrichten an den Agenten aktiviert werden können. Diese Clusters werden als die Facetten (facets) des Agenten bezeichnet. Dabei ist zu jedem Zeitpunkt das Verhalten des Agenten durch genau eine seiner Facetten bestimmt. Eine Nachricht „steckt" immer in einem Kouvert (envelope), das vom Rezipient-Agenten in einem pattern-matching-Prozeß dekodiert wird. Sobald der Rezipient die Nachricht angenommen hat, kreiert er eine Instanz der angesprochenen Operationsfähigkeiten. Jeder Agent ist von einem bestimmten Typ, der durch das Script des Agenten festgelegt wird. Soll ein Agent A mit einem Agenten B kommunizieren, so muß der Expedient-Agent A mit dem Rezipienten B bekannt sein (to be acquainted with). Diese Bekanntschaft sichern dem Expedienten Zugriffsrechte zu gewissen Operationsfähigkeiten des Rezipienten. Die Ausführung einer Instanz einer Operationsfähigkeit ist eine unteilbare (indivisible) Operation, aus der die simultane Aussendung einer beliebigen Anzahl von Nachrichten an weitere Agenten resultieren kann, mit denen der operierende Expedient bekannt ist.

In der Arbeit von Böhm et al. (1978) wird das Agentenparadigma auf das Dreiblockproblem (siehe Abb. 1) angewandt, wobei nur vorausgesetzt wird, daß ein Block (durch die ON-Relation ausgedrückt) weiß, worauf er sitzt und welcher Block auf ihm sitzt. Die Zusammenfügung der Blöcke wird dadurch bewerkstelligt, daß ein Block auf einen anderen klettern kann. Das Programm ist zwar in sequentiellem CSSA geschrieben, doch geht dadurch von der Allgemeingültigkeit des Agentenmodells nichts verloren. Der Ansatz betrachtet den Boden unter dem Wunschbrunnen (Abb. 1) als vierten Block SKIP. Alle Blöcke gehorchen dem gleichen Script BLOCK, das eine Steuerfacette CONDITIONING umschließt, die einen Steuerblock TELL für die Nachrichtengabe von Block zu Block enthält. Durch beispielsweise folgende Benachrichtigungen

/1.1 TELL((ON:)(ON ME:SKIP)) ⇔ B;
  .2 TELL((ON:SKIP)(ON ME:C)) ⇔ A;
  .3 TELL((ON:A)(ON ME:SKIP)) ⇔ C

wird die Gesellschaft der drei Agenten A, B, C zunächst in beliebiger Weise organisiert. Ziel ist jedoch die in Abb. 1 gezeigte Konstellation. Deshalb „schwenken" die Agenten in eine neue Facette

/2 SELF^ORGANIZATION

ihres Scripts. Teil von /2 ist ein Prozeßblock SOLVE, wobei durch Ausführung einer beliebigen der drei Benachrichtigungen

/3 SOLVE ⇒ A, SOLVE ⇒ B, SOLVE ⇒ C

die Konstellation in Abb. 1 herbeigeführt werden kann. Wählt man z. B. die letzte Anweisung /3, so wird SOLVE in Agent C aktiviert. Im vorliegenden Aufsatz kann der weitere Ablauf nur umgangssprachlich in enger Anlehnung an Böhm et al. (1978) skizziert werden: Block (Agent) C prüft durch Aktivierung eines weiteren Prozeßblocks SATISFIED, ob er richtig sitzt. Da dies anfänglich nicht der Fall ist, ändert C es durch Aktivierung eines Prozeßblocks TRY^GOAL. Hierbei benachrichtigt C andere Blöcke, wenn seine Oberseite frei ist, bzw. stößt sie an, ihr eigenes Problem durch TRY^GOAL zu lösen.

Zwei Eindrücke drängen sich dem CA-Designer beim Studium des Agentenparadigmas auf: Zum einen ist es der sehr anschauliche Hintergrund des Prozeßverhaltens von Agentengesellschaften, der ein multilaterales Gespräch zwischen Partnern darstellt, von denen jeder ein bestimmtes privates Ziel im Auge hat, wobei die Gesamtmotivation jedoch nur dem Programmierer bekannt ist. Entspricht darüber hinaus einem einzelnen Agenten ein Teilobjekt eines Designobjekts, so erinnert selbstorganisierendes Agentenverhalten an die Zusammenlagerung von in einer Lösung vorhandenen Teilchen. Dieses Gleichnis kann man sogar dann noch beibehalten, wenn zur Zusammenfügung von Teilen ein Manipulator als „Katalysator" zu Hilfe gerufen wird, der eventuell ein weiterer Agent ist. Zum Schluß sei die Meinung unterstützt, daß eine der bestechendsten Eigenschaften von CSSA der Besitz einer formalen Semantik ist, die in der Tradition der Fixpunktsemantik von D. Scott und anderen Forschern entwickelt wurde (Böhm et al., 1977). Durch diesen ständig präsenten mathematischen Hintergrund hebt sich das Agentenparadigma von fast allen anderen mehr handwerklichen Lösungsversuchen im CAD-Bereich und darüber hinaus in der Informatik beruhigend ab.

7. Eine formale Theorie und ein Methodenbank-Ansatz für CAD

Erfolgreiches CAD ist ein Schlüssel für die Bewältigung drückender Rationalisierungsprobleme, wahrscheinlich das Werkzeug der Wahl. Deshalb verwundert es nicht, daß man sich in vielen Ländern intensiv um die Entwicklung besserer CAD-Systeme kümmert. Die Literaturstelle Radakrishna Murty et al. (1978) berichtet über eine derartige Entwicklung. Den Begriff AED (Automated Engineering Design) haben die Verfasser von dem CAD-Altmeister D. T. Ross übernommen (Ross, 1967). AED (im Sinne der genannten Verfasser) paßt in ein Problemlösungsschema, dessen Bedeutung in den nächsten Jahren sicher zunehmen wird, nämlich die Benutzung von Methodenbanken im Rahmen von Multiprozessor-Konfigurationen mit leistungsfähigen Betriebssystemen (obgleich im erwähnten Aufsatz von Multiprocessing noch nicht die Rede ist). AED geht jeweils von einem POPS (Problem Oriented Program Support) aus, der am Problembereich orientierten Methodenbank, die außer Prozeduren ein nichtprozedurales Modell enthält. Das Eingangsdatum für einen Designprozeß besteht aus einer dem Ingenieurdenken angepaßten nichtformalen Beschreibung des Designproblems. AED formalisiert dieses Datum und führt eine automatische Durchsuchung des gespeicherten Modells durch, in deren Verlauf Programm-Moduln zusammengestellt werden, die ein übergeordneter Supervisor zum Ablauf bringt. Die rechnerische Grundvorstellung ist dabei die des Zustandsraums, in dem das gestellte Problem ein Punkt ist, der durch Anwendung von Operatoren zu einem Problemlösungspunkt verschoben wird.

Für die formale Problem- und Modellbeschreibung wurde eine interessante Datenstruktur, der M-Graph entwickelt, der die Speicherung k-stelliger Relationen zwischen Designvariablen auch für beliebiges k gestattet. Es leuchtet ein, daß ein so streng durchgeführter Ansatz dann besonders erfolgversprechend sein wird, wenn es gelingt, den Supervisor über einem Feld von parallel arbeitenden Betriebsmitteln zu organisieren.

8. Das Kombüsenparadigma

Man stelle sich einen kleinen Dampfer oder ein Spezialitätenrestaurant mit einer winzigen Küche und einem einzigen Koch vor, der um die Mittagszeit eine Vielzahl von Eßwünschen zu befriedigen hat. Dieser „Designer" vollbringt Wunderdinge an Parallelarbeit mit seinen Töpfen und Pfannen. Das Beispiel übertrage man auf einen im Dialog mit einem Rechner operierenden CA-Designer, wobei der Rechner jedoch über starke und viele kollateral betreibbare Betriebsmittel verfüge, die der Designer (um in der Marinesprache zu bleiben) beliebig „entern" kann. Eine solche Rechenumgebung dürfte vor allem für Entwurfsprozesse von Interesse sein, wo sehr rechenaktive Teilvorgänge eventuell viele Stunden zu ihrer Abwicklung benötigen. Solche Vorgänge sind z. B. gewisse Finite-Elemente-Berechnungen. Es stellt sich dann das Problem einer möglichst einheitlichen Programmier- und Kommandosprache für die „Kombüse". Hier soll ein Sprachvorschlag gemacht werden, der schon an anderer Stelle erwähnt worden ist (Nees, 1978). Die Sprache ITH (sprich wie englisch „eat"), hat eine äußerst einfache Syntax:

/1.1 („."(Parameterliste/Unterstrichener^Text)*„.")*

Ein unterstrichener Text soll auch als ein Fix bezeichnet werden. Das von Punkten eingeschlossene Konstrukt heißt eine Schablone (template), genauer Formalschablone, wenn die Parameterlisten der Schablone nur Formalparameter enthalten, dagegen Aktualschablone, wenn auch Aktualparameter vorhanden sind (die Schablone darf freie Variablen enthalten). Es ist sinnvoll, (in Klammern gesetzte) Aktualschablonen selbst als Aktualparameter zuzulassen. ITH kann als Gastgebersprache für andere formale Sprachen dienen. Auf diese Weise gewinnt man Schablonendeklarationen, wie im folgenden Beispiel:

/1   .Fläche des Kreises mit Radius r. = $r*r*pi$
/2   .Umfang des Kreises mit Radius r. = $2*r*pi$
/3.1 .Diagonale des Rechtecks mit Breite b und Höhe h. =
   .2 $sqrt(b*b + h*h)$.

Der Grundgedanke des Gebrauchs eines ITH-Systems besteht aus Rechen-, Editier-, Symbolverarbeitungs- und pattern-matching-Prozessen auf Mengen von Schablonen;

Beispieldialog:

/4.1 .assign 2.5 to r.

(Gleitpunktzahlen dürfen nicht mit einem Punkt beginnen)

/5 .print (.Kreisfläche mit Radius r.).
/6.1 Template unknown
  .2 May I propose templates?
/7 .yes.
/8 1: .Fläche des Kreises mit Radius r.
/9 .assign 1 to r .. perform (1).
/10 3.14159.

Die Zeilen /6, 8, 10 werden vom System ausgegeben. In /9 bezieht sich die zweite Eins auf die in /8 vom System ausgegebene (dialog-lokale) Schablonennummer. Das Entern von zwei Kollateralen kann folgendermaßen aussehen:

/11 .give all templates with „Kreis".
/12.1 1: .Fläche des Kreises mit Radius r.
  .2 2: .Umfang des Kreises mit Radius r.
/13 .assign 7 to r .. collate (1,2) in S.

Hier übergibt in /13 die zweite Aktualschablone die in /12 ausgewiesenen Schablonen an Betriebsmittel. Die Werte der Schablonen werden im Speicher S gesammelt.

Wie das im vorhergehenden Abschnitt erläuterte System beruht auch ITH auf der Idee einer intelligenten Methodenbank.

9. Ausblick

Die Erkenntnis, daß kollaterale Prozesse schwieriger zu programmieren und organisieren sind als sequentielle, gilt auch bei den CAD-Fachleuten als Gemeinplatz. Ebenso treffend ist jedoch auch hier eine Beobachtung, auf die Wolfgang Händler in Vorträgen eindringlich hingewiesen hat, daß der Mensch nämlich bei Versuchen geistiger Durchdringung raumzeitlichen Parallelgeschehens möglicherweise besonders leicht in „Denkblöcke" gerät. Dies ist vermutlich auch ein Grund dafür, daß sich für Parallelrechnen bis heute eine allgemein verwendbare, hinreichend gut durchschaubare, lehr- und erlernbare Sammlung von Programm-, Steuer- und Datenkonstrukten nicht herausgeschält hat. Bei CAD gesellt sich dazu die Schwierigkeit, daß die physikalischen Prinzipien (z. B. Mechanik, Elektrodynamik), die den zu entwerfenden Objekten zugrundeliegen, so außerordentlich verschiedenartig sind.

Der vorliegende Aufsatz wollte insbesondere den an CAD interessierten Informatikern einige Ansätze nahebringen, die zur Zeit diskutiert werden. Es bleibt abzuwarten, welche begrifflichen Schemata sich fruchtbar weiterentwickeln und durchsetzen werden. Zweifellos haben auf längere Sicht die Vorschläge die größten Überlebenschancen, die mit einem gesunden theoretischen Unterbau aufwarten können.

Literatur

Böhm, H. P., Fischer, H. L., Raulefs, P.: CSSA: Language concepts and programming methodology. Proc. ACM SIGART-SIGPLAN Symposion on Artificial Intelligence and Programming Languages. Rochester, N.Y., August 1977.

Böhm, H. P., Fischer, H. L., Raulefs, P.: Dialogues in actor-nets. SEKI-77-04/Proc. AISB-GI Conf. Artificial Intell., 1978.

Ernst, D.: New trends in the application of process computers. Plenarvortrag anläßlich des 7. IFAC-Weltkongresses. 12. bis 16. Juni 1978 in Helsinki. Sonderdruck der Siemens AG.

Fischer, H. L., Raulefs, P.: Design rationale for the interactive programming language CSSA for asynchronous multiprocessor systems. SEKI-BN-79-09/Institut für Informatik III. Universität Bonn, Bonn 1980.

Gaines, B. R.: 3.65 Simulation of natural systems. Computing Reviews, ACM, April 1975.

Grossman, D. D., Taylor, R. H.: Interactive generation of object models with a manipulator. IEEE Transactions on Systems, Man, and Cybernetics SCM-8 (1978).

Hendrix, G. G.: Modeling simultaneous actions and continuous processes. Artificial Intelligence – An International Journal 4 (1973).

Howein, W.: Methoden und Möglichkeiten der Datenverarbeitung. Planung und Abwicklung von leittechnischen Ausrüstungen für verfahrens- und kraftwerkstechnische Projekte mittels EDV. Arbeitsgemeinschaft des VDE-Bezirksvereins. Frankfurt am Main, vom 24. November bis 15. Dezember 1975 (Vollmeyer, A., Hrsg.). Frankfurt am Main: Selbstverlag des VDE-Bezirksvereins.

Klapp, E.: Stand und voraussichtliche Entwicklung rechnerunterstützter Methoden (CAD/CAM) in der Verfahrensindustrie mit Ausblick auf Qualitäts- und Kostenstruktur. In: Methoden der Informatik für rechnerunterstütztes Entwerfen und Konstruieren (Gnatz, R., Samelson, K., Hrsg.). (GI-Fachtagung, München, 1977.) Berlin-Heidelberg-New York: Springer 1977.

Lowrance, J. D., Friedman, D. P.: The Hendrix model of simultaneous actions and continuous processes: An introduction and implementation description. Technical Report No. 33, June 1975. Computer Science Department, Indiana University, Bloomington, Indiana.

Miller, M. L., Goldstein, I. P.: SPADE: A grammar based editor for planning and debugging programs. Artificial Intelligence Laboratory, Cambridge, Mass., December 1976. U.S. Department of Commerce, National Technical Information Service.

Miller, M. L., Goldstein, I. P.: Structured planning and debugging – A linguistic theory of design. Gleiches Datum und Quelle wie vorhergehender Aufsatz.

Miller, M. L., Goldstein, I. P.: Overview of a linguistic theory of design. Gleiches Datum und Quelle wie vorhergehender Aufsatz.

Miller, M. L., Goldstein, I. P.: Overview of a linguistic theory of design. Artificial Intelligence Laboratory, Cambridge, Mass., February 1977. U.S. Department of Commerce, National Technical Information Service.

Nees, G.: Vielzweckdialogsprachen unter besonderer Berücksichtigung der Vielzwecksprache ITH für die Technik. Techniken des Dialogs (Kupka, I., Hrsg.). 1. Treffen 1977 des German Chapter of the ACM am 29. und 30. April 1977 in Hamburg. München-Wien: 1978.

Nees, G.: Struktur und Organisationsform von CAD-Systemen aus der bisherigen Praxis. CAD-Fachgespräch (Proceedings) bei der GI-Jahrestagung, Berlin 1978. Forschungs- und Arbeitsberichte des Fachgebietes „Graphisch-interaktive Systeme" (Encarnacao, J., Straßer, W., Hrsg.), Nr. GRIS 78-3. Technische Hochschule Darmstadt, Fachbereiche Informatik.

Nees, G.: CAD als Universalansatz – Für und Wider. In: Rechnergestützte Aktivitäten – CAD (Händler, W., Nees, G., Hrsg.). Mannheim-Wien-Zürich: 1980.

Nilsson, N. J. (ed.): Progress Report Artificial Intelligence – Research and Applications, May 1975. Stanford Research Institute, Menlo Park, Ca.

Radhakrishna Murty, V., Raju, K. N., Bashmakov, I. A.: A formal theory for automation of engineering design. Proc. International Conference Interactive Techniques in Computer Aided

Design (ACM, Universita degli Studi di Bologna, IEE, A.I.C.A.). Bologna, September 21 – 23, 1978.

Rieger, C., Grinberg, M.: The declarative representation and procedural simulation of causality in physical mechanisms. Technical Report 513, March 1977. Department of Computer Science, University of Maryland, Maryland.

Ross, T. D.: The AED approach to generalized computer aided design. MIT., Proceedings ACM National Meeting, 1967.

Sutherland, I. E.: SKETCHPAD: A man-machine graphical communication system. Massachusetts Institute of Technology, Lincoln Laboratory. Technical Report No. 296, 30 January 1963, Lexington, Mass.

Wilhelms, H.: Perspektiven der Rechneranwendung in Entwicklung, Konstruktion und Fertigung. Vortrag auf der Jahresversammlung der VDI-Ausschüsse ADB/ADKI am 26. Oktober 1971 in Düsseldorf. (Sonderdruck der Siemens AG.)

Woods, W. A.: Transition network grammars for natural language analysis. Comm. ACM 13 (1970).

Dr. G. Nees
Unternehmensbereich Energietechnik
Siemens AG
D-8520 Erlangen
Bundesrepublik Deutschland

Computing, Suppl. 3, 141 – 148 (1981)
© by Springer-Verlag 1981

A Program System of Parallel Processes for Understanding Continuous Speech

H. Niemann and H.-W. Hein, Erlangen

Abstract – Zusammenfassung

A Program System of Parallel Processes for Understanding Continuous Speech. A system concept is shown which enables several independent processes, each having specialized knowledge about one aspect of a complex real world pattern, to cooperate in parallel, analyzing and understanding this pattern automatically.

A software environment is introduced, providing an experimenter with tools to define different system configurations and to develop reasonable control strategies for them.

Intended is a usage for the automatic understanding of continuously spoken german sentences. The principles of the various knowledge modules which will be needed for this pattern analysis task are given also.

Ein Programmsystem von parallelen Prozessen zum Verständnis kontinuierlicher Sprache. Es wird ein Systemkonzept vorgestellt, bei dem mehrere unabhängige Prozesse parallel zusammenarbeiten können, um ein komplexes Muster der realen Welt automatisch zu analysieren und zu verstehen. Jeder Prozeß besitzt dazu spezielles Wissen über einen Aspekt des Musters.

Die Softwareumgebung, die es einem Experimentator erlaubt, unterschiedliche Konfigurationen festzulegen und geeignete Kontrollstrategien für diese zu entwickeln, wird beschrieben.

Da eine Verwendung für das automatische Verstehen fließend gesprochener deutscher Sätze vorgesehen ist, werden die Prinzipien der verschiedenen Wissensmodule, die man bei diesem Problem der Musteranalyse benötigt, ebenfalls dargelegt.

1. Introduction

In many everyday situations one would like to speak to an automatic system instead of pushing buttons or typing words on a keyboard. An important reason is the evidence that speech is the preferred means of human communication [1]. Recognition of speech already can be done well in cases, where the number of words is rather small and unchanging, and the analyzing routine can be adapted to a constant group of speakers [2, 3].

But much research has to be done in building up a system, to which an unrestricted number of people can speak in a natural fluent manner, using many different words. Such a system will need good linguistic models of the speaker independent features of human natural speech. Today such models are available only partially and then often not formalized; therefore, they are difficult to transform into algorithms and speech understanding research first has to develop derivatives of them for computing purposes.

As is known from the difficulties with automatic translation, linguistic models are certainly very language dependent, but formalisms and methods of writing them down may be transferable. Much research on this area was already done in USA [4, 5].

Besides models, there is need for processing abilities, lying above those already existing. Human speech signals are very fuzzy patterns and their analysis usually will produce at every step many possible interpretations, all to be handled in further steps. In spite of this huge amount of computation a useful system must understand and react in real time. Intelligent understanding strategies, in particular those using parallelism are thought to cope with the problem of complexity [6].

In our institute we are developing a system using both linguistic models and parallel processing to manage the speaker independent understanding of continuously spoken german sentences. The general approach is drawn from the experiences of the ARPA Speech Recognition Project (1971 – 1976), especially from the Carnegie-Mellon University HEARSAY-II system [7]. Parallel processing will be simulated within an experimental software environment, built up also for developing and measuring purposes. But at least one of the resulting speech understanding configurations is planned to be implemented on a real parallel computer, as soon as one is available.

The task of understanding connected speech may be viewed as a problem of pattern analysis (another problem of this kind is the analysis of images [8]). In pattern analysis one deals with a complex entity which cannot be classified as a whole – the classification approach is feasible in recognition of isolated words, but not in understanding connected speech. In this case one has to obtain simpler constituents from the complex entity and analyze (describe) it in terms of the simple constituents. This is done by putting them together to form larger units, repeatedly through certain levels of abstraction, up to an overall description. In understanding of spoken sentences the main levels are: Phone, word, sentence structure (syntax), and sentence meaning (semantics).

2. Concept of Understanding

The general concept adopted for the speech understanding system is shown in Fig. 1. The system consists of four main components:

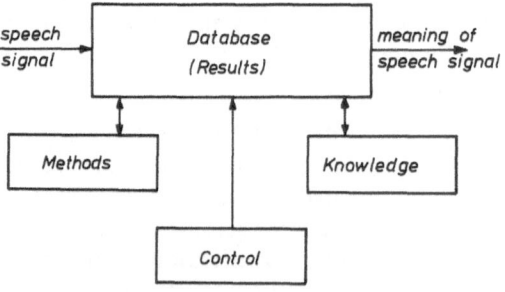

Fig. 1. Concept of speech understanding

a) A database which contains recent results of analysis, obtained so far during working on utterances of connected speech.

b) A module (or modules) containing methods for processing of utterances.

c) A module (or modules) containing knowledge about syntactic, semantic, and pragmatic (task-specific) properties of utterances.

d) A module which executes control.

Results of analysis may be phones extracted from a parametric representation of speech, words generated from phones, or sentences built up from words. At the end of analysis the database will contain a – hopefully correct – sentence, extracted from the speech signal which was the initial input to the database.

During analysis the intermediate results which are obtained, may be viewed as hypotheses about the utterance. These contain various alternatives of possible labels for simple constituents, their localization within the pattern, and different levels of abstraction.

We distinguish methods and knowledge, although the border is not clear cut. By methods we name algorithms which contain low-level knowledge, that is they are fairly independent of the particular task encountered in speech understanding. By knowledge we name algorithms which use the particular syntax, semantics, and task-specific (pragmatic) information. The distinction is useful in order to separate activities for developing the modules. On the other hand, both types of modules may also be considered uniformly as modules cooperating in speech understanding. The main concept is to modularize the system, not to name the modules. Since we have independent modules and do not want to specify a particular system structure or strategy of analysis in advance, another component – the control module – is introduced. It will be discussed below. A general view of the system is, therefore, a set of experts (the various modules implementing particular algorithms) operating on a common database.

This last view of the system also clarifies the role of the control module. Initially we have the database containing the speech signal. In this state of the system (the state being given by the contents of the database) a set of operations is applicable. These operations have to be imagined as possibly parallel and repeated accesses of experts to the database. Execution of an operation will add new results to the database, thereby transforming the present state of the system to a new state. Again, the new state may be transformed by an operation to another new state, and so on. The task of the control module is to select, for any input utterance, a suitable sequence of operations which finally will result in a correct understanding of the input.

Since control is treated as an independent module, it is easily possible to change the control strategy and to change the sequence of operations. It is obvious that the set of possible states may be represented by a graph, and the control module has to find a successful path through the graph leading from the initial state (input speech signal) to a goal state (a correct understanding of the input). The operational decisions of the execution control module (and the database modifications made from experts, too) mainly will be driven by quality scores. The scores are given to hypotheses by the creating expert or by other experts at verification time. Because there is no general need to proceed strictly bottom-up, each expert of course may produce new intermediate results by verifying or putting together results of others and also by making alternative guesses about parts of the signal. The score of a new hypothesis is calculated out of the score of hypotheses which are used to create it, and out of the experts' special knowledge.

To find a successful path to understanding of the input, it is important to give the control module a strategy which uses the hypotheses scorings in an intelligent way. To avoid deadlocks it has to track several alternative paths in parallel. But to optimize recognition time it always should keep on paths, where the involved hypotheses are of the better scored ones.

Understanding should be done, if a hypothesis is created at the highest abstraction level, which spans the whole speech signal and is scored good enough. An automatism which guarantees the first found being the best possible optimizes computation time and is reported by Woods [9].

3. Approach to System Implementation

It is not possible to develop powerful strategies for the execution control module and related scoring policies for the different expert modules without intensive experimenting. The control strategies are needed to enable understanding processes to converge rapidly and with a high probability to the right interpretation of an input speech signal. To explore them it is important to have an experimental system of various software tools:

a) a special dialog system,
b) a universal database system,
c) a knowledge pool for speech understanding.

The dialog system allows a human experimenter to watch any involved module during a running speech signal analysis. Via terminal the experimenter can compose a distinct understanding system structure out of stored modules and then start it to analyze speech data. The speech data, parametrized spoken sentences, is not computed at realtime but taken out of a pool of preprocessed speech inputs. This allows in general any repetition of experiments. Further it makes possible various comparisons between performance of different structured understanding systems. The dialog system besides enables the experimenter to stop the analysis at any point of interest to extract status information out of his working model. This can be statistics about the hypotheses in the database of results, groups of hypotheses themselves, protocols of certain expert modules, and measured consumptions of processing time from every active module. All status information can be output easily on screen or paper, in printed or graphic manner. Finally the dialog system permits persons to interact with an understanding process as additional "expert modules". This feature will be used to test some knowledge without having programmed algorithms. Later evaluation of those experiments may then lead to the development of a new expert module.

A database system with data definition language and query language is important in the state of experimenting. It helps staying flexible with respect to the structure of the database of results. Further it supplies all accessing expert modules with a standardized interface to the database. This releases all implementors of expert modules from thinking about problems of concurrent data access, data protection, private regions or memory management. If one imagines that the expert modules will be programmed by various people, often specialized to the concerned expert knowledge, a common query language for the database of results will be the main integrating factor for a composed speech understanding system. For our project we develop a database system which is not specialized anyhow and whose design will follow the relational approach [10]. It provides us with all possibilities in changing the database to any structure that will come out of the experiments as an efficient one.

The other application of the database system is given with the establishing of a broader knowledge pool about speech and language properties. Larger amounts of knowledge data, accumulated in the course of time can be structured and administrated thus properly. A point of most significance is that programmed editing tools operating on the knowledge pool, can be introduced into the dialog system mentioned before. Further it is possible to design expert modules suited in two parts, one having a certain algorithm and the other an exchangeable knowledge part. With that an experimenter can compose and test understanding systems not only of different structure but also with modules using graded knowledge "weight".

4. Types of Knowledge

The systems built in the frame of the experimental system will all belong to the kind of parallelized expert systems. In connection with speech understanding certain types of expert knowledge will be needed anyway, others optionally. The main part of a possible configuration is shown in Fig. 2.

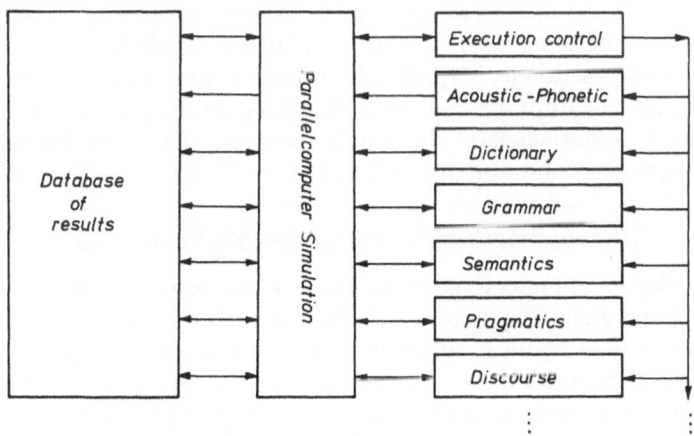

Fig. 2. Structure of a speech understanding system

This and the following chapter give an introduction to the principles and contents of the diverse expert modules. The knowledge mentioned in this chapter is thought to be elementary.

a) Acoustic-Phonetic Module

After quantizing and digitizing the speech signal parameters are extracted, which allow its segmentation into voiced, unvoiced, and silent parts, the segmentation of the voiced parts into vocals and voiced consonants etc. There is extra experimental research done at our institute, based on numerous publications on this area [11, 12], to develop a reliable and speaker independent acoustic-phonetic expert. His output will be a string of segments. For each segment will be given some classifications into phones, together with their matching score. Several parameter extraction algorithms have been programmed and research now concentrates on finding the right mixture for a reasonable phonetic segmentation of german speech and, in close connection with that, on designing a proper classificator for phonetic transcription of the segments.

b) Dictionary Module

The next level above that of phonetic segments is the word level. A dictionary expert matches the known words against the segment string, beginning in parts where the alternatives in the string are few and the first score is high. This will generate word islands into the continuous flow of speech. A dynamic programming algorithm derived from that of Viterbi [13] and made suitable for the special situation at the phonetic level does the matching. Result of a match is a score for similarity. The word knowledge of the dictionary expert is given in phonetic symbols. It is prestructured in means of the used similarity measure (phonetic metric), so the search for the best fitting word would converge much faster than otherwise.

c) Grammar Module

Given some word island, a grammar expert can start proposing classes of words that may occur in between. Elements of these hypothetical classes can be verified afterwards by the dictionary expert. The syntactic knowledge of the grammar expert will be given within the concept of frames [14] using syntactic classes also known by the dictionary expert. The mainly top-down parsing techniques must be direction independent and able to start at any word in a correct sentence.

d) Pragmatic Module (Task Specific Knowledge)

The general concept of understanding works task independent even if naturally the knowledge of the dictionary expert will include the task specific words, and the grammar expert may know some extra sentence structures. Nevertheless all the needed information about the world model and the context, in which the spoken sentences have to be understood is given with a task expert module.

The first task expert in this project concerns the german Intercity-Train-System. Its world model consists of concepts about spatial and temporal laws of nature, of geographic knowledge, timetables and fares. Information retrieval demands about this are expected as contents of incoming speech signals.

5. Further Modules

It may be the result of experiments that the foreseen levels of understanding are too far from another and there have to be some in between, connected with new expert modules, whose type of knowledge will be thus specified.

Anyway it is already known what modules one needs to expand a speech understanding system to a full speech communication interface for automatic systems. Very important is that, with the exception of the synthesis module, they all can be used intensively to support the understanding process also.

In practice, one spoken sentence has not to be seen isolated but as a part of a dialog between man and machine. The knowledge of certain discourse patterns, together with the history of the actual one, may be very helpful to understand speech signals because it is often foreseeable "what comes next". Furthermore, in many cases it is possible for the computer to be the initiative communication partner.

It is also possible to define besides the task dependent knowledge additional and more general concepts for meanings of words and sentences. They will be used from a semantics expert in the understanding process for proposing words and syntactic structures, and for verifying parsed sentences as "making sense". With the same semantic concepts an answer generation module can transform all what the machine wants to express into a natural sentence down to word level.

An acoustic synthesis module then should be able to finish a text-to-speech synthesis of the computers german output sentences.

6. Concluding Remarks

Besides developing a system for understanding connected speech a major concern of our research is to have available a large software system for experiments in pattern analysis in general. It is expected that the explored control concepts for expert systems and the overall ability to specify knowledge databases will be useful for other areas of pattern analysis, too.

References

[1] Chapanis, A.: Interactive human communication. Scient. American 232, 36–42 (1975).
[2] De Mori, R.: Recent advances in automatic speech recognition. Proc. 4. J. Conf. on Pattern Recognition, Kyoto, Japan, pp. 106–124 (1978).
[3] Ainsworth, W. A., Green, P. D.: Current problems in automatic speech recognition. In: Pattern recognition: Ideas in practice (Batchelor, B. G., ed.), pp. 365–396. New York: Plenum Press 1978.
[4] Bates, M.: The theory and practice of augmented transition network (ATN) grammars. In: Natural language communication with computers (Lecture Notes in Computer Science, Vol. 63), (Goos, G., Hartmanis, J., ed.), pp. 191–259. Berlin-Heidelberg-New York: Springer 1978.
[5] Walker, D. E. (ed.): Understanding spoken language. New York: North-Holland 1978.
[6] Fennell, R. D., Lesser, V. R.: Parallelism in artificial intelligence problem solving: A case study of HEARSAY-II. IEEE Transactions C-26, 98–111 (1977).
[7] Klatt, D. H.: Review of the ARPA speech understanding project. J. Acoust. Soc. Am. 62, 1345–1366 (1977).

10*

[8]   Niemann, H.: Digital image analysis. In: Recent advances in digital image processing (Stucki, P.,
       ed.), pp. 77 – 122. New York: Plenum Press 1979.
[9]   Woods, W. A.: Shortfall and density scoring strategies for speech understanding control, Report
       No. 3303. Cambridge: Bolt Beranek & Newman Inc. 1976.
[10] Date, C. J.: An introduction to database systems, 2nd ed. Reading, Mass.: Addison-Wesley 1977.
[11] Schafer, R. W., Rabiner, L. R.: Parametric representations of speech. In: Speech recognition
       (Reddy, D. R., ed.), pp. 99 – 150. New York: Academic Press 1975.
[12] Makhoul, J.: Linear prediction in automatic speech recognition. In: Speech recognition (Reddy,
       D. R., ed.), pp. 183 – 220. New York: Academic Press 1975.
[13] Forney, G. D.: The Viterbi algorithm. Proc. IEEE **61**, 268 – 278 (1973).
[14] Bobrow, D. G., et al.: GUS, a frame-driven dialog system. Artificial Intelligence **8**, 155 – 173
       (1977).

Prof. Dr.-Ing. H. Niemann
Dipl.-Inf. H.-W. Hein
Lehrstuhl für Informatik 5 (Mustererkennung)
Universität Erlangen-Nürnberg
Martensstrasse 3
D-8520 Erlangen
Federal Republic of Germany

Computing, Suppl. 3, 149 – 157 (1981)

Micro-Modules Implementation of a Learning Pattern-Recognition System

H. Rohrer, Campinas, **H. Schreiber,** and **V. Sigmund,** Erlangen*

Abstract – Zusammenfassung

Micro-Modules Implementation of a Learning Pattern-Recognition System. A Brazilian/German computer architecture project of a special purpose multi-microprocessor system implemented by using a set of micro-modules is described. The system is organized as a macro-pipeline proposed by Händler [7]. High performance at a low cost, an arbitrary configurability and expandibility, and potential reliability are the main features of such systems. The modules are interconnected by multiport access to the blocks of the distributed main memory. A nine module system for a learning classification process used in pattern recognition, previously simulated and evaluated on three conventional general purpose computers, is presently being built up in Erlangen. The design of the modules consisting of the 16-bit-microprocessor Intel 8086 and specifically designed multiport memories is described, together with the intermodule communication protocol of the system.

Mikro-Moduln-Implementierung eines lernenden Mustererkennungssystems. Ein brasilianisch-deutsches Rechnerarchitekturprojekt eines mit Mikro-Moduln implementierten Spezialzweckrechners wird beschrieben. Der Rechner ist wie eine Makropipeline nach Händler [7] organisiert. Derartige Rechner bieten eine hohe Leistung zum niedrigen Preis, erhöhte Zuverlässigkeit und sind beliebig konfigurierbar und erweiterbar. Die Moduln sind durch Multiport-Speicherzugriff zu den Blöcken des verteilten Hauptspeichers verbunden. Der Entwurf der Moduln eines in Erlangen gegenwärtig gebauten 9-Moduln-Mustererkennungssystems, bestehend aus den 16-Bit-Mikroprozessoren Intel 8086 und spezifischen Multiport-Speichern, wird beschrieben, sowie das Kommunikationsprotokoll zwischen den Moduln.

1. Introduction

Modular computer architecture at various levels of computer design has already proved to be useful in manufacturing, applications, research and education (cf. Clark [1], Parker and Siewiorek [2]). As semiconductor technology has evolved, standard module sets have advanced from circuit elements to gates and flip-flops, to register-transfer modules and finally to PMS-level modules (cf. Fuller, Siewiorek and Swan [3]). As a result, various multi-microprocessor systems have been projected, designed or even built in the last years. Their main design objectives are high performance at a low cost, potential reliability and sometimes a certain degree of freedom with regard to the configurability and expandibility of the system. The most advanced project in this direction is the experimental multi-microprocessor computer system Cm* built and running at the Carnegie-Mellon University in Pittsburgh, U.S.A. (cf. Fuller et al. [4]). Cm*-systems consist of an arbitrary

* This research was performed in part during the stay of the second and third author at the University of Campinas, supported by the Cooperation Contract between the Internat. Büro of the GMD Bonn and the Conselho National de Desinvolvimento Científico e Technológico, Brasilia.

number of computer modules connected by a hierarchical system of time-shared busses to form a network which reflects the interprocessor communication requirements of the application. They are primarily intended for special purpose systems, though they also can be used to implement a general purpose computation facility [3]. At the Institut für Mathematische Maschinen und Datenverarbeitung in Erlangen, Germany, design objectives and aims similar to the Cm* project resulted in a joint project of the University of Erlangen-Nürnberg with the University of Campinas, S. P., Brazil: design, implementation and evaluation of a set of LSI computer modules for user definable special-purpose multi-microprocessor systems DIRMU (Desinvolvimento e Implementação de Redes de Multiprocessadores; engl. interpretation: Distributed Reconfigurable Multiprocessor) [5], [6]. The actual system design and the present pilot implementation have been preceded by a thorough study of common structural features of machines and computations (cf. [7] to [10]), and the intended applications (cf. [11], [12]) at our institute, including simulations on conventional general-purpose computers (PDP 15 and 10, CDC 3300) accompanied by extensive hardware measurements (cf. [13] to [15]).

The proposed system consists of microprogrammable computer modules, each having the processing power of a minicomputer, local memory and provision for I/O extensions, similarly to Cm*. The main difference to Cm* is in the way the modules are interconnected. In DIRMU the processors have multiport access to memories of neighbouring modules. This solution also contributes to program locality (cf. Fuller, Siewiorek and Swan [3]) and, moreover, it should help to avoid possible congestion in data flow that can arise with the use of time-shared busses. In the case of special-purpose systems, a machine is dedicated to a particular computational structure which can therefore be directly reflected in the interconnection structure of the system. The interconnection scheme using multiport memory access allows a straightforward implementation of pipelining at the PMS-level (cf. "macro-pipelining" in Händler [7]) for data flow in such high-performance special-purpose multi-microprocessors.

In order to stress the direct relation of the computational structure of the application to the corresponding DIRMU system, we continue in Section 2 with the analysis of the structure of the learning classification process for pattern recognition, and show the corresponding nine module DIRMU system we are presently implementing. Section 3 describes the modules of this prototype system. They consist of the 16-bit microprocessor Intel 8086 and specially designed multiport memories. Microprogrammability of the modules had to been postponed to the final LSI modules, the design of which has begun in parallel to the pilot system implementation. The intermodule communication protocol of DIRMU systems is described in Section 4.

2. Structure of the Application and Machine

The learning classification process shortly described here (cf. [11] for a thorough mathematical treatment) is used for assignment of an input pattern to one of the pattern classes known to the system, or rejection of the input pattern if it does not fit to any known class.

It consists of the following basic tasks:

1. Input and coding: control of the pattern input — e.g. an interactive input with the use of a light pen and a graphic terminal — and coding of the submitted pattern, e.g. as a matrix of values representing the darkness and color of screen points.

2. Pattern matching: computation of the distances between the submitted pattern and each stored template that represents a pattern class known to the system; thus the set of stored templates is the image of the external world in the system.

3. Decision making: comparison of the distances, and decision about the class of the submitted pattern or rejection of the pattern.

4. Learning: correction of the template representing the resulting pattern class, chosen in phase 3; this correction takes into account possible differences between the template and submitted pattern.

The learning phase provides for the initial establishment of templates as approximations to submitted patterns of each class, and also makes the system's image of the external world adaptive.

A more refined model of this classification process uses several different criteria in the pattern matching phase, e.g. the occurrences of convex or concave curves in hand-written letters. In other words, several different measures are used in the computation of the distances between the submitted pattern and templates.

Since all these distance computations are independent of each other, we get m parallel subtasks 2.1 to 2.m as the pattern matching phase with m different criteria. In this refined system not only the templates representing the allowed pattern classes but also the pattern matching criteria themselves are subject to learning. Let us for example assume that for one of these criteria the point matrix of the screen is partitioned in disjunct subsets which are searched for subpatterns of the submitted pattern. It can become apparent in the learning process that for all patterns, one of these subsets is more important than the remaining subsets of the screen points. Then the measured distance of the corresponding part of the submitted pattern and template should be more decisive than the distances of the remaining parts, e.g. by taking an appropriately weighted sum over the subsets of the screen partition in the decision making phase 3 as a resulting "semi-distance" between pattern and template according to the corresponding pattern matching criterium. If the weights mentioned above are probabilities, the "semi-distance" is the mathematical expectation of the distances between the submitted pattern and template over the subsets in consideration [11].

A new task, *criteria correction*, performs this learning phase; in the above example, the weight factors for the computation of resulting distances — as a part of the decision making task number 3 above — would be corrected after each decision, by comparing the result with the measured distances in each subset of screen points.

The learning process can also show that one of the pattern matching criteria 2.1, ..., 2.m gives for certain patterns more accurate results than the other criteria. This can be used as a decision aid in "undecidable" cases, where different criteria would propose different classes for the submitted pattern.

Thus a new task, *criteria evaluation*, takes the intermediate decisions (i.e. measured distances) of pattern matching criteria 2.1, ..., 2.*m* and the feedback information from the final decision phase 3 as its arguments, evaluates the criteria, and passes the result as a decision aid to the decision making phase 3. The mathematical model of the system actually applied (cf. [11]) uses two evaluation algorithms in parallel in this phase, and uses the results of this evaluation also in the criteria correction phase. The latter can be viewed as an interaction of the parallel pattern matching tasks during the process of their learning, since the "criteria correction" task described earlier would change only each criterium independently of each other.

The resulting classification process consisting of the mentioned tasks and their data dependencies is shown in Fig. 1.

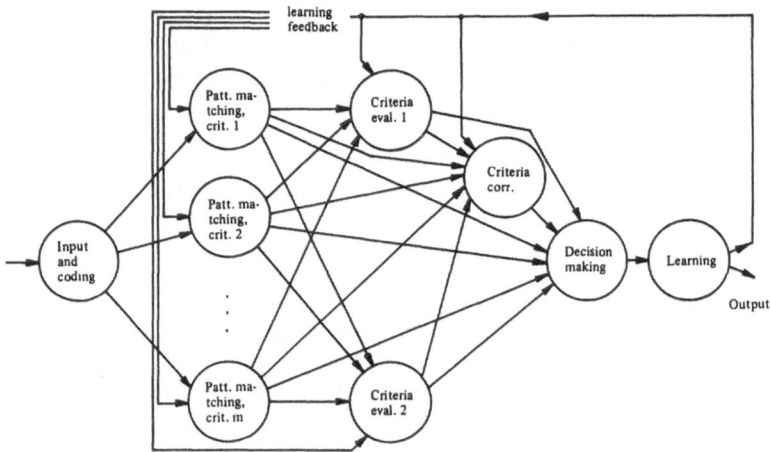

Fig. 1. Structure of the learning classification algorithm (pattern recognition)

Now, as mentioned in the previous section, a high-performance special-purpose multi-microprocessor system can reflect this structure directly in hardware, to the extent it is economically feasible. If we use computer modules as nodes of Fig. 1, each having a microprocessor and local memory, and form the interconnection structure (shown by the arrows) by using multiport memory access of the processors to the neighbouring modules — as proposed for DIRMU systems —, the "largest" system for the application would be a configuration isomorphic to the graph in Fig. 1. This system could execute a fast repeated input and classification (or rejection) of patterns, forming a pipeline-network (at the PMS-level, or macropipeline [7]) with feedback. It is also immediately obvious that if we "coalesce" two or more nodes or arrows in the graph, we get a smaller (and cheaper) system, but, in general, the performance will be slower. A trivial system consists of a single node.

The tasks represented as nodes in Fig. 1 require different amounts of computation. Also the arrows of Fig. 1 represent data streams of quite different intensities. If we design a corresponding DIRMU system using only one kind of computer modules – this is the case in our prototype system –, then tasks which represent simple computations can be coalesced without performance penalty.

The algorithm has been simulated on conventional general-purpose computers, subject to extensive hardware measurements. The information about the execution times and data flow in the system has led us to the nine module configuration shown in Fig. 2. It uses four different criteria in the parallel pattern matching phase. In comparison to the graph in Fig. 1, the tasks "decision making" and "learning" has been coalesced to a single module. In order to save interconnection paths, the parameters from the "pattern matching" task to "criteria correction" are passed through the tasks "criteria evaluation", and the parameters from the task "learning" to the "pattern matching" tasks are passed through "input and coding".

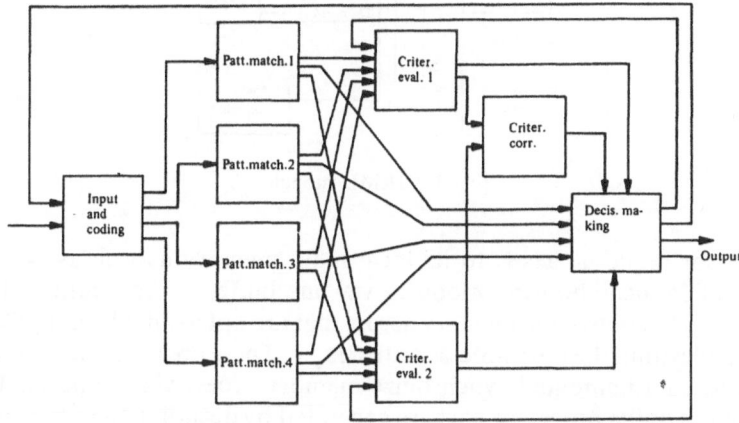

Fig. 2. DIRMU system for the learning classification

3. Prototype Modules

The structure of the prototype modules is shown in Fig. 3. It is a dual bus system with a processor bus controlled by the CPU and a memory bus controlled by a multiport controller.

The processor part consists of the 16-bit microprocessor Intel 8086 with its bus controller 8288, wait-state generator and further support circuits required for its operation. The module's private memory consists of 16K bytes EPROM and 4K bytes RAM for system initialization and monitor routines and tables. A keypad and LED display are useful for the inspection of register and memory contents, and for single-step execution under control of the monitor program of the Intel system design kit SDK-86 [16]. A CRT display terminal or a host computer can be connected to any module through its serial I/O-port during system testing and debugging. Only the latter feature will be provided in the final DIRMU modules. A mass storage device or a host computer can be connected to the module through its parallel I/O-port.

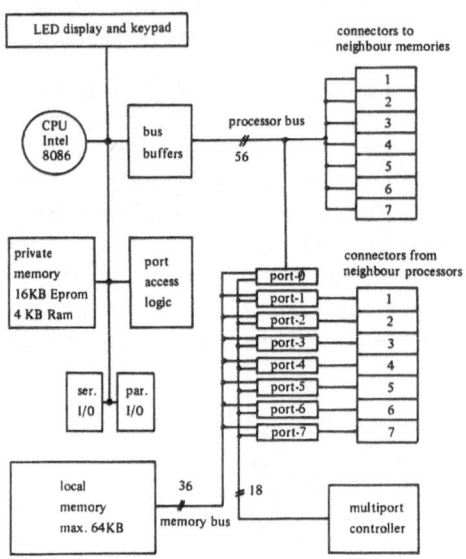

Fig. 3. DIRMU module

The processor requests access to its local main memory as well as to the main memories of its neighbouring modules via bus buffers. The additional control signals needed to control the memory access that are not available in the 8086/8288 are generated within the port-access control logic. These are the hand-shake signals necessary to coordinate and synchronize memory access via the ports. The port request signals in the processor part are generated by decoding the uppermost four address bits of the 8086. Only eight processor access ports of the 16 possible are used at present. 32 lines of the processor bus are used for separate 16-bit data and addresses.

A multiport read/write memory with eight access ports is used as a local main memory of each module. The port number zero serves for the access of the corresponding local processor, ports number 1 to 7 are used for the connections to the processor ports of the neighbouring modules as required by the structure of the application (cf. Section 2). The local main memory stores the application program code defining the operation of the module (module's task) and also serves as a module's buffer for data flow through the system. This program code can be loaded by a serial loader program (cf. [16]) residing in the private EPROM of the processor through the serial *I/O*-port. Alternatively, a system bootstrapping could be applied, where the application programs of all modules are loaded through the fixed system input (cf. Fig. 2) and spread over the configuration. If several modules perform the same subtask, they can use reentrant code located in one of them or in their common direct neighbour. A drawback of this solution is that instruction fetch of a processor has to compete with the memory accesses of the neighbouring modules to its local main memory. The port access logic at the processor part and the multiport controller at the memory part of the prototype modules cause a memory access delay that will require at least one 8086 wait state even in case of a single access request at a time. We consider therefore also the solution in which a larger private memory of the processor stores the application program code. EPROMs containing the code could be directly plugged into the processor board.

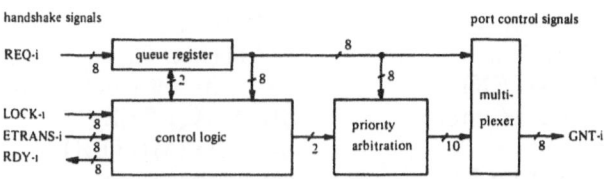

Fig. 4. Multiport controller

The memory access is controlled on a request/grant basis by the multiport controller shown in Fig. 4. We denote with REQ-i the access request signal to the multiport controller incoming through the memory port i. It has been generated by the processor port access logic of the processor connected to this memory port. Multiple simultaneous requests to memory are saved in a queue register. The control logic in Fig. 4 activates the priority arbitration part that decides which request will be granted. The round-robin strategy is used. The grant signal GNT-i of the controller activates the corresponding memory port number i, and at the same time a ready signal RDY-i is sent to the processor that receives memory access. Other requesting processors – which do not receive RDY signal – enter the 8086 wait states. The port access logic of the served processor answers with an end-of-transfer signal ETRANS as soon as the memory access of the processor has finished, and the multiport controller grants memory access to the next processor selected by the priority arbitration logic. If the request has been accompanied by the LOCK signal of the processor – which can be forced by the corresponding prefix in front of any 8086 instruction –, consecutive memory accesses are granted to this processor as long as its LOCK signal is active.

The 1 M byte address space (i.e. 20 bit address) of the 8086 is partitioned in 16 blocks of 64K bytes each. One block is used for the processor's private EPROM and RAM, the remaining 15 blocks can be used for the local main memories of the modules accessible by the processor, including its own local main memory. In our pilot implementation only 8 blocks are used.

4. Intermodule Communication Protocol of DIRMU Systems

Data flow through a DIRMU system is a typical example of the producer/consumer problem which is simply solved by the use of general semaphores. We show the case of a single producer P and a single consumer C with the use of a buffer for up to N data sets to be passed:

semaphore	initial value	comment
MUTEX	1	controls the mutually exclusive buffer access
FREE	N	counts free places in the buffer
FULL	$\emptyset$	counts full places in the buffer

```
P:                              C:
  ⋮                               ⋮
produce data set                WAIT(FULL)
WAIT(FREE)                      WAIT(MUTEX)
WAIT(MUTEX)                     read data set from the buffer
write data set into             SIGNAL(FREE)
the buffer                      SIGNAL(MUTEX)
SIGNAL(FULL)                    consume data set
SIGNAL(MUTEX)                     ⋮
  ⋮
```

The 8086 LOCK prefix serves as convenient means to implement the standard WAIT and SIGNAL operations on a semaphore S:

WAIT(S):
```
      LOCK DEC S        ;   lock S; S := S − 1; unlock S
LOOP MOV AL, S
      TEST AL, ZERO     ;   } if S < ∅, then loop
      JB LOOP
```

SIGNAL(S):
```
      LOCK INC S        ;   lock S; S := S + 1; unlock S.
```

Without the use of the LOCK prefix no deadlocks could occur at the instruction level of the intercommunication protocol, since a processor in the 8086 wait state (waiting for a memory access) cannot hinder any other processor. Deadlocks due to the LOCK prefix or deadlocks at the programming level of the communication protocol could appear in DIRMU systems at places where feedback joins the pipeline (cf. Fig. 2). In the pilot configuration, a programmable interval counter/timer is used in such a case in order to avoid infinite waiting.

5. Conclusion

The complete pilot pattern recognition system shown in Fig. 2 is due to be operable in July 1981. The design of the final set of LSI DIRMU modules runs in parallel and will incorporate the experience with the prototype system. The following additional features are in consideration [5]:

microprogrammable processor, so that the modules could be tailored to special processing modes (non-numeric processing, associative processing)

special instructions for data exchange such as "broadcast" and "collect" as well as instructions for processor intercommunication

module synchronization/communication phase as a part of the basic system cycle containing the usual instruction fetch/execute cycle of each processor.

The DIRMU system is aimed as a modular system kit for user specified PMS-pipeline implementation of any application. Our present work includes the design of a DIRMU implementation of two-dimensional computations of chemical reactors – essentially the integration of a system of ordinary differential equations and the simplex method of minimization – used at the Institute for Technical Chemistry of the University of Erlangen-Nürnberg.

Acknowledgement

We are obliged to Professor W. Händler for valuable advice during the work and Mr. R. K. Bell for useful comments on this paper.

References

[1] Clark, W. A.: Macromodular computer systems. AFIPS Conf. Proc. **30**, 335 – 336 (1967).
[2] Parker, A. C., Siewiorek, D. P.: Educational and industrial applications of register transfer modules. In: EUROMICRO 1976, Second Symposium on Micro Architecture (Sami, M., Wilmink, J., Zaks, R., eds.), pp. 221 – 230. Amsterdam: North-Holland 1976.
[3] Fuller, S. H., Siewiorek, D. P., Swan, R. J.: Computer modules: An architecture for large digital modules. First Ann. Symp. on Computer Architecture 1973. IEEE **1973**, 231 – 237.
[4] Fuller, S. H., et al.: Multi-microprocessors: An overview and working example. Proc. of the IEEE **66**, 216 – 228 (1978).
[5] Händler, W., Rohrer, H.: Gedanken zu einem Rechner-Baukasten-System, Projektunterlagen des DIRMU-Projekts, Oktober 1977. Univ. Erlangen-Nürnberg, reprinted in Elektronische Rechenanlagen **22**, 3 – 13 (1980).
[6] Händler, W., Schreiber, H., Sigmund, V.: Computation structures reflected in general purpose and special purpose multi-microprocessor systems. Proc. of the 1979 Internat. Conf. on Parallel Processing. IEEE **1979**, 95 – 102.
[7] Händler, W.: The concept of macro-pipelining with high availability. Elektronische Rechenanlagen **15**, 269 – 274 (1973).
[8] Händler, W.: On classification schemes for computers in the post-von-Neumann-era. G.I. (Gesellschaft für Informatik) 4. Jahrestagung, Berlin, 1974, pp. 439 – 452. Berlin-Heidelberg-New York: Springer 1975.
[9] Händler, W., Hofmann, F., Schneider, H. J.: A general purpose array with a broad spectrum of application. In: Computer Architecture, Workshop of the G.I., Erlangen, May 1975 (Händler, W., ed.), pp. 311 – 335. Berlin-Heidelberg-New York: Springer 1976.
[10] Sigmund, V.: Parallel compiled interpretation. Proc. of the 1977 Internat. Conf. on Parallel Processing. IEEE **1977**, 16 – 25.
[11] Rohrer, H.: A supervised network on adaptive automata for pattern recognition. Arbeitsberichte des IMMD, Universität Erlangen-Nürnberg, Vol. 8, no. 8, 1975, pp. 1 – 41.
[12] Drewes, B.: Implementation of a structural pattern recognition system. Cf. [11], pp. 43 – 80.
[13] Schreiber, H., Thomas, B., Wolf, F.: Beschreibung eines synthetischen Jobmix für verschiedene Benchmark-Tests. Lecture Notes in Computer Science **8**, 218 – 232 (1974).
[14] Klar, R., Schreiber, H., Widjaja, H.: Messungen mit dem Zählmonitor II. Arbeitsberichte des IMMD, Universität Erlangen-Nürnberg. Vol. 8, no. 8, 1975.
[15] Schreiber, H.: Hardware-Messung und Analyse des Ablaufgeschehens im Rechnerkern. Arbeitsberichte des IMMD, Universität Erlangen-Nürnberg. Vol. 11, no. 7, 1978.
[16] SDK-86, MCS 86 System Design Kit, User's guide. Santa Clara: Intell Corporation 1978.

Prof. Dr. H. Rohrer
Inst. da Matemática, Estàtistica
e Ciância de Computacâo
Univ. Campinas
C.P. 1130
13100 Campinas, SP
Brazil

Dr. H. Schreiber and
Dr. V. Sigmund
Institut für Mathematische Maschinen
und Datenverarbeitung
(Informatik III)
Universität Erlangen-Nürnberg
Martensstrasse 3
D-8520 Erlangen
Federal Republic of Germany

Computing, Suppl. 3, 159—171 (1981)

Ein Modell für diskrete Systeme mit reellem Zeitparameter

A. Schmitt, Karlsruhe

Zusammenfassung — Abstract

Ein Modell für diskrete Systeme mit reellem Zeitparameter. Die bisher bekanntgewordenen System- und Prozeß-Modelle verfügen ähnlich wie die Petri-Netze nicht über einen reellen Zeitparameter, was in manchen Situationen nachteilig ist. Ausgehend vom Modell des Moore-Automaten wird daher eine Verallgemeinerung erarbeitet, bei der keine Taktung mehr erfolgt, sondern eine reelle Zeitachse zugrunde gelegt wird. Solche direkt aus Moore-Automaten hervorgehenden Elementar-Systeme können zu komplexen Systemen zusammengeschaltet werden. Ein Algorithmus für die genaue Simulation komplexer, rückgekoppelter Systeme wird angegeben. Der Algorithmus kann z. B. dazu benutzt werden, um insbesondere Zeitprobleme in großen Schaltwerken aufzudecken. Einige offene Fragen über das neue Systemmodell werden diskutiert.

A Model of Discrete Systems with Real Time Parameter. Previously known system- and process models including Petri-nets do not contain a real time parameter. In some situations this is disadvantageous. Starting with the Moore automaton model a generalization is achieved which does not process its input on a step by step basis, but on a continuous time axis. These so-called elementary systems can be connected together to form complex systems. An algorithm for the exact simulation of such complex systems including feedback is presented. Amongst other things the algorithm can be used to discover timing problems in complex switching circuitry. Several open questions related to the new system model are discussed.

1. Einleitung

Der Prozeß-Begriff hat im zurückliegenden Jahrzehnt in der Informatik eine immer größere Bedeutung erlangt. In vielen komplexeren Rechnersystemen und auch bei der Bewältigung größerer organisatorischer Aufgaben kann nämlich mit dem klassischen Algorithmus-Begriff nur noch eine sehr unvollkommene Modellierung der notwendigen Funktionsabläufe erzielt werden. So bestehen z. B. neuere Betriebssysteme auch für recht kleine Rechner in ihrem Kern aus einem Prozeß-Verwalter. Dieser erfüllt die zentrale Aufgabe, alle als Einzel-Prozesse abzuwickelnden Aktivitäten zu koordinieren und zu überwachen. Hand in Hand mit der praktischen Bedeutung des Prozeß-Begriffes hat sich auch eine umfangreiche, meist theoretische Literatur entwickelt. So gewannen auch die Petri-Netze erst in den siebziger Jahren nachhaltiges wissenschaftliches Interesse, obwohl sie bereits 1962 definiert und eingeführt wurden.

Der entscheidende Unterschied zwischen einem Algorithmus-Ablauf und einem Prozeß-Ablauf besteht darin, daß Algorithmen — zumindest nach klassischer Diktion — keine kommunikativen Vorgänge mit einer Umwelt abwickeln. Der theoretische Begriff der Berechenbarkeit, wie er z. B. auch auf der Basis der Turing-

Maschine normalerweise entwickelt wird, basiert z. B. stets auf dem Begriff der berechenbaren Funktionen. Berechnungen einer Turing-Maschine erfolgen so, daß eine Konfigurationsfolge durchlaufen wird, bis eventuell ein Endzustand erreicht wird. Während die Maschine jedoch arbeitet, wird nur die auf dem Speicherband abgelegte Information berücksichtigt und keineswegs irgendwelche sonstige Information aus der Umwelt. Dieses ist ein wesentliches Kennzeichen von Algorithmen im klassischen Sinn. Bei den Prozessen ergeben sich dagegen zusätzliche kommunikative und synchronisierende Beziehungen zu anderen Prozessen der Umwelt.

In der Literatur hat es sich eingebürgert, nur das Ablaufgeschehen — also die Folge der durchlaufenen Zustände, Operationen und ausgelösten Ereignisse — als *Prozeß* zu bezeichnen (Deussen [1]). Außerdem liegt einem informationsverarbeitenden Prozeß in aller Regel auch eine Definition dessen zugrunde, wie der Prozeß funktioniert. Das ist z. B. ein Programm, eine digitale Schaltung usw. Diese Definition bzw. die physikalische Realisierung, die gewissermaßen Prozesse erzeugt, wollen wir als *System* bezeichnen. Das steht in gutem Einklang mit dem normalen Sprachgebrauch, reden wir doch auch von Betriebssystemen, Rechensystemen, Semi-Thue-Systemen usw. Selbstverständlich können im Sinne der obigen Festlegungen auch viele Automaten als Systeme bezeichnet werden.

Untersuchungen über Prozeßstrukturen werden gewöhnlich so durchgeführt, daß der Zeitparameter aus dem System und den resultierenden Prozeßabläufen entfernt ist. Das wird durch den Wunsch begründet, die Funktionsweise und die Leistungen eines komplexeren Systems invariant von der Zeit zu gestalten. Bei der Untersuchung von Betriebssystemstrukturen — aber nicht nur hier — ist dieses Vorgehen sehr günstig. Ein typisches, inzwischen weithin bekanntes Systemmodell ohne Zeitparameter sind z. B. die Petri-Netze [2].

Nun gibt es bei der Systemmodellierung aber auch Situationen, wo der Zeitparameter nicht einfach vernachlässigt werden sollte. Das betrifft z. B. die Schaltwerks-Konstruktion und -Analyse. Außerdem ist es vom theoretischen Standpunkt aus unbefriedigend, daß in der Literatur praktisch nur Beschreibungsmethoden ohne Zeitparameter untersucht werden. Daher wird in dieser Arbeit ein Systemmodell für komplexe Prozesse eingeführt, das mit einem reellen Zeitparameter ausgestattet ist und ansonsten aber nur über diskrete Signal- und Zustandsmengen verfügt. Eine erste Untersuchung dieses Systemmodells zeigt, daß insbesondere elementare Schaltwerke sehr allgemein und wirklichkeitsgetreu modelliert werden können. Es zeigt sich auch, daß die Simulation komplexer Systeme recht übersichtlich möglich ist, da ein nicht sehr umfangreicher Simulationsalgorithmus angegeben wird. Eine ganze Reihe interessanter Fragen kann jedoch im Rahmen dieser Arbeit nicht beantwortet werden. Darunter fallen z. B. Fragen der Lebendigkeit und Robustheit von Systemen mit Zeitparameter.

Ähnliche Funktionsmodelle, wie sie hier eingeführt werden, sind aus dem Gebiet der temporären Logik bekannt. So hat z. B. Sifakis [3] logische Funktionen mit reellem Zeitparameter eingeführt und ausführlich untersucht, die als ein Spezialfall des hier eingeführten Modelles gelten können. Dagegen ist die Arbeit von Ramchandani [4] über sogenannte "timed Petri nets" nicht direkt mit unserem

Ansatz zu vergleichen. Auch die sequentiellen (getakteten) booleschen Gleichungen etwa im Sinne von Even und Meyer [5] zielen in eine ganz andere Richtung.

2. Elementare diskrete Systeme

Das Systemmodell mit Zeitparameter wird einsichtiger, wenn die wichtigsten Forderungen quasi als Axiomensystem zusammengestellt werden, die schließlich zu der hier vorgestellten Definition geführt haben. Die Definition sollte insbesondere die Realitäten widerspiegeln:

(1) Das Modell für die Zeit sind die reellen Zahlen.

(2) Jede Informationsänderung (einschließlich Zustandsänderungen) benötigt Zeit, es gibt also keine zeitlosen Vorgänge.

(3) Zustände und Signalmengen von Systemen sind endlich.

(4) In jedem endlichen Zeitintervall sind nur endlich viele Zustands- und Ausgangssignal-Änderungen möglich.

(5) Jedes System ist mit endlich viel diskreter Information und einer endlichen Menge reeller Zahlen beschreibbar.

Mit dem klassischen Automatenmodell von Moore [6] als Leitbild wurde schließlich folgende Definition entwickelt:

Definition 1. Ein Quintupel $S = (X, Y, Z, \delta, \tau, \mu)$ heißt *Elementar-System*, wenn gilt:

(1) X, Y und Z sind endliche Mengen, wobei X Menge der Eingabesignale, Y Menge der Ausgabesignale, Z Menge der Zustände.

(2) δ ist eine Abbildung $\delta: Z \times X \to Z$, die Zustands-Fortschalt-Abbildung.

(3) τ ist eine Abbildung $\tau: Z \times X \to R_+$ in die nichtnegativen reellen Zahlen R_+, genannt die Reaktionszeit-Abbildung, für die

$$\forall z \in Z \; \forall x \in X (\tau(z, x) = 0 \to \delta(z, x) = z)$$

gilt. (Diese Bedingung besagt, daß die Reaktionszeit nur dann 0 sein kann, wenn ohnehin keine Zustandsänderung eintritt.)

(4) μ ist eine Abbildung $\mu: Z \to Y$, die Ausgabe-Abbildung.

Ein solches Elementar-System ist eine eigenständige funktionale Einheit. Es verarbeitet Eingabesignale und erzeugt dadurch einen Zustandsübergangs-Prozeß. Der Ausgabeprozeß ist wegen der einfachen Gestalt von μ direkt vom Zustandsprozeß abgeleitet. Leider ist die genaue Definition der Funktionsweise nicht mehr so einfach wie bei endlichen Automaten möglich. Denn die Prozesse spielen sich jetzt auf der reellen Zeitachse ab, was gegenüber getakteten Systemen erhebliche zusätzliche Probleme mit sich bringt. (Die getakteten Systeme, die ja von der Automatentheorie her wohlbekannt sind, haben als Zeitmodell die natürlichen Zahlen). Die definierten Elementar-Systeme verhalten sich ähnlich wie die klassischen Moore-Automaten, bei denen das Eingabesignal im Takt t keinen Einfluß auf das Ausgabesignal im Takt t, sondern frühestens auf die Automatenausgabe im

Takt $t+1$ hat. Die τ-Abbildung legt dabei fest, wie lange ein Eingabesignal ununterbrochen am Eingang anliegen muß, um eine Zustandsfortschaltung zu bewirken. Das bedeutet also: Wenn im Zustand z das Signal x für die Zeitdauer $\tau(z,x) \in R_+$ oder auch länger am Eingang des Systems anliegt, so schaltet das System genau nach der Zeit $\tau(z,x)$ in den Zustand $\delta(z,x)$ um. Liegt das Signal x nicht lange genug an, so erfolgt kein Zustandsübergang. Systeme werden also in gewisser Hinsicht als träge betrachtet, was zur Folge hat, daß zu schnelle Änderungen der Eingabe wirkungslos sind.

Definition 2. Eine Abbildung $f\colon R_+ \to X$ heißt reguläre diskrete Zeitfunktion über X, wenn gilt:

In jedem endlichen Intervall $(t_0, t_n]$ von R_+ gibt es endlich viele Werte $t_1, t_2, \ldots, t_{n-1}$ sowie eine Folge $x_1, x_2, \ldots, x_n$, so daß gilt:

$$\forall i(i = 1(1)n)\ \forall t(t_{i-1} < t \leqslant t_i)(f(t) = x_i).$$

Reguläre diskrete Zeitfunktionen werden im folgenden einfach Zeitfunktionen genannt.

Ohne in Zukunft ausdrücklich darauf hinzuweisen, nehmen wir an, daß es sich bei der Eingabe für Systeme stets um reguläre diskrete Zeitfunktionen handelt. Außerdem legen wir ein für allemal fest, daß Änderungen einer diskreten Größe auf der Zeitachse stets so erfolgen: Im Zeitpunkt der Änderung bleibt noch der alte Wert formal bestehen. Die Zeitintervalle, in denen ein Signal einen bestimmten Wert hat, sind also links offen und rechts abgeschlossen.

Die genaue Spezifikation der Funktionsweise von Elementar-Systemen läßt sich am einfachsten durch einen sequentiellen Algorithmus angeben, der Elementar-Systeme simuliert.

Definition 3. Ein Elementar-System $S = (X, Y, Z, \delta, \tau, \mu)$ gemäß Definition 1 möge sich zum Zeitpunkt $t = 0$ im Zustand $z_0 \in Z$ befinden. Der Eingabeprozeß für das System möge durch eine Zeitfunktion f über X gegeben sein. Diese sei durch zwei Folgen

$$x(1),\ x(2), \ldots \qquad \in X$$
$$t(0) = 0,\ t(1),\ t(2), \ldots \qquad \in R_+$$

definiert, wobei für $t(i-1) < t \leqslant t(i)\ f(t) = x(i)$ gilt. Dann erzeugt der unten angegebene sequentielle Algorithmus zwei Folgen

$$z(1), z(2), \ldots \qquad \in Z$$
$$tz(1), tz(2), \ldots \qquad \in R_+,$$

die analog wie oben erläutert, eine Zeitfunktion über Z bestimmen. Diese Zeitfunktion ist der Zustands-Prozeß des Systems, wenn dieses im Anfangszustand z_0 mit dem Eingabeprozeß f gespeist wird.

Erläuterung zu dem Algorithmus:

Treal = Realzeit-Parameter der Simulation
$x$akt = das seit der Zeit Treal anliegende x-Signal
Tx = Zeitdauer, während der $x$akt (seit Treal) bereits anliegt
Z = aktueller Zustand

(*Initialisierungen*)

$$Treal := 0; \ Z := z_0; \ j := 1;$$

$$Tx := t(1); \ xakt := x(1); \ i := 2;$$

While True Do
    Begin (*Zustandsfortschaltungen, falls möglich*)
      If $\tau(Z, xakt) = 0$ **Then** (*Sonderfall $\delta(z, x) = z$*)
        Begin
            $Treal := Treal + Tx;$
            $Tz(j) := Treal$
            $z(j) := Z;$
            $j := j + 1;$
            $Tx := 0$
        End
      Else
      While $\tau(Z, xakt) \leqslant Tx$ **Do** (*reguläre Zustandsfortschaltung*)
        Begin
            $Treal := Treal + \tau(Z, akt);$
            $tz(j) := Treal;$
            $z(j) := Z;$
            $j := j + 1;$
            $Tx := Tx - \tau(Z, xakt);$
            $Z := \delta(Z, xakt);$
        End;

    (*Erfassung eines Eingabe-Schrittes*)

    If $xakt = x(i)$ **Then Begin** $Tx := Tx + t(i) - t(i - 1);$
                                      $i := i + 1;$
                            End
                    Else Begin (*Wechsel in der Eingabe*)
                    $Treal := Treal + Tx;$
                    $tz(j) := Treal;$
                    $z(j) := Z;$
                    $j := j + 1;$
                    $Tx := t(i) - t(i - 1);$
                    $xakt := x(i);$
                    $i := i + 1;$
                    End;
    End;

Der Ausgabeprozeß ergibt sich aus dem erzeugten Zustandsprozeß, indem für $j - 1, 2, \ldots$ der Zustand $Z(j)$ durch $\mu(Z(j))$ ersetzt wird.

Beispiel. Ein Modulo-4-Zähler kann wie folgt durch eine Tabelle spezifiziert werden:

Z	μ	0	1
0	0	0, 0	1, 0.2
1	1	1, 0	2, 0.3
2	2	2, 0	3, 0.2
3	3	3, 0	0, 0.5

Daraus liest man z. B. ab: $Z = \{0, 1, 2, 3\}$, $X = \{0, 1\}$, $Y = Z$, $\delta(2, 1) = 3$ sowie $\tau(2, 1) = 0.2$.

Der Eingabeprozeß

$$X: \quad 0 \quad 1 \quad 0 \quad 1 \quad 0 \quad 1 \ldots$$
$$R_+: 0.3 \; 0.9 \; 1.7 \; 2.4 \; 2.7 \; 2.9 \ldots$$

erzeugt folgenden Zustandsprozeß, falls der Automat sich zum Zeitpunkt 0 im Zustand 0 befindet:

$$Z: \quad 0 \quad 0 \quad 1 \quad 2 \quad 2 \quad 3 \quad 0 \quad 0 \quad 1$$
$$R_+: 0.3 \; 0.5 \; 0.8 \; 1.7 \; 1.9 \; 2.4 \; 2.7 \; 2.9 \ldots .$$

Das eingeführte Systemmodell kann als eine Verallgemeinerung des Moore-Automaten auf reelle Zeit betrachtet werden. Es wird sich später noch zeigen, daß die meisten realen Effekte in digitalen Schaltungen, wie z. B. Hazards, rückgekoppelte reale Gatter usw., problemlos modelliert werden können. Das Modell ist zunächst deterministisch, was unter anderem dazu führt, daß die sich ergebenden Zustandsprozesse von ihrer Struktur her uninteressant sind. Das ändert sich im nichtdeterministischen Fall, der sich ergibt, wenn die Abbildung δ in die Gestalt $\delta: Z \times X \to 2^Z$ gebracht wird, wobei 2^Z die Potenzmenge von Z darstellt. Diese Entwicklung wird in dieser Arbeit nicht weiter verfolgt.

3. Aufbau zusammengesetzter Systeme aus Elementar-Systemen

Im Gegensatz zu Algorithmen können Prozesse in großem Umfang mit ihrer Umgebung Kommunikation betreiben, wodurch sich die Möglichkeit ergibt, komplexe Systeme zusammenzusetzen. Aus vielen Bereichen der Automatentheorie ist jedoch bekannt, daß für einen gegebenen Formalismus, wie z. B. die Mealy-Automaten oder die stochastischen Automaten, folgendes Gesetz gilt:

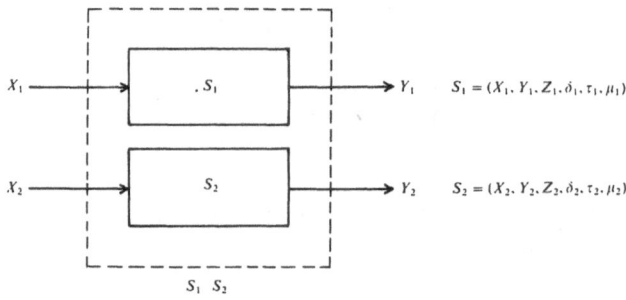

Abb. 1

Wenn man einen oder mehrere Automaten zu einem neuen, größeren Automaten zusammenschaltet, so ist das zusammengesetzte System mit dem gleichen Formalismus beschreibbar wie die einzelnen Bestandteile. Für die oben eingeführten Elementar-Systeme läßt sich zeigen, daß ein zusammengesetztes System in der Regel nicht mehr als ein großes und komplexes Elementar-System aufgefaßt werden kann. Um dies zu beweisen, betrachtet man zunächst den einfachsten Fall einer Zusammenschaltung, nämlich die reine Parallelschaltung zweier Systeme S_1, S_2 gemäß Abb. 1.

Die Parallelschaltung $S_1//S_2$ führt offensichtlich zu einem neuen System, welches $X_1 \times X_2$ als Eingabe-Signalmenge und $Y_1 \times Y_2$ als Ausgabe-Signalmenge aufweist.

Satz 1. *Die Parallel-Schaltung $S_1//S_2$ zweier durch Abbildungen δ_i, τ_i, μ_i ($i = 1, 2$) im Sinne von Definition 1 darstellbarer Elementar-Systeme kann im allgemeinen nicht mehr als ein einzelnes komplexeres Elementar-System dargestellt werden. Das gleiche gilt auch für die Serienschaltung, für Schaltungen mit Rückkoppelungen usw.*

Beweis. Es genügt, die Behauptung durch ein Gegenbeispiel zu belegen. S_1 und S_2 mögen identisch zu dem Elementar-System aus Beispiel 1 sein. Betrachte auf beiden Eingangsleitungen. den Eingabeprozeß

$$X: \qquad 0 \qquad\quad 1 \quad \dots$$
$$R_+: \quad 0.1+\varepsilon \quad 0.3+\varepsilon \dots \qquad (\varepsilon \geqslant 0).$$

Das jeweils zum Zeitpunkt $T_{real} = 0$ im Zustand $z = 0$ gestartete System liefert offensichtlich zum Zeitpunkt $0.3 + \varepsilon$ eine Änderung der Ausgabe. Da bei dem System $S_1//S_2$ sich stets dann eine Ausgabeänderung ergibt, wenn mindestens eines der Teilsysteme die Ausgabe ändert, kann durch kleine Änderungen in der Eingabe erreicht werden, daß sich in beliebig kurzen Zeitabständen die Ausgabe von $S_1//S_2$ ändert. Die Elementar-Systeme gemäß Definition 1 haben diese Eigenschaften nicht, denn die Werte $\tau(z, x)$ haben — abgesehen von den Spezialfällen $\tau(z, x) = 0$ — ein von 0 verschiedenes Minimum, τ_{min}. Für diesen Wert τ_{min}, der gemäß

$$\tau_{min} := \text{Min } \tau(z, x),$$
$$(z, x) \in Z \times X$$
$$\tau(z, x) \neq 0$$

definiert ist, gilt wegen der Endlichkeit der Menge $Z x X$ stets $\tau_{min} > 0$. Es gilt außerdem, daß zwischen je zwei aufeinanderfolgenden Änderungen des Zustands und damit der Ausgabe des Elementar-Systems mindestens die Zeitspanne τ_{min} verstreicht. Da das oben eingeführte ε beliebig positiv gewählt werden kann, ist damit bewiesen, daß das System $S_1//S_2$ im allgemeinen nicht mehr als Elementar-System dargestellt werden kann. Da diese Beweisführung offensichtlich für alle Teilsysteme S_1 und S_2 gilt, bei denen durch die Eingabe eine Ausgabe-Änderung angestoßen werden kann, gilt die bewiesene Aussage für praktisch alle nicht-trivialen Elementar-Systeme S_1, S_2.

Mit dem gleichen Beweis-Prinzip läßt sich ohne größere Schwierigkeiten zeigen, daß auch die System-Schaltungen von Abb. 2 in der Regel nicht als Elementar-

Systeme dargestellt werden können, obwohl die einzelnen Teilsysteme nach Voraussetzung elementar sind. Offen bleibt die Frage, ob es nicht auch komplexere Zusammenschaltungen von Elementar-Systemen gibt, die sich insgesamt wieder als Elementar-Systeme erweisen – unabhängig von der speziellen Natur der Bestandteile.

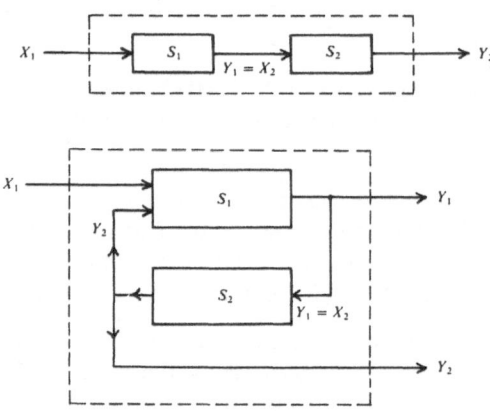

Abb. 2. S_1, S_2 Elementar-Systeme, die Zusammenschaltungen sind im allgemeinen nicht mehr elementar, vergleiche Satz 1

Aus dem negativen Resultat des Satzes 1 wird deutlich, warum in Definition 1 der Terminus „Elementar-System" gewählt wurde. Dieser Begriff ist in der Tat sinnvoll, zumal das weitere Interesse sicherlich mehr den zusammengesetzten Systemen als den einzelnen Elementar-Systemen gilt. Man kann aus Satz 1 auch noch den Schluß ziehen, daß zusammengesetzte Systeme prinzipiell allgemeinere Prozesse erzeugen können als die Elementar-Systeme.

4. Genaue Simulation komplexerer zusammengesetzter Systeme

Obwohl in Satz 1 festgestellt wurde, daß zusammengesetzte Systeme sich im allgemeinen nicht mehr mit Elementar-Systemen gleichsetzen lassen, wurde das tatsächliche Verhalten solcher zusammengesetzter Systeme nicht formal definiert. Vielmehr wurde von der Vorstellung ausgegangen, daß auch bei reeller Zeitachse das Fortleiten von Signalen so lange zeitlos erfolgt, wie die Information nicht von einem Teilsystem verarbeitet wird. Das gilt auch für Rückkoppelungen. Insbesondere beim Vorliegen von Rückkoppelungen muß jedoch sorgfältig untersucht werden, ob das System nicht in eine widersprüchliche Situation hineinläuft oder die Funktionsweise sonstwie undefiniert wird. Um diese offenen Punkte zu klären, soll ein Algorithmus angegeben werden, der die Funktionsweise von n miteinander verschalteten Elementar-Systemen genau simuliert. Unter einer genauen Simulation verstehen wir eine solche Simulation, die sämtliche beteiligten Parameter exakt und nicht etwa nur näherungsweise liefert. Wir betrachten demgemäß n elementare Systeme $S_1, S_2, \ldots, S_n$, deren Signalmengen X und Y im allgemeinen Fall die Gestalt eines kartesischen Produktes, wie in Abb. 3 angedeutet, haben.

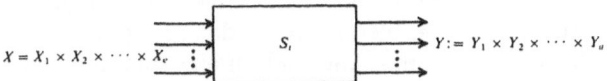

Abb. 3. Elementar-System S_i mit Signalmengen bestehend aus kartesischen Produkten

Ein aus Elementar-Systemen zusammengesetztes komplexes System ist dann so aufgebaut, daß

(a) die externen Eingabeleitungen in das System hineinführen und nur mit Eingabeleitungen von Elementar-Systemen verbunden sind,

(b) einige aus Elementar-Systemen austretende Ausgabeleitungen insgesamt aus dem zusammengesetzten System herausgeführt sind (Ausgabeleitungen des zusammengesetzten Systems),

(c) Ausgabe-Leitungen von Elementar-Systemen auf eventuell mehrere Eingänge von Elementar-Systemen geschaltet sind,

(d) jede einzelne Eingabe-Leitung der Elementar-Systeme entweder mit einer externen Eingabeleitung oder einer internen Ausgabeleitung (Rückkoppelung) verbunden ist.

Diese Regeln ergeben sich aus physikalischen Notwendigkeiten, denn eine Leitung kann z. B. nicht von zwei verschiedenen Signalquellen gespeist werden, ohne daß sofort undefinierte Situationen auftreten.

Um die Funktionsweise des Gesamtsystems zu verfolgen, müssen zunächst einmal alle Signale auf den externen Eingabeleitungen (nach Annahme vollständig bekannt) und auf den intern erzeugten Eingabeleitungen (Rückkoppelungen) genau verfolgt werden, was hier im einzelnen nicht programmiert werden soll. Dieser Signalverfolgungsmodul wird jedoch mit Informationen versorgt, und zwar durch den Proceduraufruf

$$\text{Zukunft}(k, z_k, T).$$

Die eingesetzten Parameter-Werte bedeuten: Beim Elementar-System mit Index k bleibt der Zustand z_k mindestens bis zur Realzeit T bestehen. Die Signalverfolgung verfügt über die μ_k-Funktionen der einzelnen Elementar-Systeme und kann daher aus den Zustandsinformationen sofort deren Ausgabe ermitteln. Mit der Funktion

$$\text{Input}(k, x_k, T) \to \text{Zeitangabe}$$

wird bei dem Signalverfolgungsmodul angefragt, wie lange, gemessen vom Zeitpunkt T aus, das Eingabesignal x_k noch bei System k anliegen wird (es liegt zum Zeitpunkt T an!). Falls sich das Signal x_k ändert, so wird das neue Signal mit der Funktion

$$\text{Nextinput}(k, T) \to \text{Signalangabe}$$

angefordert. Dabei ist T der Zeitpunkt des Signalwechsels.

Eine weitere Funktion ist für die Simulation bedeutsam:

$$\text{Stabil}(k, z_k, x_k, T) \to \text{Zeitangabe}$$

liefert als Ergebnis die Zeitspanne, die das Elementar-System mit Index k noch mindestens im Zustand z_k verbleibt, wenn das Eingabesignal x_k bereits die Zeitspanne T anliegt. Das Resultat kann durch eine allerdings nicht ganz triviale Analyse der Abbildungen δ_k und τ_k berechnet werden. Der einfache Aufruf

$$\text{Stabil}(k, z_k)$$

ist äquivalent zu $\text{Stabil}(k, z_k, x_k, 0)$.

Um den angekündigten Simulationsalgorithmus formulieren zu können, werden neben den oben erläuterten Funktionen für jedes Elementar-System S_k ($k = 1, \ldots, n$) folgende Variable initialisiert und geführt:

z_k = Zustand des Systems mit Index k,
$Treal_k$ = Realzeit, bis zu der System k simuliert ist,
x_k = aktuelles Eingabesignal für System k,
Tx_k = Zeitraum vor $Treal_k$, während dem x_k bereits (unverändert) anliegt.

T_0 und „Schaltzeit" sind Hilfsvariable. Die Abbildungen δ_k und τ_k gehören jeweils zu dem System S_k.

Algorithmus.

(0) Initialisierungen:

$Treal_k := 0;\ Tx := 0;$ $\forall k(k = 1, \ldots, n)$
$z_k :=$ Anfangszustand für Teilsystem k; $\forall k(k = 1, \ldots, n)$
Zukunft$(k, z_k, \text{Stabil}(k, z_k))$; $\forall k(k = 1, \ldots, n)$
$x_k :=$ Nextinput$(k, 0)$; $\forall k(k = 1, \ldots, n)$
$k := 0;$

(1) $k := k + 1;$ Falls $k = n + 1$, setze $k := 1.$

(2) Bestimme die (bis zu diesem Augenblick bekannte) Zeitdauer T_0 für die sich die Eingabe x_k auch nach dem Zeitpunkt $Treal_k$ nicht ändern wird:

$$T_0 := \text{Input}(k, x_k, Treal_k);$$

(Zum Zeitpunkt $Treal_k$ liegt stets die Eingabe x_k an.)

(3) Falls $T_0 = 0$, so ermittle das unmittelbar nach dem Zeitpunkt $Treal_k$ vorliegende Eingabesignal:

$$x_k := \text{Nextinput}(k, Treal_k);$$
$$Tx_k := 0;$$

Weiter bei (1).

(4) Falls $\tau_k(z_k, x_k) = 0$, so muß auch $\delta_k(z_k, x_k) = z_k$ gelten, und es ist auszuführen:

$$Treal_k := Treal_k + T_0;$$
$$\text{Zukunft}(k, z_k, Treal_k + \text{Stabil}(k, z_k))$$
$$Tx_k := 0;$$

Weiter bei (1).

(5) Falls $Tx_k + T_0 < \tau_k(z_k, x_k)$, so ist auszuführen:

$$Treal_k := Treal_k + T_0;$$
$$Tx_k := Tx_k + T_0;$$
$$Zukunft(k, z_k, Treal_k + Stabil(k, z_k, x_k, Tx_k));$$

Weiter bei (1).

(6) Falls $Tx_k + T_0 \geqslant \tau_k(z_k, x_k)$, so ist auszuführen:

$$Schaltzeit := Treal_k - Tx_k + \tau_k(z_k, x_k);$$

(Zu diesem Zeitpunkt findet ein Zustandsübergang statt.)

$$Treal_k := Schaltzeit;$$
$$Tx_k := 0;$$
$$Zukunft(k, z_k, Schaltzeit);$$
$$z_k := \delta_k(z_k, x_k);$$
$$Zukunft(k, z_k, Treal_k + Stabil(k, z_k));$$

Weiter bei (1).

Ende des Algorithmus.

Eine Analyse des Algorithmus zeigt, daß er in der vorliegenden Gestalt nicht terminiert, da keine Endzeit für die Simulation vorgegeben ist, was aber leicht zu korrigieren wäre. Außerdem könnte die primitive Schleife (1) sicher dadurch verbessert werden, daß nur jeweils solche Systeme S_k mit minimalem Wert $Treal_k$ abgearbeitet werden. Die Korrektheit des Algorithmus ist formal nicht an-zweifelbar, da er ja anstelle einer viel zu komplizierten Definition für das Verhalten zusammengesetzter Systeme steht. Die einzige, noch wirklich offene Frage lautet daher: Kann der Algorithmus beim Vorliegen unglücklicher Umstände auf der Zeitachse stecken bleiben?

Satz 2. *Der angegebene Algorithmus hat folgende Eigenschaft: Jeder vorgebbare Wert für* $Treal_k \in T_+$ *wird in endlich vielen Simulationsschritten übertroffen.*

Beweis. Offensichtlich bilden die verschiedenen Werte, die eine Variable $Treal_k$ annimmt, eine monoton wachsende Folge. Um den Satz zu beweisen, muß gezeigt werden, daß keiner dieser Folgen konvergiert. Wenn nun angenommen wird, daß bei einer Simulation einige der Elementar-Systeme, z. B. diejenigen mit Index $k_1, k_2, \ldots, k_r$, tatsächlich in das Konvergenzproblem hineinlaufen, so bedeutet dies, daß sich für die Werte $Treal_{k_1}, \ldots, Treal_{k_r}$ unüberwindbare Schranken ergeben. Die Eingabe für diese Systeme kann also höchstens bis zu den Zeiten $Treal_{k_1}, \ldots, Treal_{k_r}$ ermittelt werden. Es interessieren nun die Systeme, deren Grenzwerte $Treal$ minimal sind. Es seien dies die Systeme $k_1, k_2, \ldots, k_s$. Jedes dieser Systeme kann offensichtlich deshalb nicht über die Zeit T_{min} hinaus weitersimuliert werden, weil es Eingangssignale vom Ausgang dieser $Treal$-minimalen Systeme bezieht (Rück-koppelung), denn sonst wäre der Grenzwert T_{min} sofort überwindbar. Mindestens eines dieser Systeme muß bei der Simulation unmittelbar vor dem Konvergenz-punkt unter den Fall (5) fallen, denn bei Fall (4) und (6) ergibt sich folgende Aussage: Es gibt ein $\varepsilon > 0$, so daß $Stabil(k, z_k)$ stets größer ist als ε, und zwar für alle

Parameter-Kombinationen. Nur ein unter Fall (5) fallendes Teilsystem kann also verhindern, daß die Eingabe über den Konvergenzpunkt T_{min} hinaus bekannt wird. Für dieses System ist dann aber der Konvergenzpunkt T_{min} gleichzeitig auch ein Zeitpunkt, wo es den Zustand gemäß (6) wechselt. Wenn also die Eingaben für alle Systeme bis zum Zeitpunkt T_{min} bekannt sind, so bewirkt der Fall (6) ein Fortschreiten über diesen kritischen Punkt hinaus, womit der Satz 2 bewiesen ist.

Die Existenz eines sequentiellen, von einem Zeitparameter unabhängigen Simulations-Algorithmus für beliebig komplexe, parallel arbeitende Systeme wirft eine grundsätzlich wichtige Frage auf: Wenn die Anzahl n der beteiligten Elementar-Systeme in Beziehung gesetzt wird zum Rechenaufwand (= Zeitkomplexität) des sequentiellen Simulations-Algorithmus, welcher Simulationsverlust ist dann gegeben? Die Beantwortung dieser noch offenen Fragen steht in unmittelbarem theoretischem Zusammenhang mit Fragen der Rechnerarchitektur. Falls komplexe Systeme mit einem hohen Ausmaß an interner Kommunikation mit der Zeitdehnung n = Anzahl der Teilsysteme sequentiell simuliert werden können, wären komplexere Systeme ökonomisch nicht erstrebenswert. Ergibt sich hingegen eine Zeitdehnung $f(n)$ mit $f(n) > n$, so wären komplexere Systeme mit hohem Grad an Parallelarbeit ökonomischer als rein sequentielle Systeme – zumindest bei typischen parallel abwickelbaren Aufgaben. Der angegebene Algorithmus hat eine Zeitdehnung von n im günstigsten Fall (n nicht miteinander kommunizierende Elementar-Systeme). In ungünstigen Fällen (n vollständig miteinander kommunizierende Teilsysteme) ergibt sich der Wert n^2. Konkrete Schlüsse sollten aus diesen Werten noch nicht gezogen werden, da es ja möglich ist, daß ein besserer Algorithmus existiert. Es sollte der Vollständigkeit halber erwähnt werden, daß getaktete Systeme mit ganzzahligem Zeitparameter stets mit der Zeitdehnung n sequentiell simuliert werden können. Das gleiche gilt für Petri-Netze, wobei bei diesen die Anzahl der durchschnittlich im Netz bewegten Markierungen die Rolle von n übernimmt.

5. Zusammenfassung und Ausblick

Die eingeführten diskreten deterministischen Systeme mit reellem Zeitparameter führen zu Systemen und Prozessen, die im Vergleich zu Petri-Netzen noch wenig abstrakt sind. Der reelle Zeitparameter eröffnet Möglichkeiten der Modellierung, wo die gewöhnliche Automatentheorie oder die Prozeß-Theorien versagen. So ist es möglich, mit zwei als Elementar-Systeme definierten NOR-Gattern durch die bekannte Rückkoppelung (z. B. Klar [7], Seite 118) ein RS-Flip-Flop zu erhalten, ohne daß irgendwelche besonderen Annahmen zu machen wären. Das so modellierte Flip-Flop verhält sich sehr wirklichkeitsgetreu. Mit einem einzelnen rückgekoppelten NOR kann z. B. ein Oszillator aufgebaut werden. Komplexere Beispiele von größerem Interesse erhält man, wenn z. B. asynchrone Kommunikation zwischen zwei Systemen auf Handshaking-Basis modelliert wird.

Neben solchen, aus didaktischen Gründen sicher nicht uninteressanten Schaltungen interessieren aber in der Hauptsache die komplexen, aus vielen Einzelteilen zusammengesetzten Systeme. Der vorgestellte Simulations-Algorithmus erscheint geeignet, auch sehr umfangreiche Systeme in kurzer Zeit durchzuspielen. Da es sich um eine genaue Simulation ohne Näherungen irgendwelcher Art handelt, sind die Ergebnisse auch entsprechend interpretierbar. Allerdings wirft das neue Systemmodell weit mehr Fragen auf, als im ersten Schritt beantwortet werden können. Da ist zunächst der Wunsch, die große Bedeutung des Zeitparameters durch konstruktive Maßnahmen zurückzudrängen. Bei den hier vorgestellten Systemen ist der Begriff der τ-Invarianz von Interesse: Ein zusammengesetztes System heißt τ-stabil, wenn kleine Änderungen an den τ-Werten die logischen Leistungen des Systems nicht verändern. Der Zusammenhang mit Bauteile-Toleranzen ist unmittelbar einsichtig.

Für nichtdeterministische Systeme stellen sich eine ganze Reihe von Fragen, die aus der Theorie der Petri-Netze bekannt geworden sind, z. B. die Frage nach der Lebendigkeit und nach der Erreichbarkeit bestimmter Situationen. Auch die Äquivalenz zu anderen Modellen wird noch näher zu untersuchen sein.

Literatur

[1] Deussen, P.: Description of Processes. Proceedings of the ECI73 (Davos), pp. 11 – 17. North-Holland 1974.
[2] Petri, C. A.: Grundsätzliches zur Beschreibung diskreter Prozesse. In: 3. Colloquium über Automatentheorie, Oktober 1965, Hannover (Händler, W., Peschl, E., Unger, H., Hrsg.). Basel: Birkhäuser 1967.
[3] Sifakis, J.: Modèles temporels des Systèmes Logiques. Thèse docteur ingénieur informatique, Université de Grenoble, 1974.
[4] Ramchandani, C.: Analysis of Asynchronous Concurrent Systems by Timed Petri Nets. PhD Thesis, Department of Electrical Engineering, MIT, Cambridge, Mass., 1973.
[5] Even, S., Meyer, A. R.: Sequential Boolean Equations. Trans. IEEE on Computers **18**, 230 – 240 (1969).
[6] Moore, E. F.: Gedanken-Experiments on Sequential Machines. Automata Studies, Ann. Math. Studies (Princeton) **34**, 129 – 153 (1956).
[7] Klar, R.: Digitale Rechenautomaten, 2., erweiterte Aufl. Berlin: Walter de Gruyter 1976.

Prof. Dr. A. Schmitt
Institut für Informatik I
Universität Karlsruhe
Postfach 6380
D-7500 Karlsruhe 1
Bundesrepublik Deutschland

Computing, Suppl. 3, 173—180 (1981)

Algebraic Specification of the Software Controlling a Parcels Distribution Machine

H. J. Schneider, Erlangen

Abstract — Zusammenfassung

Algebraic Specification of the Software Controlling a Parcels Distribution Machine. The algebraic method of software specification has proved its worth in many examples closely related to mathematical problems. In this paper, the method is applied to the development of the software controlling a parcels distribution machine. We show how to derive the axioms from the verbal problem formulation. Our example differs from those often cited in the literature because of the necessity to specify the synchronization between hardware and software.

Algebraische Spezifikation der Steuerungssoftware für eine Paketverteilanlage. Die algebraische Methode zur Spezifikation von Software hat sich bei vielen mathematisch formulierbaren Beispielen als wertvoll erwiesen. In diesem Aufsatz wird sie auf die Entwicklung der Steuerungssoftware für eine Paketverteilanlage angewandt. Wir zeigen, wie die Axiome aus der verbalen Problembeschreibung abgeleitet werden können. Unser Beispiel unterscheidet sich von den in der Literatur oft zitierten, weil die Synchronisation zwischen Software und Hardware bei der Spezifikation berücksichtigt werden muß.

1. Introduction

Dijkstra and many others have pointed out that the degree of complexity the human intellect is able to understand, is much smaller than the complexity of today's software systems [2]. Specifying and implementing such systems, we have to reduce the degree of complexity by dividing the problem into several smaller problems such that each part may be comprehended by one person at all stages of the software development. If necessary, this decomposition must be continued through several levels until easily handled units result. Often, a reduction of complexity may be obtained by abstraction: On each level, only these properties of the objects and operations are considered, which are relevant to this level; other properties are neglected, especially those resulting from implementation details. This is contrary to the "classical" application-programmers' practice of defining representation details first. The method causes the programmer to manipulate or read an object only via the operations defined on its type. This way of programming was first suggested by the class concept of SIMULA and later on studied by Liskov and Zilles in great detail [10].

2. Specification of the Syntax and Semantics

The specification of a data type must include the syntax and semantics of the operations defined on its objects. The syntactic specification assigns an identifier and the type both of the arguments and of the value to each operation. This declaration may be given using the well-known mathematical notation as well as a programming language notation. We consider the very common example of the queue and the mathematical notation:

$$
\begin{aligned}
\text{CREATE\_QUEUE:} &\qquad\qquad\qquad \to \text{queue} \\
\text{ADD:} &\qquad \text{queue} \times \text{element} \to \text{queue} \\
\text{FIRST:} &\qquad\qquad\qquad \text{queue} \to \text{element} \\
\text{REMOVE:} &\qquad\qquad\qquad \text{queue} \to \text{queue} \\
\text{EMPTY:} &\qquad\qquad\qquad \text{queue} \to \text{boolean}
\end{aligned}
$$

The exclusive use of functions whose arguments cannot be altered (i.e. call by value), substantially facilitates mathematical formulation. Nevertheless, this technique sometimes results in an inconvenient and obscure programming style. Guttag, Horowitz, and Musser have shown how to discard this restriction without giving up the mathematically more convenient handling of functions [7]. So far, we have defined the syntactic rules according to which the operations may be applied, not their semantics. In spite of our simple example, the choice of suggestive identifiers does not prevent misunderstandings even in specifying familiar data types.

For some years, different methods to specify semantics have been developed. We must distinguish the operational methods from the algebraic or axiomatic ones. Operational methods use an abstract machine and the set of its states; the semantics of each operation is described by the state transitions which the operation effects. Guttag called special attention to the fact that this method is similar to programming, and programmers easier succeed in interpreting the specification. On the other hand, he rightly pointed out that this method often tempts one to take into account unnecessary details. These details prejudge the implementation both by restricting the number of allowable solutions and by making the proof of correctness more difficult because the unnecessary properties must be verified [4]. The algebraic method avoids these difficulties. As is the custom in algebra, a set of axioms is defined which describe the relation between the operations. This set of axioms must only be complete with regard to the problem specification and include all properties used at the specification level under consideration. Completeness in the mathematical sense is not necessary, but may be of interest because it is able to exclude unexpected situations (and therefore augments the reliability of the specified software) and renders possible the intentional omission of uninteresting properties.

If we specify the queue, the only property we have to define is the FIFO-property. For this, Guttag stated the following axioms

$$
\begin{aligned}
\text{EMPTY(CREATE\_QUEUE)} &= \text{true} \\
\text{EMPTY(ADD}(q,e)) &= \text{false} \\
\text{FIRST(ADD}(q,e)) &= \textbf{if } \text{EMPTY}(q) \textbf{ then } e \\
&\quad\ \textbf{else } \text{FIRST}(q) \textbf{ end if} \\
\text{REMOVE(ADD}(q,e)) &= \textbf{if } \text{EMPTY}(q) \textbf{ then } \text{CREATE\_QUEUE} \\
&\quad\ \textbf{else } \text{ADD(REMOVE}(q),e) \textbf{ end if}
\end{aligned}
$$

Furthermore, it must be mentioned that

FIRST(CREATE_QUEUE) and REMOVE(CREATE_QUEUE)

lead to errors.

Inspecting this example in more detail, we find that we have not defined a single data type, but a set of identically structured data types. The set parameter is the type of the queue elements. This point of view is of importance in designing re-usable software.

Guttag gave two important arguments in favour of the algebraic specification [4]. As mentioned before, it is possible to define communication between several components of a software system without anticipating the details of data storage. These may optimally be scheduled at a later project phase, knowing frequency and mode of access. The second argument is the use in formally verifying the program. The implementation of the system agrees with the specification if and only if the implementation of the operations fulfil each axiom, i.e. if it is a homomorphic image of the heterogeneous algebra given by the axioms. In addition to the usual top-down segmentation, the verification of the whole system is horizontally structured by considering one axiom after the other.

How can we systematically find the relations between the operations? For this, we have to remember that there are two different classes of operations, called V-functions and O-functions by Parnas [12]. V-functions return values, but do not change the objects. O-functions operate on the objects. Because a V-function is the only way to get some information about the objects, the semantics of each operation is completely defined if we state the effects it has on subsequent calls of the V-functions. In our example, FIRST and EMPTY are V-functions, CREATE_QUEUE, ADD, and REMOVE are O-functions. We have to consider the three O-functions and to define which value the V-functions should yield afterwards.

The algebraic method was applied to a larger compiler example by Guttag, Horowitz, and Musser [8] and to a non-mathematically oriented problem, e.g. by Denert [1].

3. Application to the Parcels Distribution Machine

3.1. Problem

As an example we consider the software controlling a parcels distribution machine. The structure of the machine is given in Fig. 1. The parcels arriving at the entry station, are marked by a code defining the target station. The controller reads this code and directs the distribution stations which inform it of the passing of each parcel. The distribution stations are not able to read the code again or to identify the parcel in any other way after it has left the entry station.

Designing the controller which is to be realized by software, we assign parallel software processes to the stations. The communication between them is established by queues: All data about parcels processed by the software of a station, but not yet processed by the software of the following station, are placed in the queue of this second station.

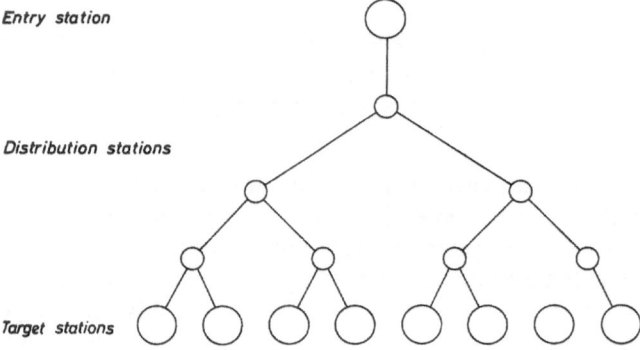

Fig. 1. Structure of the parcels distribution machine

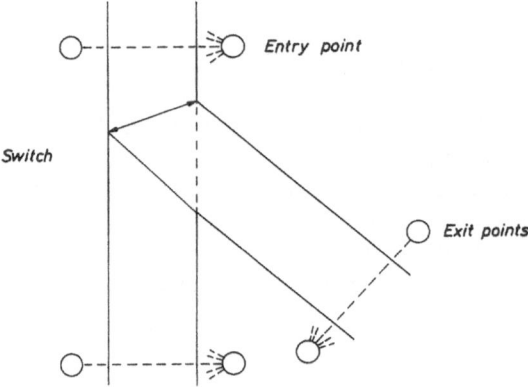

Fig. 2. Structure of a distribution station

Fig. 2 shows the structure of a distribution station. There are photocells at the entry point and at the exit points. These are able to recognize the passing of each parcel with certainty, even if the parcels closely follow one another. The messages from these photocells are evaluated by the software system which determines the control instruction for the next switch from the data read at the entry station. The control instruction may not be sent out until the distribution station is free of parcels. Because the entry station may send parcels with the same target station closely after one another, providing for a safety distance only between parcels with distinct targets, several parcels may be in the same station. If the switch must be shifted, but the parcel has already reached the entry point before its predecessor has left the station (due to differences in speed), shifting does not occur; the parcel follows its predecessor, and an error message is printed out.

3.2. The Data Type "Distribution Station"

The functions defining the data type diststat (= distribution station), are:

$$\begin{aligned}
\text{NEW\_STAT:} &\qquad \text{position} \rightarrow \text{diststat} \\
\text{SHIFT:} &\qquad \text{diststat} \times \text{position} \rightarrow \text{diststat} \\
\text{EMPTY\_STAT:} &\qquad \text{diststat} \rightarrow \text{boolean} \\
\text{POSITION:} &\qquad \text{diststat} \rightarrow \text{position}
\end{aligned}$$

where

$$\text{position} = \{\text{left}, \text{right}\}.$$

NEW_STAT and SHIFT are O-functions, EMPTY_STAT and POSITION are V-functions.

If we consider how to change the result of EMPTY_STAT, we find two other O-functions which are not called at any point of the algorithmic part of the process assigned to the station, but by interrupt processes assigned to the entry and exit points of the station:

$$\begin{aligned}
\text{ENTRY:} &\qquad \text{diststat} \rightarrow \text{diststat} \\
\text{EXIT:} &\qquad \text{diststat} \rightarrow \text{diststat}
\end{aligned}$$

We define the semantics of these functions in specifying the consequences the O-functions induce on an subsequent call of a V-function.

a) Consequences on EMPTY_STAT:

$$\begin{aligned}
\text{EMPTY\_STAT(NEW\_STAT}(p)) &= \text{true} \\
\text{EMPTY\_STAT(SHIFT}(d,p)) &= \text{EMPTY\_STAT}(d) \\
\text{EMPTY\_STAT(ENTRY}(d)) &= \text{false} \\
\text{EMPTY\_STAT(EXIT(ENTRY}(d))) &= \text{EMPTY\_STAT}(d)
\end{aligned}$$

The reader should notice:

(1) We initialize the distribution station with one of the positions, but do not fix it in the definition.

(2) We assume SHIFT to be used only if the distribution station is empty. If we want to ensure this by definition, we must define EMPTY_STAT and SHIFT as hidden procedures as proposed by Guttag, Horowitz, and Musser [7] and make available only an operation TEST_SHIFT in the interface.

b) Consequences on POSITION:

$$\text{POSITION(NEW\_STAT}(p)) = p$$

$$\text{POSITION(SHIFT}(d,p)) = \begin{cases} p & \text{if EMPTY\_STAT}(d) \\ \text{POSITION}(d) & \text{otherwise} \end{cases}$$

$$\text{POSITION(ENTRY}(d)) = \text{POSITION}(d)$$

$$\text{POSITION(EXIT}(d)) = \text{POSITION}(d)$$

3.3. Synchronization

If the switch is to be shifted, the distribution station must be empty. Otherwise, the software process must wait until preceding parcels have left the station. At the same time, the process must observe whether the announced parcel arrives at the entry point. We need an OV-function

$$\text{WAIT: diststat} \rightarrow \text{diststat} \times \{\text{entry, exit, already\_arrived}\}$$

which waits for a parcel passing the entry or exit point and then reports this event, or reports immediately that the parcel had already arrived when the operation was called.

Because the software process of each station must have finished the treatment of a parcel reaching the entry point of this station, this is a suitable point to prevent divergence between software and hardware. Therefore, we must call an operation

$$\text{WAIT\_ENTRY: diststat} \rightarrow \text{diststat} \times \{\text{entry, already\_arrived}\}$$

after shifting the switch, or if we cannot shift. This operation may be either described by the previously defined WAIT:

$$\text{WAIT\_ENTRY} = \textbf{repeat } S := \text{WAIT};$$
$$\textbf{until } S \neq \text{exit } \textbf{end repeat}$$

or independently defined in an analogous way. We prefer the second possibility because the first one includes details of implementation.

WAIT is both a V-function as well as an O-function. Specifying sequential processes, Guttag, Horowitz, and Musser recommend its decomposition into two components [7]

$$\text{WAIT}(d) = (\text{WAIT}_1(d), \text{WAIT}_2(d))$$

where

$$\text{WAIT}_1\text{: diststat} \rightarrow \text{diststat}$$

is an O-function,

$$\text{WAIT}_2\text{: diststat} \rightarrow \{\text{entry, exit, already\_arrived}\}$$

is a V-function. If we consider both components separately in the module interface, a new problem arises: WAIT operates immediately on the data structure representing the station, but control will not be returned until the result of WAIT_2 has been determined. In the calling process both components must always appear immediately following one another, but within the module the operations ENTRY and EXIT may occur between the components. This is contrary to sequential problems. This special aspect must be taken into consideration if we specify the effect the O-function WAIT_1 has on the V-function WAIT_2:

$$\text{WAIT}_2(\text{ENTRY}(\text{WAIT}_1(\text{NEW\_STAT}(p)))) = \text{entry}$$
$$\text{WAIT}_2(\text{WAIT}_1(\text{ENTRY}(\text{NEW\_STAT}(p)))) = \text{already\_arrived}$$
$$\text{WAIT}_2(\text{EXIT}(\text{WAIT}_1(\text{NEW\_STAT}(p)))) \quad = \text{exit}$$

$WAIT_1$ has no immediate effect on the other V-functions:

$$POSITION(WAIT_1(d)) = POSITION(d)$$
$$EMPTY\_STAT(WAIT_1(d)) = EMPTY\_STAT(d)$$
$$EMPTY\_STAT(EXIT(WAIT_1(d))) = EMPTY\_STAT(EXIT(d))$$

Furthermore, we must consider the fact that a call of WAIT must correspond to each ENTRY. It would be wrong to write

$$ENTRY(WAIT_1(NEW\_STAT(p))) = NEW\_STAT(p)$$

because this ignores the effect on EMPTY_STAT. This equality is true only in combination with a subsequent $WAIT_2$:

$$f(ENTRY(WAIT_1(NEW\_STAT(p)))) = f(NEW\_STAT(p))$$

where f denotes one of the following functions:

$$f(d) = \begin{cases} WAIT_2(ENTRY(WAIT_1(d))) & \text{or} \\ WAIT_2(EXIT(WAIT_1(d))) & \text{or} \\ WAIT_2(WAIT_1(ENTRY(d))). \end{cases}$$

In this example, we need not consider the discussion brought about by a paper of Majster because f may be replaced by a finite number of cases [11].

4. Conclusion

This paper was initiated by a working group which compared several specification methods using the same problem: the parcels distribution machine. The author was in doubt whether the algebraic method would be able to solve the problem. The first attempt seemed to confirm this because the synchronization and the possibility of operations being interrupted conflict with the mathematical concept of an operation as an indivisible action. The solution described above was the third attempt.

Finally, we can state that the method of examining the effects the O-functions cause, yields a very good test whether the problem is completely described. The same idea is used in a more operationally oriented way by Keramidis and Mackert [9]. The path expressions, used by Flon and Haberman, are another means to ensure the completeness of specification [3].

References

[1] Denert, E.: Software-Modularisierung. Informatik-Spektrum **2**, 204–218 (1979).
[2] Dijkstra, E. W.: Notes on structured programming. In: Structured Programming. New York: Academic Press 1972.
[3] Flon, L., Haberman, A. M.: Towards the construction of verifiable software systems. ACM SIGPLAN Notices **11** (1976). Special Issue Conf. on Data, pp. 141–148.
[4] Guttag, J. V.: Abstract data types and the development of data structures. Communications Assoc. Comput. Mach. **20**, 397–404 (1977).
[5] Guttag, J. V., Horning, J. J.: The algebraic specification of abstract data types. Acta Informatica **10**, 27–52 (1978).
[6] Guttag, J. V., Horowitz, E., Musser, D. R.: The design of data type specifications. Proc. 2nd Internat. Conf. Software Engineering, San Francisco, 1974, IEEE Conf. Proceedings, pp. 414–420.

[7] Guttag, J. V., Horowitz, E., Musser, D. R.: Some extensions to algebraic specifications. ACM SIGPLAN Notices **12**, 63–67 (1977).

[8] Guttag, J. V., Horowitz, E., Musser, D. R.: Abstract data types and software validation. Communications Associat. Comput. Mach. **21**, 1048–1064 (1978).

[9] Keramidis, S., Mackert, L.: Specification and implementation of parallel activities on abstract objects. Proceedings 4th Internat. Conf. Software Engineering, München, 1979. IEEE Conf. Proceedings, pp. 203–211.

[10] Liskov, B. H., Zilles, S. N.: Programming with abstract data types. ACM SIGPLAN Notices **9**, 50–59 (1974).

[11] Majster, M. E.: Limits of the "algebraic" specification of abstract data types. ACM SIGPLAN Notices **12**, 37–42 (1977).

[12] Parnas, D. L.: A technique for the specification of software modules with examples. Communications Associat. Comput. Mach. **15**, 330–336 (1972).

[13] Spitzen, J. M., Levitt, K. N., Robinson, L.: An example of hierarchical design and proof. Communications Associat. Comput. Mach. **21**, 1064–1075 (1978).

[14] Wirth, N.: Towards a discipline of real-time programming. Communications Assoc. Comput. Mach. **20**, 577–583 (1977).

Prof. Dr. H. J. Schneider
Lehrstuhl für Programmiersprachen
Universität Erlangen-Nürnberg
Martensstrasse 3
D-8520 Erlangen
Federal Republic of Germany

Computing, Suppl. 3, 181 – 191 (1981)

On Cellular Automata with a Finite Number of State Changes

R. Vollmar, Braunschweig

Abstract – Zusammenfassung

On Cellular Automata with a Finite Number of State Changes. The number of state changes is introduced as a complexity measure for the recognition of languages in cellular automata. The relation of the simplest class – i.e. the one with a constant number of changes per single automaton – to the Chomsky hierarchy is investigated and a comparison with sequential tape complexity is made.

Über Zellularautomaten mit beschränkter Änderungskomplexität. Die Anzahl der Zustandsänderungen jedes Einzelautomaten wird als Maß für die Komplexität bei der Erkennung von Sprachen in Zellularautomaten eingeführt. Die einfachste dadurch definierte Klasse von Sprachen, die mit konstanter Änderungszahl pro Einzelautomat, wird bezüglich ihrer Lage in der Chomsky-Hierarchie untersucht, und es wird eine Verbindung zur sequentiellen Bandkomplexität hergestellt.

0. Introduction and Motivation

Investigating the behaviour of cellular automata (ca) usually time, space, state set and template size are considered as complexity measures (cf. e.g. [1]).

The notion of information transmission is among others defined by Nishio [2]. With respect to the (spatial-temporal) partitioning of computations this notion seems very important.

If a real ca (of a fixed size) is used to recognize words which do not fit (i.e. which are longer than the ca), a first approach can be a partitioning of the words into blocks of an appropriate length. Transitions are done with such a block until an information exchange with at least one neighbouring block becomes necessary; in this case a stockpiling must take place. Other blocks are processed, and in doing so, in general accesses to intermediate results of other blocks are necessary. But at which points should the words be cut? It seems to be an obvious approach to choose such points where the smallest information exchanges occur. This corresponds to a small number of state changes of the neighbouring automata of such a cut point (automaton) during the recognition process in an "appropriate" ca.

Therefore it would be desirable to find methods to compute for a given language the points characterized by the minimum of state changes during the recognition process, respectively to find algorithms (for ca) resulting in "convenient" points.

In this article a modified goal is aspired: Which languages are elements of the class of languages recognizable by ca with a constant number of state changes (per single automaton)? At a first glance for such languages it seems unimportant at which points the sections are made. But a more thorough consideration reveals this motivation as dubious: The exchange of blocks also depends on the temporal sequence of the state changes.

The advantage of this class is the possibility to recognize easily – by counting the number of changes – the moment from which on a block (subword) may be processed independent of the neighbouring blocks.

1. Definitions and Notations

First some important definitions are given formally whereas the remaining notions are introduced informally; explicit definitions may be found in [1].

Starting point is a one-dimensional cellular automaton $\mathscr{A} = (A, 1, N, F)$. It may be imagined as a chain (the second component of the quadruple fixes the dimension) of finite automata with the state set A where the connections are characterized by the neighbourhood index N. In this article without loss of generality, the so-called von Neumann template H_1 is assumed, which is characterized by the connection of each automaton with its two immediate neighbouring automata. The global transition function F describes the global change of the ca possible in one transition step. At succeeding moments the state of each automaton depends in a deterministic way on its own state and on the states of the neighbouring automata specified by the so-called local transition function. The parallel application of the local transition function to each automaton corresponds to one global transition.

To use ca as language recognizers some further definitions are needed: Let $L \subseteq W'(X)$ [1] be a formal language. A word w, for which is to recognize whether $w \in L$ or not, is coded symbol per symbol as a chain of states within a simple-connected region of single automata, called retina. The retina is bounded by two automata (the so-called border automata) which are initially preset with a specific state, the border state, which is characterized by the fact that this state is never changed by applications of the global transition function.

The first automaton of the retina, the accept automaton, shows the result of the recognition: The state set A contains states α and ω; if the accept automaton assumes α, then $w \in L$, if it assumes ω this corresponds to $w \notin L$. If an automaton ever assumes state α or ω, then this state can never be changed by F.

Such a ca is called a ca-recognizer (for the language L). The covering of the retina and of the border automata with states at time $t = 0$ is denoted as the initial configuration c_0, or if necessary, as the initial configuration attached to w. α and ω may not occur in c_0. Starting with c_0 by repeated application of the global transition function F a sequence of configurations $c_0, c_1, \ldots$, a so-called propagation $\langle c_0 \rangle$ is generated. The deterministic (and "complete") transition behaviour of the ca implies for a given c_0 the existence of a unique propagation, which is considered as non-terminating; but it may become stable.

During the recognition process the length of the retina remains fixed. Therefore it is easy to show that this class of ca recognizes the class of deterministic context-sensitive languages. Analogously to the linear bounded automata for each word

---

[1] $W'(X)$ denotes the set of words over X without the empty word.

a "fitting" retina is given; therefore the size of the retina and the length of the word to analyze are in each case equal.

In the following it is assumed that for a given word $w = w^1 \cdots w^n$ with $n \geq 1$, the symbol w^i $(1 \leq i \leq n)$ is coded to the state of the automaton with coordinate i – simply called the automaton i. The current state of the automaton i at time t is denoted $c_t(i)$ (see also above).

Definition 1. Let $\mathscr{A} = (A, 1, N, F)$ be a ca, $w \in W'(X)$, c_0 the initial configuration attached to w, and $f: \mathbb{N} \to \mathbb{N}^2$ a function.

a) The number of state changes (or simply changes) of an automaton i $(1 \leq i \leq n)$ is defined by

$$\ddot{a}(i) := \#\{t/c_t(i) \neq c_{t+1}(i)\}\ ^3.$$

b) The number of changes for the propagation $\langle c_0 \rangle$ is defined by

$$\ddot{a}(c_0) := \sup_{1 \leq i \leq n} \{\ddot{a}(i)\}.$$

c) A propagation $\langle c_0 \rangle$ is called f-change-bounded if the following holds:

$$\ddot{a}(c_0) \leq f(n).$$

Remark to c). In general the "behaviour" of a propagation does not only depend on the complexity of the ca but also on the length n of the given word, which is equal to the size of the retina.

Definition 2. Let $\mathscr{A}$ be a recognizer for the language $L \subseteq W'(X)$, and let w, c_0, f be as in Definition 1.

a) $\mathscr{A}$ is called f-change-bounded, if the following holds: $\forall w \in W'(X)$: $\langle c_0 \rangle$ is f-change-bounded.

b) A language L is called f-change-bounded, if the following holds:

$$\exists\ \text{ca-recognizer } \mathscr{A} \text{ for } L: \mathscr{A} \text{ is } f\text{-change-bounded.}$$

c) The class of f-change-bounded languages is denoted by $\ddot{\text{A}}\text{ZA}(f)$.

Also a definition about the time complexity of ca-recognizers is needed.

Definition 3. Let $\mathscr{A}$ be ca-recognizer for $L \subseteq W'(X)$, and let w, c_0, f be as in Definition 1.

a) A propagation $\langle c_0 \rangle$ is called f-time-bounded, if the following holds:

$$\min\{t/c_t(1) \in \{\alpha, \omega\}\} \leq f(n).$$

b) $\mathscr{A}$ is called f-time-bounded if the following holds:

$$\forall w \in W'(X): \langle c_0 \rangle \text{ is } f\text{-time-bounded.}$$

A simple, but efficient tool will be modified crossing sequences (following Hennie [3]).

---

2 $\mathbb{N}$ denotes the set of natural numbers (without zero).
3 $\#M$ denotes the cardinality of M. Also $|M|$ is used.

The initial part $c_0, c_1, \ldots, c_l$ of $l + 1$ elements of a propagation is denoted $\langle c_0 \rangle |_l$ and called l-propagation. The "spatial" restriction of a propagation containing the automata $i, i + 1, \ldots, j$ with $1 \leqslant i < j \leqslant n$ is denoted $\langle c_0(i,j) \rangle$ and called propagation section; analogously to l-propagations, $\langle c_0(i, j) \rangle |_l$ is introduced and called l-propagation section. For $i = 1, \ldots, n$ $\langle c_0(i, i) \rangle$ is identified with $\langle c_0(i) \rangle$.

In an obvious manner the concatenation of propagations (of the same length) is introduced and denoted by the concatenation of the corresponding expression; the resulting (connected) chain of automata has to be enclosed by border automata.

Definition 4. Two l-propagation sections $\langle c_0(i, k) \rangle |_l$ and $\langle c_0(m, n) \rangle |_l$ are called equal if the following conditions hold:

$$k - i = n - m$$

and

$$\forall t \in \{0, 1, \ldots, l\} \colon \forall j \in \{0, 1, \ldots, k - i\} \colon c_t(i + j) = c_t(m + j).$$

Analogous definitions are used for propagation sections.

Lemma 1. *Let $\mathscr{A}$ be a ca-recognizer. For a given c_0 let $\langle c_0(i, i + 1) \rangle$ and $\langle c_0(j, j + 1) \rangle$ be two propagation sections which are equal and $1 \leqslant i \leqslant n - 3, 3 \leqslant j \leqslant n - 1$, where $n \geqslant 4$ and $j > i + 1$. Let*

$$c_0' := \langle c_0(1, i) \rangle |_0 \langle c_0(j + 1, n) \rangle |_0.$$

Then holds

$$\langle c_0'(1) \rangle = \langle c_0(1) \rangle.$$

An analogous result holds for l-propagation sections.

Proof. Since $\mathscr{A}$ has template H_1 and since the propagation sections are equal, after the cutting off at each moment the states of the automaton neighbouring to the automata i and $j + 1$ have not changed with respect to those of the intact propagation. (Naturally for the other automata there are a fortiori no changes). Therefore also the behaviour of the first automaton does not change.

Remarks. 1) Analogous results also hold for two other types of cutting off.

2) The equality of the propagation sections of single automata does not imply a corresponding statement.

3) An analogous assertion also holds for an iterated insertion of the propagation sections cut off.

Lemma 2. *Let $\mathscr{A}$ be a ca-recognizer. Let $w, \bar{w} \in W'(X)$ with $|w| = n$ [4], $|\bar{w}| = \bar{n}$, and let c_0 and $\bar{c}_0$ be the initial configurations attached to w and $\bar{w}$, respectively.*

Let $\langle c_0(i, i + 1) \rangle$ and $\langle \bar{c}_0(j, j + 1) \rangle$ be equal propagation sections with $1 \leqslant i \leqslant n - 1$ and $1 \leqslant j \leqslant \bar{n} - 1$.

---

[4] For a word w, $|w|$ denotes the length of w.

With the notations

$$c'_0 := \langle c_0(1, i) \rangle |_0 \langle \bar{c}_0(j + 1, \bar{n}) \rangle |_0$$

$$\bar{c}'_0 := \langle \bar{c}_0(1, j) \rangle |_0 \langle c_0(i + 1, n) \rangle |_0$$

hold:

$$\langle c'_0(1) \rangle = \langle c_0(1) \rangle \quad and \quad \langle \bar{c}'_0(1) \rangle = \langle \bar{c}_0(1) \rangle.$$

A similar result holds for l-propagation sections.

The proof is analogous to that of Lemma 1.

Therefore propagation sections $\langle c_0(i, i + 1) \rangle$ determine in a unique way the information to be transmitted to the accept automaton from the automata $i + 2, \dots$.

2. Results

By an example, among others, it is shown that even obvious procedures are leading to different results concerning the number of state changes.

	a	a	a	b	a	a	a	a	

$t = 0$

	a	a	a	b	a'	a	a	a	
				a					

$t = 1$

	a	a	a	b	a'	a'	a	a	
		a	$-$	a					

$t = 2$

	a	a	a	b	a'	a'	a'	a	
		a	$-$	a	$-$	a			

$t = 3$

	a	a	a	b	a'	a'	a'	a'	
	a	$-$	a	$-$	a	$-$	a		

$t = 4$

Fig. 1. On the processing of the ca-recognizer $\mathscr{A}_1$

Let

$$L := \{a^n b a^n / n \in \mathbb{N}\}.$$

A ca-recognizer $\mathscr{A}_1$ for L works in the following obvious manner:

The a-subword right of b [5] is "shifted" to the left (until the left border is reached) and then it is checked for equality. Simultaneously to this process initially a checking signal starts from the right border, which tests whether the word is of type $W'(\{a\})\{b\}W'(\{a\})$. The acceptance of the given word depends among others on the positive result of this test, i.e. this signal guarantees the correct processing of the complement set of L (with respect to $W'(\{a, b\})$).

It may be helpful to imagine each automaton to be partitioned into two tracks to perform the shifting. The automaton representing the symbol b successively pulls the a-subword on its right: In its second track the state a and a "blank" state alternate (see Fig. 1 as a drawing of some successive configurations).

In the "center automaton" representing b $0(n)$ [6] changes occur.

For the further process of recognition only a constant number is needed; thus the sketched ca-recognizer $\mathscr{A}_1$ for L is f-change-bounded with $f = 0(|w|)$.

A "simpler" ca-recognizer $\mathscr{A}_2$ for L works in the following manner: From both automata immediately neighbouring to the border automata signals are started which move towards the center. If the two signals arrive simultaneously in the neighbourhood of b and they did not check any b on their way, this means that the given word is $\in L$; in this case a signal is sent to the accept automaton to put it into the state α; in the other case the state ω is assumed. Therefore $\mathscr{A}_2$ is const-change-bounded (with const $= 2$) and it holds: $L \in \text{ÄZA(const)}$.

The two following procedures are sketched under the aspects of the "change constructibility" which is definable in an obvious manner: A ca-recognizer, which is $0(|w|^2)$-change-bounded, simulates a linear bounded automaton with a tape of length $|w|$, which again is subdivided into two tracks. Using the representation of square numbers as the sum of odd numbers on one of the tracks $|w|^2$ steps are performed. Between each two such steps on the second track a complete passing through of the tape with alternating changes of the inscription occurs.

In an easy way an exponential number of changes is reached: $|w|$ automata are considered as one register in which it is count to base β. This counting process is stopped as soon as the register is filled. In the automaton representing the lowest valued digit $0(\beta^{|w|})$ changes occur.

A first result about the position of the class ÄZA(const) in the Chomsky hierarchy is easily derived.

Proposition 1. Besides all regular languages, ÄZA(const) contains languages from $\mathscr{L}_2 \backslash \mathscr{L}_3$ and from $\mathscr{L}_1 \backslash \mathscr{L}_2$.

Proof. Since the class of regular languages is closed under the operation of reflection, the corresponding ca-recognizer can simulate a deterministic finite automaton which runs from the right border to the accept automaton and puts it into the corresponding state. Therefore regular languages are elements of the class ÄZA(1).

---

[5] Instead of "the automaton representing x" for the sake of simplicity sometimes only the notation "x" is used.

[6] $f = 0(g)$ means that there exists a $c \in \mathbb{N}$, such that almost everywhere $f \leqslant c \cdot g$ holds.

The language L of the above example is a representant from $\mathscr{L}_2 \backslash \mathscr{L}_3$.

As an example from $\mathscr{L}_1 \backslash \mathscr{L}_2$ $L' := \{a^n X b^n Y c^n / n \in \mathbb{N}\}$ is considered. In principle a ca-recognizer for L' works similar to that one for L sketched above: From the left border of a^n and from the right border of b^n, and from the left border of b^n and from the right border of c^n two different pairs of signals are started to meet, respectively. If they meet simultaneously respectively in X and Y, certain states are assumed; from Y a signal runs to X and then dependent on the state of X a signal runs to the accept automaton. Simultaneously at the right border a signal is started that tests for $W'(\{a\})\{X\}W'(\{b\})\{Y\}W'(\{c\})$.

For the following a statement about the connection between time- and change-boundedness is needed.

Lemma 3. *Let $\mathscr{A}$ be an f-change-bounded ca-recognizer. Then $\mathscr{A}$ is $f(|w|) \cdot |w|$ time-bounded.*

Proof. If two successive elements of the propagation $\langle c_0 \rangle$ are equal, i.e. if there exists a $t \geqslant 0$ such that $c_t = c_{t+1}$, then because of the deterministic behaviour of $\mathscr{A}$, $\langle c_0 \rangle$ remains stable, i.e. in this case for all $i \geqslant 0$ holds $c_t = c_{t+i}$.

As long as in each element of the propagation at least *one* automaton changes its state, the propagation is not stable. This implies for an f-change-bounded propagation $\langle c_0 \rangle$: There exists a t with $t \leqslant f(|w|) \cdot |w|$ such that $c_t = c_{t+1}$ holds.

ÄZA(const) consists of infinitely many classes ÄZA(k):

Proposition 2. For each $\kappa \in \mathbb{N}$ there exist $\lambda \in \mathbb{N}$, such that holds: There are languages $L \in$ ÄZA(λ), which are not elements of ÄZA(κ).

Proof. This is proved by considering languages of the following type:

For $\lambda \in \mathbb{N}$ let

$$L_\lambda := \{a_1^{j_1} a_2^{j_2} \cdots a_\lambda^{j_\lambda} c \bar{a}_\lambda^{j_\lambda} \bar{a}_{\lambda-1}^{j_{\lambda-1}} \cdots \bar{a}_1^{j_1} / j_l \in \mathbb{N}, \; 1 \leqslant l \leqslant \lambda\}.$$

a) Corresponding to the above-mentioned method a ca-recognizer for L is constructed as follows: Starting at the first (last) symbols of the a_j- $(\bar{a}_j$-) subwords (special) signals s_j ($\bar{s}_j$) run to the right (left). Simultaneously at the right border a checking signal is started which tests the given word whether it is of type $W'(\{a_1\})W'(\{a_2\}) \cdots W'(\{a_\lambda\})\{c\}W'(\{\bar{a}_\lambda\}) \cdots W'(\{\bar{a}_1\})$.

If the signals belonging to one another meet c simultaneously in the correct sequence (s_{k+1} and $\bar{s}_{k+1}$ before s_k and $\bar{s}_k$), and the checking signal and $\bar{s}_1$ arrive simultaneously, then an acceptance signal is sent to the accept automaton.

In any other case the signals (with the exception of the checking signal) are stopped, and the checking signal causes the accept automaton to assume state ω. Therefore $L_\lambda \in$ ÄZA($\lambda + 1$).

b) For certain $\kappa \in \mathbb{N}$ L_λ is not an element of ÄZA(κ): Lemma 3 implies that a κ-change-bounded ca-recognizer for L_λ $\mathscr{A}_\kappa = (A_\kappa, 1, N, F_\kappa)$ (where again N determines a von Neumann template) would be K-time-bounded with $K := \kappa \cdot |w|$.

The number of the different K-propagation sections $\langle c_0(i, i+1)\rangle|_K$ $(1 \leqslant i \leqslant n-1)$ may be estimated in the following way: Vectors of length K which contain at $\kappa + 1$ places elements of A_κ are considered; the other components are filled by the respectively following and at the end by the respectively preceding element. Then the K-propagation sections $\langle c_0(i)\rangle|_K$ with $\leqslant \kappa$ state changes are contained in this set of vectors. To illuminate this advance an example is given: Let $\kappa = 2$, $A_\kappa = \{a, b\}$. Then such a vector is given by $(a, \ldots, a, \underline{a}, \underline{b}, \ldots, b, \underline{b}, a, \ldots, a, \underline{a}, a, \ldots, a)$. The first inscribed $\kappa + 1$ elements are underlined. A further admissible vector would be $(a, \ldots, a, \underline{a}, a, \ldots, a, \underline{a}, a, \ldots, a, \underline{a}, a, \ldots, a)$ which represents 0 changes.

Therefore one can conclude that there are $\leqslant \binom{K}{\kappa + 1}|A_\kappa|^{\kappa + 1}$ different K-propagation sections $\langle c_0(i)\rangle|_K$ with $\leqslant \kappa$ changes, and $\leqslant \mu \cdot K^{2\kappa + 2}$ $(\mu \in \mathbb{N})$, or expressed in dependence of the length of the given words, $0(|w|^{2\kappa + 2})$, different K-propagation sections $\langle c_0(i, i+1)\rangle|_K$ with $\leqslant \kappa$ changes.

A result from [4] can be used to estimate the number of the different words of L_λ of length $2n + 1$: There are $\binom{n-1}{\lambda - 1}$ different words of the form $a_1^{j_1} a_2^{j_2} \cdots a_\lambda^{j_\lambda}$ where $j_l > 0$. The number is $0(|w|^{\lambda - 1})$.

This implies that for appropriately chosen λ the number of different words of length $|w|$ is greater than the number of different K-propagation sections.

By construction for all words of the length $2n + 1$ of L_λ holds: At n and $n + 1$ $a_\lambda c$ is placed. If there exists a κ-change-bounded ca-recognizer for L_λ, then there are at least two words $w_1, w_2 \in L_\lambda$ with $|w_1| = |w_2| = 2n + 1$ and $w_1 \neq w_2$, such that the corresponding K-propagation sections $\langle c_0^1(n, n+1)\rangle|_K$ and $\langle c_0^2(n, n+1)\rangle|_K$ are equal (this even holds if the other places are not considered!). In this case by Lemma 2 the two words which are formed by the "cross-wise" concatenation of the words w_1 and w_2 partitioned at place n, are recognized as elements of L_λ, too, and this is obviously not true.

Therefore there does not exist a κ-change-bounded ca-recognizer for L_λ.

Thus, to any $\kappa \in \mathbb{N}$ a desired language can be constructed.

The following proposition states the relation between ÄZA(const) and the class of languages accepted by nondeterministic multi-tape Turing machines with logarithmic space, the so-called class NSPACE($\log_2|w|$).

Proposition 3. ÄZA(const) $\subsetneqq$ NSPACE($\log_2|w|$).

Proof. a) First the working method of a nondeterministic Turing machine (TM) which recognizes languages of ÄZA(const) with const $= k \in \mathbb{N}$ is sketched. This is done without a formal definition of Turing machines: Starting point is a TM with an input tape and four storage (or working) tapes. The TM halts for all inputs.

Basically a const-change-bounded ca can be simulated by such a nondeterministic TM in the following way: The overall behaviour of the simulated ca is "guessed" (this is made possible by the nondeterminism) and afterwards tested for consistency with the transition function of the ca and the given input. Since too much space is needed to store the overall information, at a time only one l-propagation section of type $\langle c_0(i-1, i, i+1)\rangle|_l$ with $1 \leqslant i \leqslant |w|$ is considered (in accordance with the H_1-neighbourhood), where the left border is the starting point.

According to Lemma 3 it is sufficient to choose $l = k \cdot |w|$. The possibility to proceed in the following manner is given in substance by the fact that except at the beginning at any moment an automaton can only change its state if at least one of the three neighbouring automata has changed its state one moment before.

For each single automaton i $(1 \leqslant i \leqslant |w|)$ the corresponding state is not registered at each moment τ $(0 \leqslant \tau \leqslant l)$, but only at those moments immediately before a state change. Such a change is stored as a triple $(t_j^i, z_j^i, z_{j+1}^i)$. A triple represents the moment of the change (by a dual number), the present state, and the next state, respectively. Thus, the "relevant" behaviour of a single automaton i $(1 \leqslant i \leqslant |w|)$ is representable by a sequence $v(i)$ of triples

$$(t_1^i, z_1^i, z_2^i), (t_2^i, z_2^i, z_3^i), \ldots, (t_{m_i}^i, z_{m_i}^i, z_{m_i+1}^i)$$

where $m_i \leqslant k$. (Because of the nondeterminism of the TM $v(i)$ may not be consistent with $\langle c_0(i)\rangle$ for each computation, but for "successful" ones.)

Investigating $\langle c_0(i-1, i, i+1)\rangle|_l$ the working tapes are used in the following way: The first tape contains $v(i-1)$. The TM guesses $v(i+1)$ and writes it to the second working tape. The ith symbol of w is read from the input tape and with aid of the informations on the first and second tape the ith automaton of the ca is simulated; the resulting $v(i)$ is written to the third working tape. The fourth tape contains the sequence of triples (moments and states) which has been guessed for the automaton i during the simulation of the behaviour of the automaton $i-1$. It is now compared with $v(i)$. If the tapes 3 and 4 are equal, tape 3 is copied to tape 1 and tape 2 to tape 4.

The procedure continues with the automaton $i+1$. If the two tapes are not equal, the process stops, because a consistent simulation cannot happen.

The treatment of $i = 1$ and $i = |w|$ is naturally somewhat different: In the first case at tape 1 and in the second case at tape 2 the border state (in an appropriate coding) must occur.

To go into some details the following consistency tests (additionally to the check on equality of tape 3 and 4) must be performed (for $1 \leqslant i \leqslant |w|$):

(1) Without use of the input tape it is possible to check the following conditions:

(a) The number of state changes must be $\leqslant k$, i.e. $m_i \leqslant k$.

(b) In the sequence each third component of a triple must be identical with the second one of the successive triple and the transitions have to be consistent with the local transition function.

(2) The input tape is only read once. z_1^i must be the coding of the ith symbol to be read.

(3) Simulating the ith automaton, differences have to be computed in order to compare the moments of changes; this is also possible on the corresponding tapes.

For each change in a neighbouring automaton the earliest moment at which a state change in the automaton i can take place is determined.

It is checked whether transitions without any further influence by the neighbours may happen.

If a consistency check fails, the TM halts in a nonaccepting state. In the other case the l-propagation section $\langle c_0 \rangle|_l$ has been guessed correctly; if the given word is an element of the language to be recognized (indicated by the last state of the first automaton) the TM halts in an accepting state, otherwise in a nonaccepting state.

Since, as mentioned above, $l \leqslant k \cdot |w|$ holds, and since at most k triples per tape have to be stored, it is obvious that for an appropriate coding of the working tape alphabet the TM is $\log_2|w|$-tape-bounded.

b) The proof for the proper inclusion is analogous to that one of Proposition 2.b): The language

$$L = \{w/w = uvu \wedge u \in W'(\{a,b\}) \wedge v \in W'(\{c\}) \wedge |u| = |v|\}$$

is considered. The same argumentation yields with the same denotations the same result for the number of K-propagation sections $\langle c_0(i, i+1) \rangle|_K$, i.e. $0(|w|^{2k+2})$. But there are $0(2^{|w|})$ different words of length $3|w|$ in L.

By Lemma 1 it follows that there cannot exist a const-change-bounded ca for L.

But L is accepted in an obvious manner by a 3-head-automaton and is therefore contained in $\text{NSPACE}(\log_2|w|)$ (see e.g. [5]).

Remark. To simulate the const-change-bounded ca even a Turing machine has been used which reads the input tape only in one direction.

It may be interesting to make a comparison with a result of Hennie [3] for Turing machines: He investigates Turing machines containing the input on the single tape. If each square of the tape can only be reached k times ($k \in \mathbb{N}$) by the (single) read-write-head (which again means that for each square only a finite number of changes can occur), then only regular languages are recognizable.

The results described above confirm the intuitively stringent conjecture that, roughly formulated, with respect to state changes, parallel working has advantages against sequential procedures.

Acknowledgements

I am indebted to F. J. Brandenburg and J. G. Pecht for helpful discussions and especially to the former for the hints at the "direct" proof of Proposition 3.a).

References

[1] Vollmar, R.: Algorithmen in Zellularautomaten. Stuttgart: Teubner 1979.
[2] Nishio, H.: Heuristic use of image processing technique for theoretical studies of automata. In: Frontiers of pattern recognition (Watanabe, S., ed.), pp. 373–389. New York: Academic Press 1972.

[3] Hennie, F. C.: One-tape, off-line Turing machine computations. Inform. Control **8**, 553—578 (1965).
[4] Feller, W.: An introduction to probability theory and its applications, Vol. I, 3rd ed. (revised printing), p. 38. New York-Sydney: Wiley 1968.
[5] Greibach, S. A.: Visits, crosses, and reversals for non-deterministic off-line machines. Inform. Control **36**, 174—216 (1978).

Prof. Dr.-Ing. R. Vollmar
Lehrstuhl C für Informatik
Technische Universität Braunschweig
Gaussstrasse 11
D-3300 Braunschweig
Federal Republic of Germany

Computing, Suppl. 3, 193 – 203 (1981)

Models to Describe Those Features of Cellular Computer Nets Which Are Relevant to the Operating System

K. Wendler, Nürnberg

Abstract – Zusammenfassung

Models to Describe Those Features of Cellular Computer Nets Which Are Relevant to the Operating System. A cellular computer net seems adequate to execute user problems which have a high computational complexity and which exhibit a high degree of parallelism. The cellular net is seen as a subsystem of a hierarchical modular computer system. A structure-model and a state-model will be presented. The first describes the topological features of a cellular net which are static, the second mainly models dynamic faults and the status of allocation. Finally three alternatives for realizing cellular nets are discussed.

Modelle zur Beschreibung der betriebssystemrelevanten Eigenschaften zellularer Rechnernetze. Ausgangspunkt ist eine hierarchisch modulare Rechnerstruktur, die zur Ausführung stark parallelisierbarer, rechenintensiver Anwenderprobleme ein zellulares Rechnernetz bereitstellt. Es wird ein Strukturmodell und ein Zustandsmodell vorgestellt. Das Strukturmodell dient der Beschreibung der statischen topologischen Gegebenheiten eines zellularen Netzes, im Zustandsmodell werden vor allem dynamische Fehlersituationen und der Belegungszustand dargestellt. Schließlich werden drei Realisierungskonzepte für zellulare Netze diskutiert.

1. Introduction

The history of powerful computing systems is characterized by increasing parallelism. One of the different types of parallelism which will be discussed in this paper is the polyprocessor structure for simultaneously processing numerous instruction streams. A further tendency is to be seen in the specialization of subsystems for certain classes of functions. Well-known realized examples are the largest models of CDC with their peripheral processors and the STARAN-system [6], in which a traditional von Neumann-computer is dedicated to the functions of the operating system.

Since the technology of microprocessors appeared, the interest in the research and development of polyprocessor systems has considerably increased. Many symmetrical structures have been proposed, similar to the classical multi-processors like C.mmp [8] and Pluribus [5], as well as asymmetrical systems [1, 4] with dedicated subsystems for user- and operating system tasks.

2. Hierarchical Modular Polyprocessor Structure

2.1. The starting point of this paper is a *hierarchical modular* scheme for designing polyprocessor systems. It is derived from the class hierarchy of tasks as it is present in powerful computing systems (Fig. 1) according to the principles of parallelism and specialization [7].

The different classes of tasks:

central administration and control tasks of the operating system (*O-Tasks*),
user oriented tasks with a high computational complexity (*U-Tasks*),
data base tasks (*D-Tasks*)
control of peripheral units (*P-Tasks*), etc.

are supported by different subsystems *O-SS*, *U-SS*, *D-SS*, and *P-SS* (Fig. 2). The
subsystems may be built of a varying number of processors and types of processor.

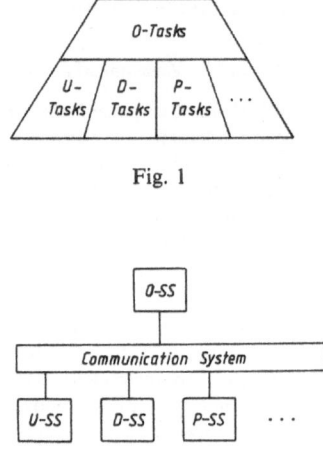

Fig. 1

Fig. 2

2.2. A net of processors in the user subsystem *U-SS* is dedicated to the parallel
execution of user tasks. Fig. 3 shows an example of a cellularly structured two-
dimensional net which is supposed to be connected like a torus. This structure
corresponds to that of the so-called *A*-processor array in the EGPA-architecture
[3].

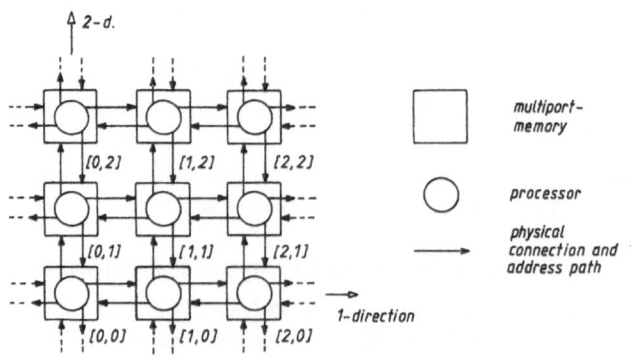

Fig. 3

The outlined structural scheme supports especially the following design objectives: modular extensibility, dynamic reconfiguration, and highly parallel execution of problems which exhibit an inherent high degree of parallelism (e.g. weather forecast).

2.3. Regarding the operating system, processors and memories, together with their connecting network, represent a *structured system of resources* which is to be supervised and used as economically as possible for realizing systems of processes. For this purpose the operating system requires a formal model of the subsystem *U-SS*. It must reflect its characteristic features which are relevant to the operating system. We are interested in a transparent model which can be implemented in an efficient way and which permits simple operations for manipulating the model. Such operations have to be executed in case of scheduler activities and reconfigurations.

Subsequently we assume that all processors and all memories of the user subsystem *U-SS* are identically structured towards the other subsystems and that they behave equally at their interfaces to them. With this assumption the interface aspects need not be considered in the models.

3. Modelling Cellular Nets

Any net can be modelled as a graph with labelled edges. The labels may represent topological features like "addressable memory is situated east of"

3.1. We are highly interested in *cellular* nets, since they present the following favourable characteristics, as will be shown:

They can be extended in a *conformable* and *modular* ('in small portions') way. Conformable in this context means that the local features do not change when an extension is performed.

A clear model can be given. It can be efficiently implemented in the operating system. The algorithms for updating the implemented model on behalf of modifications of the real net are simple.

The scheduler algorithms are not affected by net extensions.

Systems of processes can be loaded at any area of the net, because it is a homogeneous structure without edges.

Many problems with a high computational complexity (e.g. weather forecast) exhibit a cellular-like structure themselves. Therefore they can quite naturally be decomposed in a system of processes and implemented in a cellular net.

The *cells* of a cellular net are entities being composed of a processor, a memory, and some ports which enable the communication with other cells and with the environment of the net too. Within a cell the memory is always addressable by the corresponding processor. This general feature of a cell does not have to be modelled individually. It is further assumed that all cells are functionally identical. That in particular means that for all cells the number and the type of ports and also the memory size are the same.

3.2. The characteristics of the structure and addressability of a cellular net are clearly represented in the *cellular structure-model*. The features of a cellular net being composed of processors and memories will be specified by means of this model.

Definition 1. A *cellular structure*, briefly called *C-structure*, is a 5-tuple

$$C = (d, w, Z, S, A) \tag{1}$$

with characteristics as follows:

a) The *dimension d* of the C-structure is a finite natural number. The *width w* is a finite vector, $w \in \mathbb{N}^d$. Z is the set of *logical cells*

$$Z = Z_1 \times \cdots \times Z_d, \quad \text{with } Z_i = \{0, 1, \ldots, w[i] - 1\} \text{ for } 1 \leqslant i \leqslant d. \tag{2}$$

The *local connectivity S* and the *local addressability A* are finite sets of vectors $S = \{s_1, \ldots, s_m\}$ and $A = \{a_1, \ldots, a_n\}$ respectively, with

$$s_j \in \mathbb{Z}^d \backslash o_d \quad \text{for} \quad 1 \leqslant j \leqslant m \quad \text{and} \quad a_j \in \mathbb{Z}^d \backslash o_d \quad \text{for} \quad 1 \leqslant j \leqslant n. \tag{3}$$

o_d stands for the *d*-dimensional *zero*-vector.

b) $$\forall s(s \in S \rightarrow \exists s' | s' \in S \wedge s' = -s). \tag{4}$$

c) $$A \cup (-A) \supseteq S. \tag{5}$$

d) $$w[i] \geqslant \max(\pi[i](S \cup A)) - \min(\pi[i](S \cup A)) + 1 \quad \text{for} \quad 1 \leqslant i \leqslant d. \tag{6}$$

$\pi[i](M')$ is the projection of M' onto the *i*th component, with $M' \subseteq M$ and $M = M[1] \times \cdots \times M[d]$.

The elements of Z represent the cells of the net. S and A describe the *local* characteristics of connectivity and addressability. They are identical for all cells. The set of cells to which a given cell z is physically connected, is called *connected neighbourhood CN(z)*. It is calculated according to the following rule which is implicit to the model:

$$CN(z) = \{z \oplus s_1, z \oplus s_2, \ldots, z \oplus s_m\}. \tag{7}$$

$z \oplus s_j$ denotes the vector-addition of the vectors z and s_j, modulo the components of the width w. The modulo operation implicitly models the local homogeneity which is very important for cellular nets. A ring-shaped closed cellular net is modeled by a C-structure of the dimension $d = 1$, a net closed to a torus by a 2-dimensional C-structure, and so forth.

The *positive* and *negative addressable neighbourhood* $AN_+(z)$ and $AN_-(z)$ are calculated accordingly:

$$AN_+(z) = \{z \oplus a_1, z \oplus a_2, \ldots, z \oplus a_n\}, \tag{8}$$

$$AN_-(z) = \{z \ominus a_1, z \ominus a_2, \ldots, z \ominus a_n\}. \tag{9}$$

$AN_+(z)$ represents which cells can be addressed by z, $AN_-(z)$ describes by which cells z can be addressed.

It is essential to make a difference between the physical connectivity and the addressability, since memory requests can be put through even to not directly connected cells when implemented adequately (see Chapt. 6). The attribute (4) is necessary, as the physical connectivity is of a reflexive nature. (5) says that when two cells are connected, this implies the addressability at least in one direction. Attribute (6) is to guarantee the homogeneity and the modular extensibility, as will be shown later.

Example. The cellular net of Fig. 3 is modelled by the C-structure $\mathbf{C} = (d, w, Z, S, A)$ with $d = 2$, $w = (3, 3)$, $Z = \{(\circ, \circ), \ldots, (2, 2)\}$ and $S = A = \{(1, 0), (0, 1), (-1, 0), (0, -1)\}$. The connected neighbourhood of cell $z = (0, 1)$ for example is $CN(z) = \{(1, 1), (0, 2), (2, 1), (0, 0)\}$.

Theorem. *Any C-structure is homogeneous in the sense that*

$$\forall z(z \in Z \to |CN(z)| = |S| \wedge |AN_+(z)| = |AN_-(z)| = |A|) \tag{10}$$

holds.

Proof (indirect). Assume that there is a $z \in Z$, for which $|CN(z)| \neq |S|$ is valid. Then also $|CN(z)| < |S|$ holds because of definition (7). Hence at least one pair of vectors $s_1 \in S$, $s_2 \in S$ must exist for which $z \oplus s_1 = z \oplus s_2$ is valid. But for this $\exists i (1 \leqslant i \leqslant d \wedge |s_1[i]| + |s_2[i]| = w[i])$ is required, which is in contrast to condition (6). The proofs for $AN_+(z)$ and $AN_-(z)$ are analogous.

Definition 2. Two C-structures

$$\mathbf{C}_1 = (d_1, w_1, Z_1, S_1, A_1) \quad \text{and} \quad \mathbf{C}_2 = (d_2, w_2, Z_2, S_2, A_2)$$

are called *conformable* to each other, if and only if

$$d_1 = d_2 \wedge S_1 = S_2 \wedge A_1 = A_2$$

is valid.

This means that conformable C-structures have the same dimension and the same local characteristics.

Definition 3. A C-structure $\mathbf{C}_2 = (d_2, w_2, Z_2, S_2, A_2)$ is called *modularly extended* with respect to a C-structure $\mathbf{C}_1 = (d_1, w_1, Z_1, S_1, A_1)$, if and only if $\mathbf{C}_1$ and $\mathbf{C}_2$ are conformable to each other and

$$\exists i (1 \leqslant i \leqslant d \wedge w_2 = w_1 + l_d^i)$$

is valid. l_d^i denotes the d-dimensional vector, the ith component of which has the value *one* and the remaining components have the value *zero*.

Apparently for any C-structure $\mathbf{C} = (d, w, Z, S, A)$ there exist exactly d different modular extensions. A two-dimensional C-structure for instance can be modularly extended by adding one more line or one more column.

Definition 4. A C-structure $\mathbf{C} = (d, w, Z, S, A)$ is called

simple reflexive	in case	$A = S$,
simple irreflexive	in case	$A \cup (-A) = S \wedge A \cap (-A) = \emptyset$,
simple	in case	$A \cup (-A) = S$,
not-simple	in case	$A \cup (-A) \supset S$.

$$\tag{11}$$

4. Classes of Cellular Structures

With reference to the theory of cellular automata we can also define *grid types* for cellular polyprocessor nets. Let z be a d-tuple, $z \in \mathbb{Z}^d$. $\bar{z}$ and $/z/$ are defined by

$$\bar{z} = \sum_{i=1}^{d} |z[i]|, \qquad /z/ = \max(\{|z[i]| \,|\, 1 \leqslant i \leqslant d\}).$$

The most important grid types are:

$$H_k^{(d)} = \{z \,|\, 0 < \bar{z} \leqslant k\},$$

$$J_k^{(d)} = \{z \,|\, 0 < /z/ \leqslant k\},$$

$$K_k^{(d)} = \{z \,|\, 0 < \bar{z} \leqslant k \wedge \forall i(1 \leqslant i \leqslant d \rightarrow z[i] \geqslant 0)\},$$

$$L_k^{(d)} = \{z \,|\, 0 < /z/ \leqslant k \wedge \forall i(1 \leqslant i \leqslant d \rightarrow z[i] \geqslant 0)\}.$$

Example. Each element of a grid type in Fig. 4 is represented by a point in $\mathbb{R}^2$. The element o_d which does not belong to any grid type, is blacked. It represents the local origin.

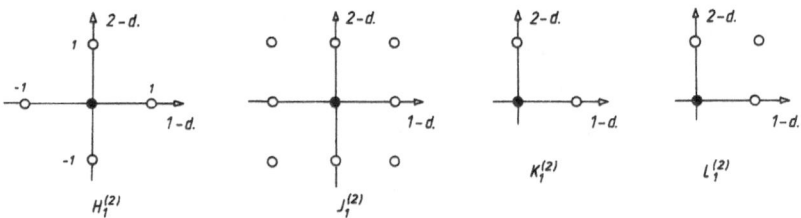

Fig. 4

Example. The C-structure of Fig. 3 thus can briefly be described by

$$\mathbf{C} = (2, (3,3), Z, H_1^{(2)}, H_1^{(2)}).$$

Because of condition (4) only the $H_k^{(d)}$- and $J_k^{(d)}$-grid type, but not the other two may define the local connectivity. If S and A appear with $S = A = H_k^{(d)}$, as for instance in the example above, or with $S = A = J_k^{(d)}$, they define a simple reflexive C-structure. If $S = H_k^{(d)}$ and $A = K_k^{(d)}$ is valid, we have a simple irreflexive C-structure.

5. State-Model for Cellular Nets

A C-structure only comprehends size and topological features of a net which is free of hardware errors. The *cellular state-model* additionally includes references to descriptions of the cells and of the presently realized systems of processes. It also reflects failures caused by hardware errors and the status of allocation. When defining the model we assumed that the processors of the net are used in a *single-programming mode*. For each system of processes which is to be executed by the cellular *U-SS*, the operating system determines a *virtual cell structure*. It is a prerequisite for loading a system of processes that an adequate region in the cellular net can be exclusively allocated for its virtual cell structure. In view of the reduction of prices for microprocessors and memories it seems reasonable to claim the single-programming mode. Anyway, this mode is convenient, when powerful nets with hundreds or even more cells are used for highly parallel problems of extraordinary complexity.

Definition 5. The state of a C-structure, briefly called S-state, is a 5-tuple $S = (C, v_r, v_v, \beta_r, \beta_v)$ over labelling alphabets N_r, N_v, B_r, B_v, where

a) C is a C-structure, $C = (d, w, Z, S, A)$;

b) $v_r: Z \to N_r$ is an injective mapping onto the alphabet N_r;

c) $v_v: Z \to N_v$, $\beta_r: Z \to B_r$ and $\beta_v: Z \to B_v$ are mappings of Z onto the alphabets N_v, B_r, and B_v.

We assume that those features of the physical realization of a cell which are relevant to the operating system are stored in its data base as a *cell description*. This description includes for instance the interrupt address of the cell processor, the addresses of the processor status words etc. All these informations are gathered according to the needs of the operating subsystem O-SS. Let R denote the set of all cell descriptions.

On its creation a cell description $r \in R$ is uniquely bound to a free symbol of N_r. N_r is the invariant set of names for cell descriptions.

Let V denote the set of all descriptions of virtual cell structures which either are already realized in the C-structure or which wait for their realization. On its creation a *virtual structure description* $v \in V$ is uniquely bound to a free symbol of N_v. N_v is the invariant set of names for virtual structure descriptions. A $v \in V$ will never be bound to the element *nil* included in N_v.

The set B_r depends on S and T. With $S = \{s_1, \ldots, s_m\}$ and $A = \{a_1, \ldots, a_n\}$ we have $B_r = \{faultless, faulty\}^{m+n+1}$. The set B_v is $B_v = \{free, occupied\}$.

An S-state S may be interpreted as a graph with labelled nodes and labelled edges. The labels of the edges are defined implicitly by S and A. The nodes are labelled over the alphabets N_r, N_v, B_r and B_v. The different labels of a node $n_r \in N_r$, $n_v \in N_v$, $b_r \in B_r$ and $b_v \in B_v$ have the following meaning:

n_r is the name of a cell description. Each $z \in Z$ represents uniquely a physical cell in a cellular net. Vice versa, during the process of modularly extending the net, the additional cells are temporarily not yet represented in the cellular state model. n_v is either the name of a virtual cell structure, in case the cell is allocated to a system of processes, or the value *nil*. b_r describes the *status of malfunction* of a cell itself and of its relations to the physically connected and the addressable cells. The *status of allocation* of a cell is specified by b_v. This label is obviously redundant because of $(n_v = nil \leftrightarrow b_v = free) \land (n_v \neq nil \leftrightarrow b_r = occupied)$. Nevertheless it was built into the model in order to simplify the work of the scheduler. The status of malfunction and the status of allocation must both be considered when a free area in the net is looked for to load a system of processes. Both of them can be coded to form a common pattern which may be easily identified.

An S-state will be changed on occasion of a reconfiguration or a scheduler activity. The reconfiguration may be explicitly requested to perform a modification of the physical net or it may be caused by an accidental failure. The required modifications of the S-state will be characterized without precisely specifying the related operations.

A *requested reconfiguration* is always initiated by the operating personnel when extending or reducing the physical computer net. The S-state $\mathbf{S}$ is transformed to the state $\mathbf{S}'$ by *two* steps. First $w \rightarrow w'$ and $z \rightarrow z'$ will be performed, then $v_r \rightarrow v'_r$, $v_v \rightarrow v'_v$, $\beta_r \rightarrow \beta'_r$, and $\beta_v \rightarrow \beta'_v$.

A *reconfiguration by malfunction* is started by the operating system as soon as a hardware error has been detected. While diagnosing the error and recovering the affected systems of processes, the old S-state $\mathbf{S}$, which was valid before the error occurred, is transformed to a new $\mathbf{S}'$ by $\beta_r \rightarrow \beta'_r$, $v_v \rightarrow v'_v$ and $\beta_v \rightarrow \beta'_v$. On the initiation of the operating personnel repaired components are made available to the scheduler by $\beta'_r \rightarrow \beta''_r$.

On occasion of *scheduler activities* aiming at allocating or freeing subnets the n_v- and b_v-labels of allocated or freed cells are modified: $v_v \rightarrow v'_v$ and $\beta_v \rightarrow \beta'_v$.

6. Alternative Net Architectures

Three alternatives for designing cellular nets will be described and discussed with respect to some qualitative attributes: the CM-architecture, the RM-architecture and the PM-architecture. They all are based on a virtual addressing scheme with segmentation.

6.1. The cells of a net realized according to the CM-*architecture* are Computer Modules [2] which are well known in literature. They are connected by inter-CM busses. The structure of a Computer Module CM is presented in Fig. 5(a). A CM includes a processor P, a memory M, a set of ports MAP and a $SWITCH$ which enables the communication between the individual ports as well as to the memory.

Each port contains a number of segment descriptors for translating addresses. Each port which is attached to an inter-CM bus is able to receive an address, to translate it, and then to route it either to the local memory or to another inter-CM bus via a further port. This ability is an important feature of the CM-architecture. It guarantees that a processor of a CM can even address memories which are part of CM's not directly connected.

Thus each CM of a cellular CM-net may potentially address any other CM of the net. Hence, not-simple cellular nets (according to def. 4) can be built, in the sense of def. 1, by choosing an appropriate local addressability A. But they cannot be modularly extended in the sense of def. 3, because every extension of the physical net causes a change of the local addressability A.

6.2. The RM-*architecture* is very similar to the CM-architecture. However, it does not imply the potential addressability of all memories by every processor.

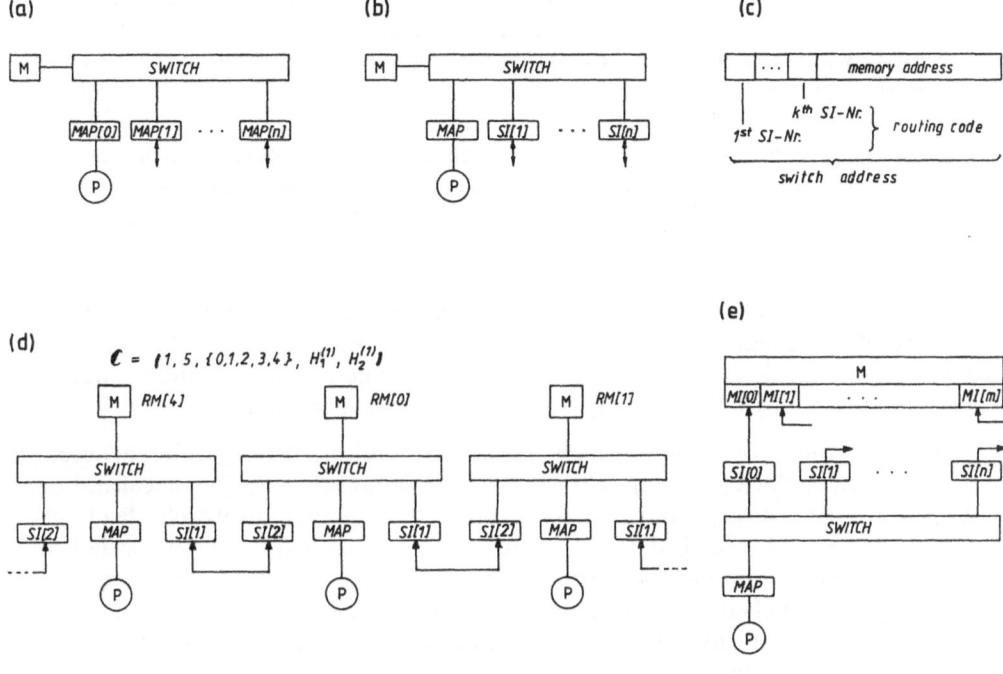

Fig. 5

A cell of an *RM*-net, briefly called *RM*-module, is illustrated by Fig. 5(b). The ports *SI* enable the communication with other *RM*'s. The port *MAP* includes a segment table with a number of descriptors. The virtual processor address is translated into a *SWITCH* address by *MAP*. The *switch address space* is the memory address space extended by the routing code (Fig. 5(c)). The routing code consists of k *SI*-numbers. The *SWITCH* routes a switch address which is offered at the port *MAP* or at a port *SI* from another *RM* either to the local memory or to an *SI*. The destination is determined by the first entry of the routing code. The value 0 means that the local memory is the destination, values $\neq$ o denote one of the *SI*'s.

The number k of the entries of the routing code is called *level depth* of the switch address. When a switch address has been received in an *SI*, an open left shift of the entries of the routing code is performed and the value 0 is loaded into the kth field. Assume a *two*-level switch address space according to the example of Fig. 5(d), then *RM*[4] can address the memory of *RM*[1] by applying a routing code (1, 1).

The level depth k determines the local addressability A. $A = H_k^{(d)}$ is valid, if *SI*-ports and bus-couplers are designed for a reflexive communication, as has been assumed so far. A cellular *RM*-net is simple for $k = 1$ and not-simple for $k > 1$.

6.3. The structure of a cell according to the *PM-architecture*, briefly *PM*-module, is represented in Fig. 5(e). Here the memory M is a multiport memory with a set of entry ports *MI*. *PM*'s communicate unidirectionally via connection lines between *SI*'s and *MI*'s.

A virtual processor address is translated into a memory address by *MAP* using a segment table. The *SWITCH* forwards the mapped address to a port *SI* which is specified by the segment table. No further mapping is done, neither in the ports *SI* nor in the ports *MI*.

6.4. In the *PM*-architecture the access time does not depend on whether the memory request concerns the local memory of the *PM*-module or a remote memory of the addressable neighbourhood. In the *CM*- and *RM*-architecture, however, the memory access time depends considerably on the number of address mappings which have to be done along the access path. Obviously the address mapping mechanism in the *CM*-architecture is more complex than in the *RM*-architecture. This results in longer access times to remote memories. In the *CM*- and *RM*-architecture additional time delays are caused when components along the access path are temporarily occupied by a request of another module.

Particularly those components which may be commonly used along different access paths cause deadlock problems in the *CM*- and *RM*-architecture. Technical and/or organizational measures have to be taken to ensure that insolvable deadlock situations will be avoided. If a *CM*- or an *RM*-net is realized as a circuit switched network, the busses connecting the modules are the critical resources. If it is realized as a message switched network, the message buffers are the bottle-neck. As *RM*-nets do not imply the universal addressability, the deadlock problems are easier to solve in *RM*-nets than in *CM*-nets.

The above discussed attributes are clearly arranged in Table 1. The data referring to the access time have to be understood in relation to the *PM*-architecture.

Table 1

Attributes		*CM*	*RM*	*PM*
Realization is possible of	simple nets		+	+
	not-simple nets	+	+	
Access time to	local memory	1	1	1
	remote memory	$\gg 1$	> 1	1
Deadlock problems		very heavy	heavy	none

Remark. Let us assume that access requests are not acknowledged in a *CM*- or *RM*-net designed as a message switched network. Then, for isolated references or when there is little contention for inter-module busses, write operations to remote memory will appear no slower than write operations to local memory. Read operations to remote memory are in any case substantially slower than read operations to local memory.

6.5. Two features of a system of processes are essential when comparing the three architectures with regard to their ability to execute parallel processes:

the degree of locality which the processes exhibit. A high degree of locality means that there are only isolated references to common data objects,

the maximum number of processes which share a data object.

Because of the single programming mode, the second feature of a system of processes determines the required size of the local addressability A. Table 2 gives qualitative information. In our opinion, a $H_1^{(d)}$-grid is an example of a small size of A, and a $H_2^{(d)}$-grid an example of a medium size of A.

Table 2

		Locality		
		High	Medium	Low
Required size	big	*CM*	*CM*	
of local	medium	*CM, RM*	*RM*	*RM, PM*
addressability	small	*RM*	*PM*	*PM*

References

[1] Arnold, R. G., Page, E. W.: A hierarchical, restructurable multi-microprocessor architecture. 3rd Annual Symposium on Computer Architecture **1976**, 40 − 45.

[2] Bell, C. G., et al.: The architecture and applications of computer modules: A set of components for digital design. Proceedings of COMPCON **73**, 177 − 180 (1973).

[3] Händler, W., Hofmann, F., Schneider, H. J.: A general purpose array with a broad spectrum of applications (Informatik-Fachberichte, Vol. 4). Berlin-Heidelberg-New York: Springer 1976.

[4] Kober, R., et al.: SMS 101 − A structural multimicroprocessor system with deadlock-free operation scheme. Euromicro Newsletter **2**, 56 − 64 (1976).

[5] Ornstein, S. M., et al.: Pluribus − A reliable multiprocessor. National Computer Conference **1975**, 551 − 559, AFIPS Press.

[6] Rudolph, J. A.: A production implementation of an associative array processor − STARAN. AFIPS FJCC **1972**, 299 − 241.

[7] Wendler, K.: Betriebssystemaspekte in hierarchisch modularen Polyprozessorsystemen − Modellierungsansätze und Koordinierungsmechanismen. Dissertation, Erlangen, 1978.

[8] Wulf, W. A., Bell, C. G.: C.mmp − A multi-mini-processor. AFIPS FJCC **1972**, 765 − 777.

Dr. K. Wendler
DATEV eG
Paumgartnerstrasse 6
D-8500 Nürnberg
Federal Republic of Germany

Computergesteuerter Fotosatz und Umbruch:
Dipl.-Ing. Schwarz' Erben KG, A-3910 Zwettl, NÖ.
Reproduktion und Offsetdruck: Novographic, Ing. Wolfgang Schmid, A-1238 Wien.